MW00617067

# The Jordanian Labor Market in the New Millennium

# The Jordanian Labor Market in the New Millennium

Edited by Ragui Assaad

OXFORD
UNIVERSITY PRESS

# OXFORD

UNIVERSITY PRESS

Great Clarendon Street, Oxford, OX2 6DP,
United Kingdom

Oxford University Press is a department of the University of Oxford.
It furthers the University's objective of excellence in research, scholarship,
and education by publishing worldwide. Oxford is a registered trade mark of
Oxford University Press in the UK and in certain other countries

© The Economic Research Forum 2014

The moral rights of the authors have been asserted

First Edition published in 2014
Impression: 1

All rights reserved. No part of this publication may be reproduced, stored in
a retrieval system, or transmitted, in any form or by any means, without the
prior permission in writing of Oxford University Press, or as expressly permitted
by law, by licence or under terms agreed with the appropriate reprographics
rights organization. Enquiries concerning reproduction outside the scope of the
above should be sent to the Rights Department, Oxford University Press, at the
address above

You must not circulate this work in any other form
and you must impose this same condition on any acquirer

Published in the United States of America by Oxford University Press
198 Madison Avenue, New York, NY 10016, United States of America

British Library Cataloguing in Publication Data
Data available

Library of Congress Control Number: 2013957078

ISBN 978-0-19-870205-4

Printed and bound by
CPI Group (UK) Ltd, Croydon, CR0 4YY

Links to third party websites are provided by Oxford in good faith and
for information only. Oxford disclaims any responsibility for the materials
contained in any third party website referenced in this work.

# Foreword

Data has always been at a premium in the region covered by the Economic Research Forum (ERF). Accordingly, ERF has been particularly keen to make dependable data available for researchers. In 1998, ERF launched its first Egypt Labor Market Panel Survey (ELMPS), which examined, among other factors, labor supply, employment, earnings and inequality, and gender and education. The data produced was deemed so important it led to another survey in 2006, and another in 2012. Those surveys in turn inspired the series to go regional; the Jordan Labor Market Panel Survey.

This volume is the result of that research. It includes the very first batch of research papers that draw on a rich and unique data set derived from the Jordan Labor Market Survey of 2010 (JLMPS 2010). Modeled after the earlier ELMPS, the JLMPS 2010 is the first wave of a planned panel, which will be carried out periodically in Jordan to ascertain the state of the labor market and of human resource development. The JLMPS 2010 was carried out by ERF in cooperation with the Jordanian Department of Statistics and the National Center for Human Resource Development of Jordan. Because ERF views the availability of microdata for researchers as an essential public good for state-of-the-art research and effective policymaking, the JLMPS 2010 data is available for public use through the ERF website (<http://www.erf.org.eg>).

While all the panels have been designed around the same axis, consistency has also been maintained by the editor, Ragui Assaad, who has led the research since the very first panel survey in 1998. Assaad was a driving force on this project, and on behalf of ERF I would like to express our appreciation to him and his team for their hard work and dedication.

The JLMPS was produced under the Research Initiative for Arab Development (RIAD) funded by the Arab Fund for Economic and Social Development and the World Bank. We would like to thank them for their financial support, along with the National Center for Human Resource Development of Jordan, which supported part of the research through its Al-Manar project, funded by the Canadian International Development Agency (CIDA).

Ahmed Galal
Managing Director,
Economic Research Forum

# Preface

Until the onset of the world financial crisis in 2008–09, the Jordanian economy was experiencing rapid rates of economic growth, averaging 8.3% per annum from 2004 to 2008. Despite this impressive growth performance, the unemployment rate remained persistently high at 12.9% in 2009, albeit having declined from a high of 15.3% in 2002. Earlier analyses of the Jordanian labor market have shown that more than half of all new jobs in Jordan were going to migrant workers in the period from 2002 to 2006 (Assaad and Amer 2008 and World Bank 2007), suggesting that there is significant labor demand in Jordan, but that for a variety of reasons, the jobs were not going to Jordanians seeking employment. The World Bank attributes this phenomenon to three mismatches in the Jordanian labor market. The first is a geographical mismatch between where the jobs are and where job seekers live. The second is a mismatch between what employers want in terms of employability skills and what Jordanian job seekers offer. This includes skills related to workplace behavior, such as effort, responsibility, absenteeism, and flexibility. The third is between the expectations of Jordanian workers about work conditions and wages and what Jordanian employers are willing to offer. While it is clear that some of these mismatches are related to the open nature of the Jordanian labor market and the ready access employers have to cheap foreign labor, they can also partly be attributed to the nature of the education system and the sorts of jobs the Jordanian economy is currently creating.

Other important issues identified by these earlier studies include (i) the very low participation rates of Jordanian females despite the closing, or even the reversal, of the gender gap in education; (ii) the low age of retirement among Jordanian males and its link to pension policies; (iii) the significant demographic youth bulge that Jordanian society is currently experiencing and its impact on education and the labor market; (iv) the inflow of large numbers of refugees from Iraq; and (v) the delay in marriage among Jordanian youth and its rising costs.

This book contributes to a more complete understanding of the Jordanian labor market by offering in-depth analyses of fresh data from a unique data source whose results are being presented here for the first time. The Jordan Labor Market Panel Survey of 2010 (JLMPS 2010) carried out by the

Economic Research Forum (ERF), in cooperation with the National Center for Human Resources Development (NCHRD), and the Jordanian Department of Statistics (DOS) provides detailed data on all aspects of the labor market in Jordan, including education, residential mobility, labor market entry, unemployment, participation in domestic work, detailed job characteristics, transitions from job to job and from work to other employment states, earnings, marriage patterns, early retirement, emigration and immigration, and work in family enterprises. This unique data set will serve as the basis of a periodic panel survey that will follow the households and individuals interviewed through time, allowing for state-of-the-art analyses of the dynamics of human capital formation and deployment in the Jordanian economy.

The JLMPS 2010 was carried out on a nationally representative sample design of 5,760 households, which resulted in a sample of 5,102 households being successfully interviewed over the period from February to April 2010, a response rate of 88.6 percent. These households contained a total of 25,969 individuals of all ages, of which 21,826 were 6 and older and responded to the detailed individual questionnaire. The sample design was a two-stage stratified cluster sample. In the first stage, 480 primary sampling units (clusters) were selected according to the principle of probability proportional to size and twelve households were randomly selected from each cluster on the basis of household lists based on the 2004 population census and regularly updated by the Jordanian Department of Statistics since then.

In what follows, we offer a brief summary of the various chapters of the book. In chapter 1, Ragui Assaad examines changes in the structure and evolution of employment in Jordan over the past quarter-century. Using the detailed retrospective questions in the JLMPS 2010, Assaad reconstructs the employment trajectories of individuals who have ever been employed. Because this data can portray new flows into the labor market and then follow these new entrants several years into their careers, they are able to highlight changes in trends much more precisely than regular quarterly labor force survey data, which simply look at stocks of workers in different segments of the labor market at different points in time. Some of the main findings are that public sector employment is declining in importance in Jordan, albeit at a slower rate in the last decade than in previous decades. Private formal employment is growing rapidly, but is becoming more temporary in nature as employers attempt to achieve greater flexibility by providing definite duration contracts or no contracts at all, while still providing social insurance coverage. This increasing precariousness of employment in the formal private sector is growing especially rapidly for female workers. Non-wage employment, whether in the form of being an employer, self-employed, or an unpaid family worker, is generally in decline in Jordan, with some limited evidence that individuals move into it after a few years of experience in informal-wage employment.

There appears to be very little mobility in Jordan between informal and formal employment in Jordan. An individual who starts his or her working life in informal employment, whether as a wage or non-wage worker tends to remain in such employment for the rest of his/her working career. The Jordanian economy appears to be generating a large number of informal jobs, most of which are being populated by foreign workers.

In chapter 2, Nader Mryyan examines the evolution of the working-age population in Jordan in terms of age composition and educational attainment. He relates these trends to the pattern of labor force participation and unemployment in Jordan. Mryyan finds that although rates of female labor force participation in Jordan are quite low, female unemployment rates are very high, especially for young women. This suggests that as education increases more young women are seeking employment, but that the labor market is not providing them with jobs that are considered socially acceptable in a conservative Middle Eastern society.

In chapter 3, Mona Amer examines the school-to-work transition among youth (15–34) in Jordan. She pays particular attention to the post-secondary and university educated and to young women who suffer the most from high unemployment rates and thus from difficulty in entering the labor market. She uses data on employment histories to determine the trajectories of young people entering the labor market and their subsequent transitions. She seeks to understand what happens to young Jordanians after completing their studies, assessing the rate at which they become active, and how long they remain unemployed until they find their first job. If they do get work, she examines the kind of jobs they get. She then examines the most prevalent job sequences following the first job, depending on what the first job is. She finds that more educated men who stay in Jordan tend to start in formal jobs in both the public and private sectors and tend to stay in these jobs for an extended period. When they do change, it is usually to get another formal employment, with most of those who change going from a private formal job to a public one or from a temporary job to a permanent one. The less educated males have difficulty obtaining formal employment outside of government. She also finds that women in Jordan are either inactive, unemployed, or working in formal employment (public or private), meaning that informal employment is almost non-existent among Jordanian women, even for the less educated, whose participation rates are very low anyway. The behavior of women with a university degree is relatively similar to that of men. Their participation rate is very high and they find their first job as quickly as men. However, they are much more affected by unemployment than men.

In chapter 4, Assaad, Hendy, and Yassine delve deeper into the gender aspects of employment in the Jordanian labor market. They find that, not only is female labor force participation in Jordan very low, but it also appears to have been relatively stagnant over the past decade. This is a seemingly paradoxical finding given the rapid rise in female educational attainment in Jordan and the highly positive association between education and participation in economic activity. The only way to resolve such an apparent paradox is to have falling participation rates among educated women over time, which are counteracted by an improving educational composition to produce flat participation rates. The authors argue that this is in fact what is happening in Jordan and that the decline in participation among educated women is due to a deteriorating opportunity structure in the Jordanian labor market. With the curtailment of public sector hiring in Jordan since the mid-1980s, opportunities for educated women are becoming more scarce. The main contribution of the chapter is therefore to document these trends with recent data and show, through careful analysis, the way in which women's employment prospects are shaped by education and marriage, and the way in which these prospects have narrowed dramatically in recent years.

In chapter 5, Mona Said investigates the evolution and structure of real hourly wages and monthly earnings in Jordan over the past two decades. Crude wage differentials are first explored by examining the differences in average hourly wages and monthly earnings across important socio-economic groups (disaggregated by gender, occupations, industry, levels of education, and sectors of ownership). Next, selectivity corrected wage equation estimates are employed to calculate sector-based and gender-based wage differentials that correct for differences in worker characteristics. Results reveal that public sector pay advantages over the private sector still exist in Jordan in 2010 but only for women. Due to rapid real wage erosion during the financial crisis, the advantage of the public sector for men turned into a disadvantage by 2010. Gender-based wage gaps remained compressed by international standards in the private sector and are either non-existent or even indicate a small premium in the public sector for women. Finally, overall hourly wage dispersion is much higher in the private than in the public sector, and it is overwhelmingly due to 'within' as opposed to 'between' socio-economic group inequality. The results confirm the importance of correcting for sector selection when estimating pay differentials in public-sector-dominated economies.

In chapter 6, Jackline Wahba documents the characteristics of outward migration and describes both current Jordanian emigrants and return migrants. She then compares immigrant workers in Jordan to Jordanian natives. Although the JLMPS 2010 underestimates both the number of emigrants and immigrants, it is still very useful in describing the main patterns of Jordanian migration. The findings suggest that Jordan is exporting high-skilled workers but importing low-skilled labor. There is evidence that immigrant workers undercut Jordanian wages. However, immigrant workers are employed in low-skilled jobs in the informal sector with very little benefits or security. On the other hand, Jordanian emigrants are able to earn at least four times the Jordanian wage when abroad and remit substantial amounts, thereby increasing the domestic reservation wages, which might give rise to behaviors similar to those in economies dependent on oil rents.

In chapter 7, Rania Salem examines how the timing and patterns of marriage have evolved in Jordan in recent years. Using retrospective reports from ever-married respondents, she describes the postponement of first marriage to successively older ages for both men and women, and traces the decline in consanguinity and the rise in nuclear-family living arrangements over time. The author finds that husbands' age seniority has fluctuated over time, but that the education gap between husbands and wives has closed over successive marriage cohorts. She also describes how these trends differ between rural and urban residents, as well as between members of different regional and socio-economic groups in Jordan. Finally, she analyzes trends in matrimonial expenditures in Jordan, finding that, contrary to popular discourse, the costs of marriage have not increased in recent years. She describes variations over time in the components of marriage costs, and examines how these differ for various socio-demographic groups.

Finally in chapter 8, Ibrahim Al-Hawarin explores the phenomenon of early retirement among men in Jordan. He examines the demographic and economic characteristics of early pension receivers and whether they tend to return to the labor market after qualifying for their pensions. He finds that nearly 85% of the living retirees at the time of the survey had retired early. He also shows that around 45% of male early pension receivers return to the labor market and occupy mostly informal jobs (i.e. ones with no health insurance, no social security, comparatively lower wages, and no paid leaves). They tend to be concentrated in a limited number of occupations, notably sales workers, drivers, and protective services workers. Economically active early pension receivers, however, appear to suffer from high unemployment rates, particularly those retiring from the private sector. The study also finds that having more education and larger family size tend to increase the propensity that early pension receivers will return to the labor market. A number of reforms of the social insurance system were carried out just at the time of the survey, partly to curb the early retirement phenomenon. An assessment of the impact of these reforms will have to await the results of the next wave of the JLMPS.

Although we have learned a great deal about the Jordanian labor market already from the first wave of the JLMPS, its true value will be revealed when a large number of researchers start making use of the public use microdata from the survey to conduct in-depth studies of various aspects of the Jordanian labor market. Even more value-added will be possible from this data when the second and subsequent waves of the panel are carried out in future years. ERF is committed to facilitating the continued collection of these data and to making the data available to the research community to support high-quality labor market research.

Ragui Assaad
December 2013

# Acknowledgements

A large number of individuals and organizations contributed to the successful completion of this book and the household survey on which it is based. The Economic Research Forum wishes to express its deep gratitude to its organizational partners in this endeavor: the Department of the Statistics (DoS) of the Hashemite Kingdom of Jordan and in particular Dr Haider Fraihat, its former director general, and Mr Basim Shanak, and Mr Mohamed Assaf, and the National Center for Human Resource Development (NCHRD) and in particular Dr Munther Masri, its former director. We are extremely grateful for the valuable contribution of Dr Nader Mryyan, director of the Al-Manar project at NCHRD, and Dr Mamdouh Al-Salamat for their role in shepherding the JLMPS 2011 survey along at every stage of its implementation. Our heartfelt thanks also go to the large number of enumerators, reviewers, supervisors, data entry operators, programmers, and managers at DoS who contributed to the success of the research.

ERF would also like to thank its own staff members who have contributed to the success of the survey and to the publication of this book. We wish to thank Mr Mohamed Yousri, finance and administration manager, Ms Yasmine Fahim, senior programs officer, Ms Mirette F. Mabrouk, director of communications, and Ms Namees Nabil, senior communications officer. ERF would also like to thank Ms Chaimaa Yassine, research assistant, for her role in preparing the data for analysis and her assistance in analyzing the data from the survey. The findings, interpretations, and conclusions expressed in this publication are entirely those of the author(s) and should not be attributed to the Economic Research Forum, members of its Board of Trustees, or its donors.

# Contents

# List of Figures

# List of Tables

# List of Contributors

**Mona Amer**, Cairo University

**Ragui Assaad**, University of Minnesota

**Ibrahim Al Hawarin**, Al Hussein Bin Talal University

**Rana Hendy**, Economic Research Forum

**Nader Mryyan**, Williams-Palmer Consulting Inc.

**Mona Said**, The American University in Cairo

**Rania Salem**, University of Toronto

**Jackline Wahba**, University of Southampton

**Chaimaa Yassine**, University of Paris

# 1

# The Structure and Evolution of Employment in Jordan

*Ragui Assaad*

## 1.1 Introduction

Despite the fact that Jordan has experienced significant economic growth in the past decade, it continues to suffer from persistently high unemployment, especially among educated youth. Despite an average annual growth rate of 6% from 1999 to 2009, the unemployment rate has hovered somewhere between 13% and 16% during this period. Unemployment is growing particularly rapidly among educated workers, whose numbers are also growing rapidly due to the rapid expansion of education in Jordan. This pattern of growth with persistently high unemployment is a long-term feature of the Jordanian economy (The World Bank 2007) but was exacerbated by the recent slowdown of growth due to the world financial crisis. GDP growth rates in 2009 decelerated markedly to just over 2% per annum after having reached nearly 8.5% in 2007. This slowdown appears to have disproportionately affected educated workers, who besides being at greater risk of unemployment are increasingly finding themselves in either temporary formal employment or in informal employment. The employment challenges faced by these increasingly educated new entrants co-exist with an economy that is creating a large number of low-quality informal jobs in construction and services that are mostly being filled by a growing legion of foreign workers.[1]

In this chapter, we use a new and original data set—the Jordan Labor Market Panel Survey of 2010 (JLMPS 2010)—to study changes in the structure and evolution of employment in Jordan over the past quarter-century.

---

[1] See Ministry of Labor and Ministry of Planning and International Cooperation (2012) for further discussion of these challenges.

The JLMPS 2010 offers significant advantages over the regular Employment and Unemployment Survey (EUS) conducted quarterly by the Department of Statistics of the Hashemite Kingdom of Jordan (DoS, various years). Although it is only the first wave of what is to be a longitudinal survey, it contains a number of retrospective questions that allow us to reconstruct entire employment trajectories, rather than to simply get a snapshot of a single point in time. The main advantage of this approach is that it allows for the examination of flows into various segments of the labor market and not simply stocks over time. Since flows are much more sensitive to changes than stocks, it is a powerful tool to study developing trends in the labor market.

The JLMPS 2010 data also offers significant advantages over the EUS in its ability to identify informal employment in its various guises, including wage and salary employment without contracts or social insurance and self-employment and unpaid family employment. It also offers a more detailed view of employment conditions including paid and unpaid leaves, the presence of health insurance, hours of work, and the type and size of economic unit in which the worker is employed.

Since JLMPS 2010 has the same sampling strategy as the EUS, it focuses exclusively on the population residing in regular households rather than in collective residential units. This makes it as likely as the EUS to under-sample the foreign worker population in Jordan. This version of the data makes no attempt to try to correct for this potential under-representation of foreign workers by using Ministry of Labor information on foreign worker licenses, and so on. The accurate estimation of the role of foreign workers in the Jordanian labor market therefore remains a challenge, although we can get some sense of what types of jobs they are likely to be concentrated in.

Some of the main findings of the JLMPS 2010 are that the formal private sector in Jordan is taking over from government as the main engine of employment growth. The share of formal private employment in the employment of new entrants to the Jordanian labor market has more than tripled from 10–12% in the mid-1980s to 36–38% in 2010. Although growing rapidly, private formal employment is becoming more temporary in nature, as employers attempt to achieve greater flexibility by providing definite duration contracts or no contracts at all. Over time, however, more than half the workers employed on temporary or no contracts manage to obtain permanent contracts. There appears to be very limited mobility between the informal and formal segments of the labor market, although many workers hired in formal firms are first hired informally for a period of time. After declining significantly since the late 1980s, government employment is now experiencing a small recovery but, unlike earlier times, many of the workers being hired by government are now coming with some experience in the private sector. This is a significant change from the 1980s, when the opposite was true, with workers getting their first job in government and then, in some cases, moving to the private sector later. Self-employment has been a low but stable part of total employment in Jordan, and is mostly accessed only after a period of time as either an informal private-wage worker or an unpaid family worker.

## 1.2 GDP Growth, Employment, and Unemployment in Jordan in the New Millennium

### 1.2.1 GDP Growth, Employment Growth, and Unemployment in Jordan

As shown in Figure 1.1, GDP growth in Jordan accelerated significantly in the second half of the past decade, before slowing significantly in 2008 and 2009 on the heels of the world financial crisis. GDP growth rates went from a healthy 4–6% in 2000–2003 to an impressive 8–8.5% per annum from 2004 to 2007. Despite this tremendous acceleration in GDP growth, unemployment rates, which were over 14% in the early part of the decade, fell only slightly to over 12%, increased again to over 14% in 2005, and then fell slowly to just over 12% at the end of the decade. This level of responsiveness of the unemployment rate to aggregate growth appears particularly weak given the very healthy growth rates achieved from 2004 to 2007.

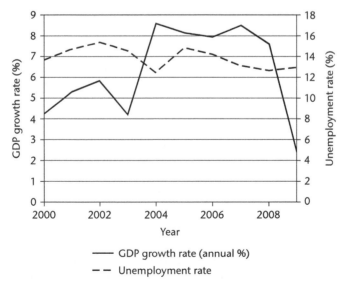

**Figure 1.1.** Jordan: GDP growth rate and unemployment rate, 2000–2009
*Source*: Department of Statistics (DoS), Hashemite Kingdom of Jordan.

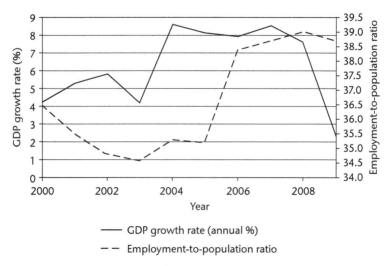

**Figure 1.2.** GDP growth rate and employment-to-population ratio over time, 2000–2010

*Source*: Department of Statistics (DoS), Hashemite Kingdom of Jordan.

While the unemployment rate was particularly sluggish in its response to economic growth, the employment-to-population ratio—which indicates how employment is growing—is more responsive, but with a significant lag. While the acceleration in growth occurred between 2003 and 2004 as shown in Figure 1.2, the employment-to-population ratio rose from around 35% to around 38.5% two years later. The 2009 slowdown in growth was not yet reflected much in the employment-to-population ratio, again because of this lagged response.

The contrasting trend in the unemployment rate and the employment-to-population ratio suggests that the Jordanian labor market seems to draw on a source of labor supply that is not coming from the pool of unemployed Jordanians. This could well be foreign workers—who are not captured very well by either the EUS or the JLMPS—or individuals who are outside the labor force and who enter in periods of high labor demand. Resolving this puzzle is one of the principle objectives of this chapter. The hypothesis that I would like to test is that the composition of the workforce is increasingly shifting towards higher education graduates who are looking for a specific kind of job, namely professional or white-collar jobs, and who are willing to remain unemployed for a time until they find such jobs. On the other hand, the economy seems to be generating lower-quality jobs that do not appeal to these graduates and that are more likely to go to foreign migrants.

Before moving to an analysis of the changing composition of the workforce and its connection to unemployment in Jordan, I examine more carefully the data on net employment growth in Jordan in recent years and the extent to which employment growth appears to be associated with the influx of foreign workers. There are three sources of data that allow us to estimate net employment growth on an economy-wide basis in Jordan, namely the EUS, the Job Creation Survey (JCS), and recently the JLMPS 2010. The EUS is the official source of data on employment and unemployment in Jordan and is conducted quarterly on a sample of about 12,000 households per quarter. The JCS is a relatively new household survey, carried out for the first time in 2007 and is carried out semi-annually on a sample of 40,000 households per round. It enquires about any new jobs, job changes, or job endings that the household experienced during the survey year. While the JLMPS 2010 is not designed to measure employment growth, we can get an estimate of net job creation by estimating the number of entries and exits into the labor market every year from the retrospective data. Figures more than a few years old should be interpreted with care, however, since some of those who exited could have died or migrated out of the country, and, therefore, disappeared from the survey sample. This could be particularly true of foreign workers in Jordan, who tend to leave the country when their jobs end. JLMPS also ignores spells of employment or non-employment that last for less than six months.

Figure 1.3 shows the net change in employment every year (relative to the year before) in both absolute numbers and as a proportion of total employment, as estimated by the three sources. While the figures fluctuate a lot from year to year and from one source to the other, we can still use them to draw some general conclusions. With the exception of 2007, when the EUS produced an unrealistically high figure, and 2009 where JLMPS produced a low figure, the estimates from the EUS and the JLMPS tend to agree with each other, suggesting a net job growth of 35,000 to 45,000 jobs per year from 2005 to 2009.[2] The estimates from JCS appear to be consistently on the high side, providing an estimate of job growth of about 70,000 jobs per year in 2007 and 2008, and 76,000 in 2009. With the exception of 2007, the EUS estimates an employment growth rate of between 3.0% and 4.1% (see Table 1.1). JLMPS 2010 estimates similar rates of growth of between 3.0% and 4.0% between

---

[2] The very high job growth estimate produced by the EUS between 2006 and 2007 appears to be the result of a change in the EUS sample, which was updated in that year using the results of the 2004 population census. This new sample seems to have a much larger proportion of Egyptians than before. Egyptians tend to have much higher employment rates than Jordanians since they are mostly single adult males coming to Jordan for work. The number of Egyptians showing up in the EUS sample more than doubles from the last quarter of 2006 to the second quarter of 2008. This is not likely to be due to a doubling of the number of Egyptians in the country. Data on work permits from the Ministry of Labor shows that the number of Egyptians on work permits in Jordan only increased by 10% from 2006 to 2007.

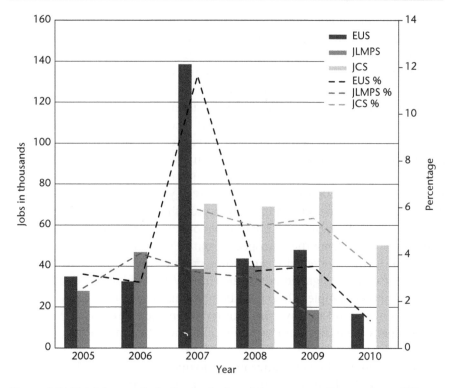

**Figure 1.3.** Net job growth in the Jordanian economy according to three different sources in thousands of net jobs per year (left axis) and as a percentage of employment (right axis)

*Note*: Figure from JCS for 2010 is based on the first half and was doubled to obtain an annual rate.

*Sources*: (i) EUS (various years); (ii) JCS (various years); (iii) JLMPS (2010).

**Table 1.1.** Employment growth in Jordan, 2005–2010

|  | All | | | Jordanians only | | |
|---|---|---|---|---|---|---|
|  | Employment | Emp. growth from prev. year | | Employment | Emp. growth from prev. year | |
|  | '000s | '000s | % | '000s | '000s | % |
| 2005 | 1158.5 | | | 1024.7 | | |
| 2006 | 1190.9 | 32.4 | 2.8 | 1055.8 | 31.2 | 3.0 |
| 2007 | 1329.4 | 138.5 | 11.6 | 1140.4 | 84.6 | 8.0 |
| 2008 | 1373.1 | 43.7 | 3.3 | 1172.7 | 32.3 | 2.8 |
| 2009 | 1421.0 | 47.9 | 3.5 | 1220.5 | 47.8 | 4.1 |
| 2010 | 1437.6 | 16.6 | 1.2 | 1240.0 | 19.5 | 1.6 |

*Source*: EUS (various years).

2006 and 2008. In contrast, the rates of growth suggested by the JCS ranged from 5.2% to 5.9% from 2007 to 2009.

The source of the discrepancy in the estimation of employment growth between the EUS and the JLMPS on the one side and the JCS on the other is not entirely apparent. All three surveys are household surveys and will therefore not be representative of the large number of foreign workers that do not live in traditional households. In any case, it is unlikely that job growth among foreign workers accounts for the difference, since, according to the 2009 JCS survey, 90% of the 69,000 net jobs created that year went to Jordanians.

### 1.2.2 The Changing Composition of the Workforce and Unemployment in Jordan

Now we move to a discussion of changes in the composition of the Jordanian labor force towards more educated groups, whose preference for formal and public-sector jobs would lead them to search longer and therefore have higher unemployment rates. This can be easily ascertained from an examination of the composition of the working age and employed populations by educational attainment shown later.[3]

As shown in Figure 1.4a, the proportion of illiterates and those who can only read and write in the working-age population has declined from about 18% to 12% over the decade. At the same time, the proportion of those with basic education has been stable at about 50% and the proportions of those with secondary and post-secondary education have either been rising slowly or stable. In contrast, university graduates are the one group whose proportion has increased rapidly from about 8% to 13% of the working-age population in only ten years.

Since participation in employment is higher among the educated, their proportion among the employed is larger than in the working-age population, but the same rising trend is apparent. While the proportion of all education groups is either declining or stable, as shown in Figure 1.4a, that of university graduates has increased from about 16% of the employed to just under a quarter (Figure 1.4b). This rapid increase in the stock of educated workers among the employed suggests that their proportion in the flow of incoming workers into the labor market is not only high, but increasing rapidly. We can ascertain this directly from the flow information available in the JLMPS 2010. Figure 1.5 shows the distribution of new entrants to the labor market by educational attainment and year of entry.

---

[3] See also Assaad and Amer (2008) for a more detailed analysis of the composition of the Jordanian workforce based on EUS data.

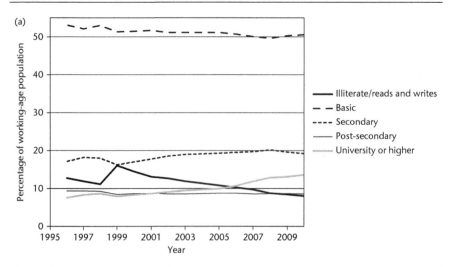

**Figure 1.4a.** Distribution of the working-age population (15–64) by educational attainment, 2000–2010

*Source*: EUS (various years).

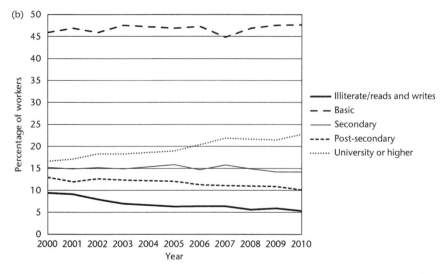

**Figure 1.4b.** Distribution of the employed population (15–64) by educational attainment, 2000–2010

*Source*: EUS (various years).

As shown in Figure 1.5, the composition of new entrants in Jordan has changed dramatically since the 1960s. In the 1960s, there was a precipitous decline in the proportion of illiterates and a rapid increase in the share of those with basic and secondary education. This rapid progress was stalled somewhat in the 1970s, but the decline in illiterates has resumed rapidly

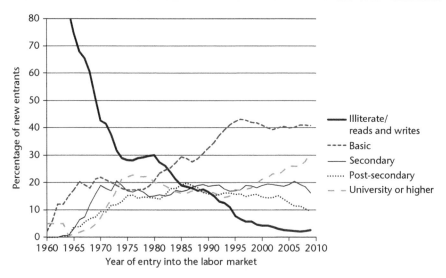

**Figure 1.5.** Distribution of new entrants by educational attainment and year of entry into the labor market, ages 15–64, Jordan
*Source*: JLMPS (2010).

since the 1980s so that now fewer than 5% of new entrants are illiterate. In the 1980s and early 1990s, the improvement in education essentially translated into the rapid growth of the share of those with basic education. However, since the mid-1990s, that share stabilized and the share of those with university degrees took off. The share of those with university degrees rose from 15% of new entrants to over 30% in less than two decades.

The rapid increase in the share of university graduates among new entrants is reflected in the share of university graduates among the unemployed, who tend to be young new entrants, and hence a better reflection of the flow into the labor market than the stock of workers. As shown in Figure 1.6, the share of those with university degrees and higher among the unemployed rose from about 12% in 2000 to over 30% in 2010.

The more rapid rise in the share of university graduates among the unemployed than among the employed translates directly into rising unemployment rates for these graduates. Figure 1.7 shows that, although the unemployment rates of all the educational groups below university level have fallen during this period, those of university graduates have risen sharply in 2000–2003 and then stabilized thereafter. However, as the composition of the workforce shifted in their direction, their higher unemployment rates in the latter period kept the overall unemployment rate high.

The inability of the Jordanian economy to absorb the growing number of university graduates is linked to the shifts that were occurring in the

9

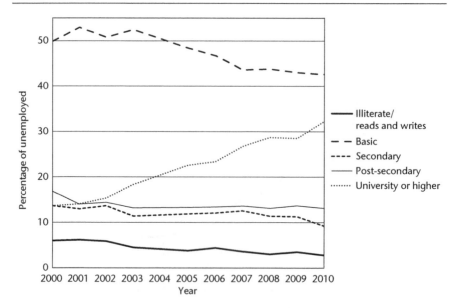

**Figure 1.6.** Distribution of the unemployed (15–64) by educational attainment, 2000–2010

*Source*: EUS (various years).

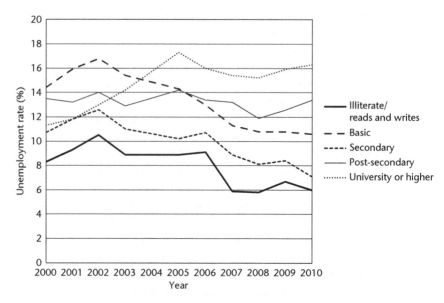

**Figure 1.7.** Broad unemployment rate (15–64) by educational attainment, 2000–2010

*Source*: EUS (various years).

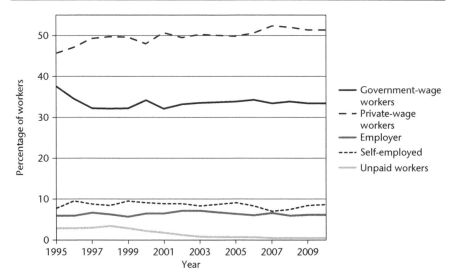

**Figure 1.8.** Distribution of employment (15–64) by type, 1995–2010
*Source*: EUS (various years).

structure of employment away from the public sector and in favor of more private-sector employment. This is an issue we will explore in great detail later in this chapter. For now, we can ascertain this fact from EUS data, which tracks the stock of workers over time by sector. As shown in Figure 1.8, the share of the government in total employment fell in the mid-1990s from 38% to about 32% and then remained at that level thereafter. Even with a fixed proportion of overall government employment and a growing share of educated workers, the probability that a given educated worker will get a government job declines significantly.

## 1.3 The Dynamics of the Jordanian Labor Market as Ascertained by JLMPS 2010 Data

In this section, we examine trends in the Jordanian labor market by taking advantage of the complete employment trajectories that JLMPS 2010 data make available, as well as the more detailed characterization of jobs that is possible from this data. We take advantage of the fact that we have similar data from the Egypt Labor Market Panel Survey of 2006 (ELMPS 06) to make comparisons with labor market trends in Egypt. Egypt went through a similar liberalization process as Jordan, but with different timing and from different starting points.

We note from the outset that the JLMPS 2010 and the EUS produce very similar results for the variables they measure in common. We show in Appendix A, a few charts comparing JLMPS 2010 results with those of the first two quarterly rounds of 2010 for the EUS, which were carried out at roughly the same time.

In this analysis, we distinguish between five types of employment, namely: (i) government employment; (ii) formal private-wage work, which includes wage and salary employment with either a legal employment contract or social insurance coverage in either the private sector or in state-owned enterprises; (iii) informal private-wage work, which includes wage and salary work in the private sector with neither a contract nor social insurance coverage; (iv) employers and self-employed individuals in the private sector; and finally (v) unpaid family workers in the private sector. In more detailed analyses, we further break down formal private-wage work into "permanent" and "temporary". Permanent formal- wage work includes indefinite duration contracts with social insurance coverage, whereas temporary formal-wage work includes definite duration contracts, as well as work with social insurance coverage but no contract. The other category includes the more precarious and temporary jobs in the private sector that nevertheless offer social insurance coverage. Figure 1.9 shows the breakdown of employment in Jordan in 2010 according to these categories and by sex.

As previously ascertained from EUS data, one-third of total employment in Jordan is in the government, just over one-fifth is in formal private-wage

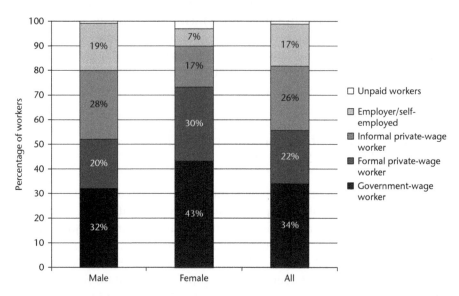

**Figure 1.9.** Distribution of employment (15–64) by type of employment and sex, 2010
*Source*: JLMPS (2010).

work, and over one-quarter is in informal private-wage work, despite significant efforts in recent years to increase the coverage of the social insurance system. Under one-fifth of employment is in own-account work as employers and self-employed workers, and a tiny fraction is in unpaid family work.

As shown in Figure 1.9, female workers in Jordan are more likely to be working for the government and more likely to be in formal-wage work than males. They are significantly less likely to be employers and self-employed workers. A further breakdown of formal employment shows that nearly all government workers (97%) have permanent contracts, whereas only 70% of formal private-sector-wage workers are permanent. Almost all employers/self-employed workers (97%) are informal in the sense that they do not have social insurance coverage, as are all unpaid family workers.

In what follows, I focus on flows into the labor market by examining the job status of new entrants by year of entry into the labor market. To smooth over year-to-year fluctuations and sampling error, I fit a trend line through the data using a six-year moving average. Later we examine the job status five and ten years after entry to distinguish between permanent changes over time versus changes in the patterns of insertion into the labor market. The advantage of this analysis is that it distinguishes changes in labor market structure that affect different cohorts of new entrants from changes that occur over workers' life-cycles as they progress in their careers.

Figure 1.10 shows the distribution of employment by type of job for the first job obtained by new entrants by year of entry from the 1960s to the 2000s for both Jordan and Egypt. The figure shows that from 1960 to the mid-1970s in Jordan, there was a continuous rising trend in the share of government employment among new entrants, with the share going from 5% in 1960 to nearly 50% in the mid-1970s. The share of government in first jobs remained high until 1990, after which it declined sharply until 2000, where it reached 25%—half of its value at the peak. There appears to be a recovery in the role of government in employing new entrants in the past decade, with the share growing to about one-third by 2010. The growing share of government in the hiring of new entrants in Jordan mirrors the experience in Egypt from the 1960s to the late 1970s. However, the reversal occurred a decade earlier in Egypt and has persisted throughout the 2000s.

The growth of government employment in the 1960s and 1970s in Jordan came at the expense of informal employment, whether in the form of informal wage employment or self-employment or unpaid family labor. Formal private-sector work was very limited and growing rather slowly until the late 1980s. However, it is very clear that when the role of government began to decline in Jordan in the mid-1980s, it was the formal private sector that took over the mantle of employment creation. The growth of its share from 10% to

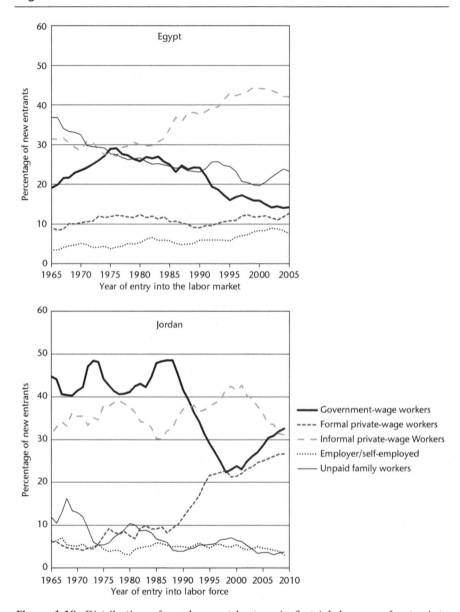

**Figure 1.10.** Distribution of employment by type in first job by year of entry into labor market, 1960–2010 (five-year moving average)

*Source*: JLMPS (2010) and ELMPS (2006).

30% of new jobs in one decade almost completely makes up for the declining share of government. Although informal private-wage work grew at first in response to the decline of government in the 1980s, its growth stabilized as that of formal private employment took off.

This picture offers a very clear contrast with the situation in Egypt, where nearly all the declining share of government was made up by the growth of informal-wage employment. Formal-wage employment in Egypt grew much more slowly than in Jordan, going from about 5% of employment in the mid-1970s when the share of government began to decline to just over 10% by 2005.

Another important contrast between Jordan and Egypt is in the growth of entrepreneurship among new entrants, as measured by the share of self-employment (and employers) in the employment of new entrants. Although this share declined in the 1960s in Jordan and remained constant at about 5% since then, it has been increasing steadily in Egypt from less than 5% in 1970 to nearly 10% in 2005.

Further insights can be gained on the changing structure of the labor market over time, by limiting our analysis to the labor market experience of educated new entrants. By focusing only on those with secondary education and above, we can see that the declining role of government in employment looms much larger in both Jordan and Egypt. As shown in Figure 1.11, over a little more than a decade from the mid-1980s to the mid-1990s in Jordan, the share of government employment among educated new entrants was halved from 60% to 30% and then remained at roughly that level throughout the 2000s. The decline in Egypt began earlier, was more gradual, but ended up being larger in magnitude, with government providing from over 70% of first jobs for educated new entrants in the 1960s to just 20% of first jobs in the 2000s. Again, the contrasting roles of formal and informal private-wage employment in Jordan and Egypt is quite clear, with the former taking up almost the entire slack in Jordan and the latter doing so in Egypt.

In concluding this discussion of the changing structure of the labor market facing new entrants, we can ascertain that Jordan was able to avoid the informalization of employment that occurred in Egypt as a result of restructuring the economy away from the public sector. As we will see below, Jordan managed to do so by making formal private employment more flexible through the use of temporary contracts, while maintaining social insurance coverage.

We now move to a deeper look that follows individuals through time as they progress through the labor market to see what can be learned about the changing structure of employment five and ten years into workers' careers for different cohorts of workers. Again, the share of each employment type in total employment at the time of entry is viewed by year of entry, but now we add the share five and ten years into the labor market. To make the figures

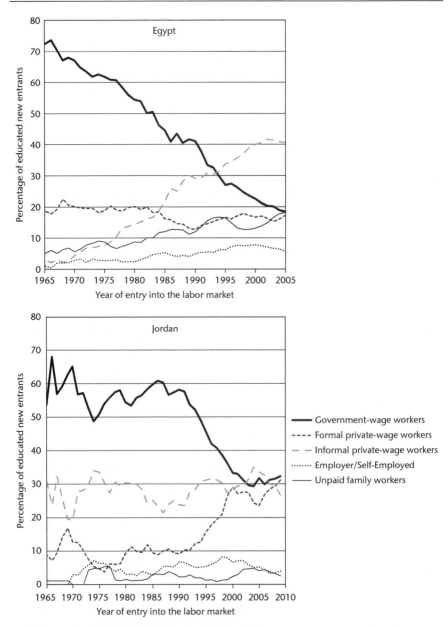

**Figure 1.11.** Distribution of employment by type in first job by year of entry into labor market for new entrants with secondary education and above, 1960–2010 (five-year moving average)

*Source*: JLMPS (2010) and ELMPS (2006).

comparable, we limit the analysis to workers who stay in the labor market for at least ten years, so as to abstract away from compositional changes due to exits from employment altogether.

We start by looking in Figures 1.12 and 1.13 at the share of the two formal sectors of employment, namely government and formal private-wage employment. From other analysis of JLMPS 2010 data, we know that there is virtually no mobility between informal and formal employment once a person has entered one of these tracks (Amer, 2014), so it is useful to examine mobility within the formal segment and within the informal segment.[4] We can see from the two figures that up to 1983 in Jordan, there was hardly any further movement once people got a first job in either of these two sectors. From 1983 to about 1990, it appears that some people who got first jobs in the government, later moved to formal private-wage employment. The opposite appears to be true after the mid-1990s, with a significant proportion of workers first starting their careers in formal private employment and then moving to government. This pattern corresponds to the time period in which the government's share of first jobs was recovering after the sharp decline it experienced from the mid-1980s to the mid-1990s. When taking into consideration these instances of delayed entry, the decline in government hiring from 1990 to 1998 is significantly attenuated, and the recovery since 1998 appears to be much stronger than by simply looking at new entrants.

The picture in Egypt is somewhat different. Until 1977 or so when the share of government was rising, most workers seemed to be starting their careers in government employment. After that, a significant proportion appeared to be starting elsewhere and then moving into government, although the share of government was declining over time, even for workers with ten years of experience. Unlike Jordan, these workers moving into government jobs did not appear to be coming from formal private-wage employment, but from informal wage employment. In the Egyptian case, informal workers also seem to have a small chance of moving into the formal private sector after five to ten years of experience. The contrast between the growth of the formal private sector in Jordan and Egypt continues to look very striking.

To understand how Jordan was able to successfully substitute formal private-sector employment for government employment and avoid the sort of informalization that occurred in Egypt, we need to delve deeper into the form that formal private employment took in Jordan. Here we make a distinction between temporary and permanent formal-wage employment. As mentioned earlier, temporary employment is either with a definite-duration contract or no

---

[4] In this analysis, we ignore mobility from informal to formal employment in the same job as it is typical of formal employers to test out workers by hiring them informally for some time and then registering them on the social insurance rolls. In this analysis, we treat these workers as formal from the start.

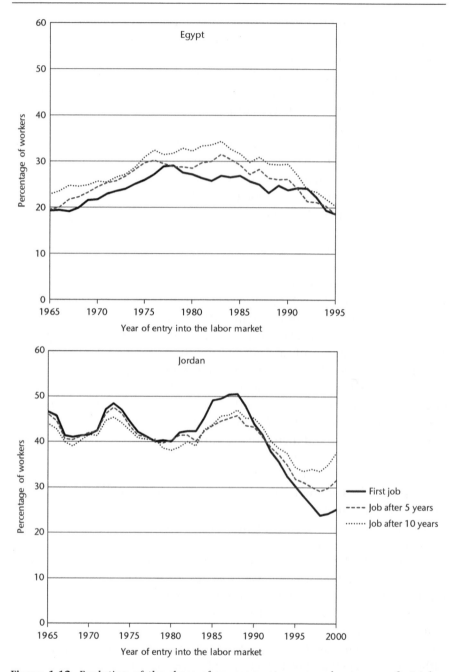

**Figure 1.12.** Evolution of the share of government-wage workers among first jobs, jobs after five years, and jobs after ten years (five-year moving average)
*Source*: JLMPS (2010) and ELMPS (2006).

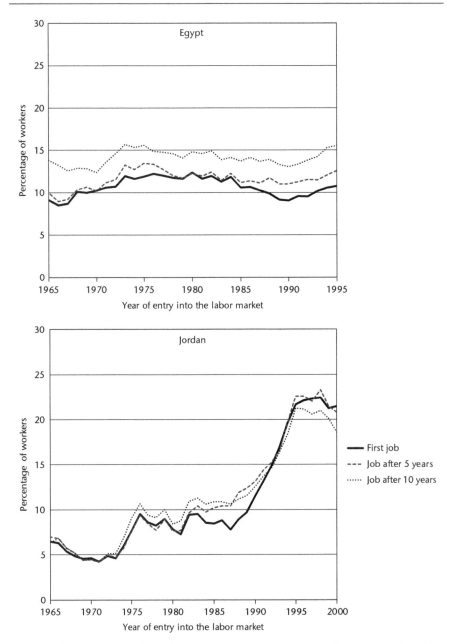

**Figure 1.13.** Evolution of the share of formal private-wage workers among first jobs, jobs after five years, and jobs after ten years (five-year moving average)
*Source*: JLMPS (2010) and ELMPS (2006).

contract, and permanent employment is with an indefinite-duration contract. Both the temporary- and permanent-wage employment categories considered here are covered by social insurance and hence are formal. Unfortunately, similar data on definite- and indefinite-duration contracts is not available for Egypt, preventing us from undertaking the Jordan–Egypt comparison.

As shown in Figure 1.14, it is temporary-wage employment that appears to be growing dramatically among new entrants in the post-1985 period, when formal private-wage employment was growing rapidly. Permanent employment grew as well among new entrants from 1985 to 1995 but more slowly, and its growth reversed in the 1995–2000 period. However, we can also see from Figure 1.14 that the share of temporary-wage employment falls significantly once workers have been in the labor market for five years and even further after ten years, and that the gap between new entrants and more experienced workers is growing over time. The opposite is true for the permanent employment category, which sees its share growing as workers spend more time in the labor market. These patterns strongly suggest that workers on temporary (or no) contracts eventually acquire permanent contracts as they gain experience. Some of these temporary workers do so within the formal private sector and some move to government, as we have seen. Again, it should be kept in mind that this analysis does not include temporary workers who withdraw from the labor force altogether, such as young women who may withdraw at marriage, since we are only considering workers who have been in the labor market for at least ten years. These results strongly suggest that the ability to hire workers on temporary contracts has allowed Jordanian private firms to flexibly grow their employment without resorting to informalization and that, eventually, most of these workers manage to obtain permanent formal employment. One point of concern however, is that the growth of permanent, formal private-sector jobs in Jordan has stagnated in recent years, even for those who have been in the labor market for ten years. This is probably due to both the recent resurgence in government employment and the increasing reliance of the private sector on temporary contracts.

Despite the rapid growth of formal private employment in Jordan, the second largest category of employment in Jordan (and Egypt) after government is informal private-wage employment; a category to which we now turn our attention. As shown in Figure 1.15, there is a tendency for workers to move out of this category a few years after entry. While the share of the category among new entrants has been rising from 1985 to about 1998, the increase is much smaller among workers who have been in the labor market for five and ten years. There is, however, no evidence in the Jordanian case that these workers have been formalizing their employment over time. In fact, the main destination of those who leave this state appears to be self-employment/ employer, as shown in Figure 1.16, a category that also receives workers from

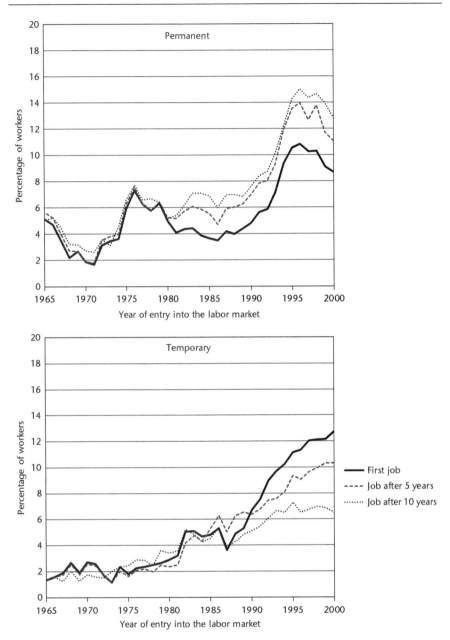

**Figure 1.14.** Evolution of the share of temporary and permanent formal private-wage workers among first jobs, jobs after five years, and jobs after ten years (five-year moving average)

*Source*: JLMPS (2010) and ELMPS (2006).

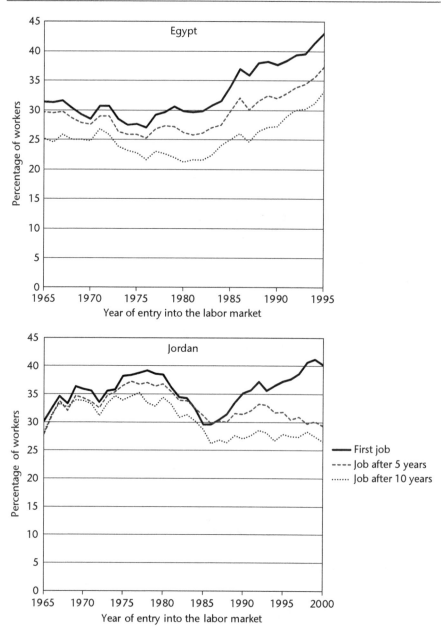

**Figure 1.15.** Evolution of the share of informal private-wage workers among first jobs, jobs after five years, and jobs after ten years (five-year moving average)
*Source*: JLMPS (2010) and ELMPS (2006).

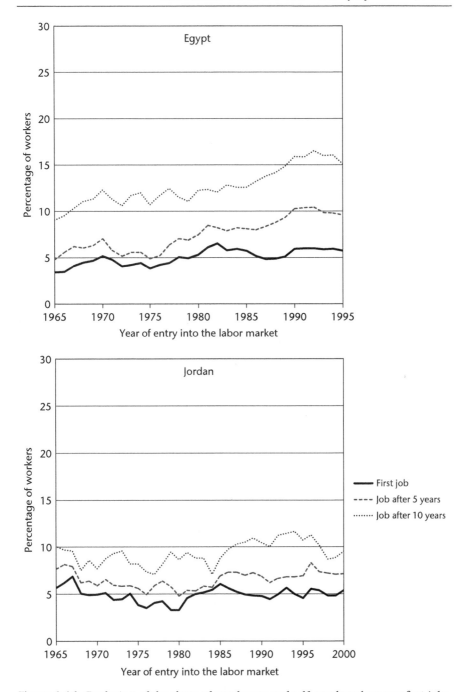

**Figure 1.16.** Evolution of the share of employers and self-employed among first jobs, jobs after five years, and jobs after ten years (five-year moving average)
*Source*: JLMPS (2010) and ELMPS (2006).

those in unpaid family work (Figure 1.17). Of the 7 to 8 percentage points of employment that appear to move into the employer/self-employed category in Jordan after ten years of experience, approximately 4–5 percentage points appear to come from informal wage work and 2–3 percentage points appear to come from unpaid family labor. In contrast, in Egypt, most of the increase in the size of the employer/self-employed category after ten years of experience appears to match exactly those who leave the unpaid family work category within ten years of starting to work. The relatively slow growth, or even stagnation, of these mostly informal categories over time also contrasts with their more rapid growth in Egypt.

## 1.4 Characteristics of Private-Wage Employment in Jordan

We focus more closely in this section on private-wage employment, including both its formal and informal subcomponents, as it is the segment of the labor market that is likely to be most dynamic in the coming period. We begin by looking at its composition by firm size and then examine the characteristics of employment and workers for different size categories. One of the issues we attempt to address is the composition of the private-sector work force by nationality, given the tendency of many private employers in Jordan to prefer foreign workers. While we acknowledge that, like the EUS, the JLMPS underestimates the number of foreign workers in the Jordanian economy, it can still provide an indication of the kind of jobs in which they are concentrated.

### 1.4.1 The Size Distribution of Firms and the Type of Employment by Firm Size

As shown in Figure 1.18, nearly one-third of private-wage employment is in establishments of fewer than five workers and just under one-half in enterprises of fewer than ten workers. If we include non-wage workers, the proportion of workers in establishments of fewer than ten workers rises to 57%. This compares to 69% in the case of Egypt. Enterprises of more than 100 workers employ about one-quarter of total private-wage employment, leaving about 30% in small and medium enterprises of 10 to 99 workers.

Figure 1.19 shows that workers in enterprises of fewer than five workers are almost entirely informal (92%). This is partly due to the fact that Jordan's current social insurance law exempts enterprises of fewer than five workers from social insurance coverage. The share of informal workers then drops steadily from 68% in the 5–9 category to 10% in the 100+ category.

Within formal-wage work, the proportion of permanent workers hovers between 60% and 65% for the intermediate size categories (5–9 to 50–99),

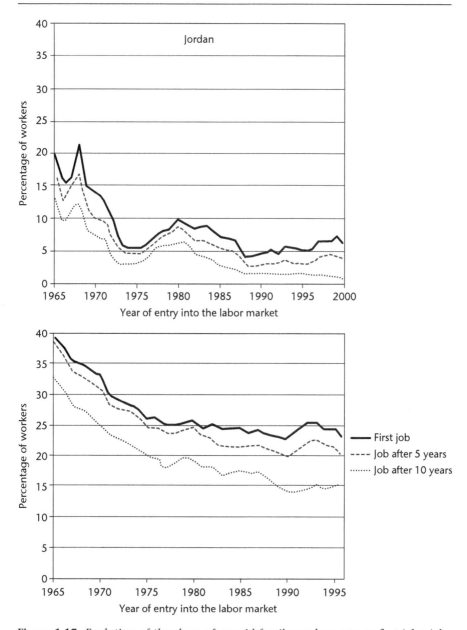

**Figure 1.17.** Evolution of the share of unpaid family workers among first jobs, jobs after five years, and jobs after ten years (five-year moving average)
*Source*: JLMPS (2010) and ELMPS (2006).

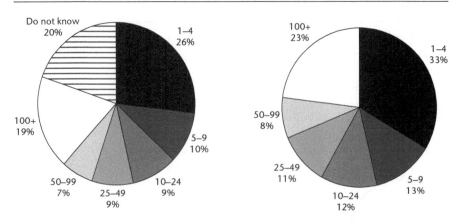

**Figure 1.18.** Distribution of private-wage employment by establishment size, 2010
*Source*: JLMPS (2010).

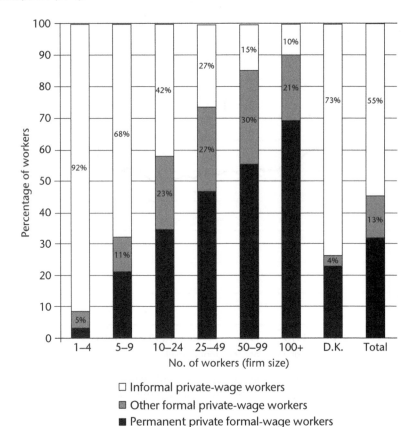

☐ Informal private-wage workers
▨ Other formal private-wage workers
■ Permanent private formal-wage workers

**Figure 1.19.** Employment structure in private-wage employment by firm size, 2010
*Note:* D.K. = don't know.
*Source*: JLMPS (2010).

but increases to 77% for the 100+ category (Figure 1.19). This suggests that while the largest firms can provide the most stable and protected forms of employment, they still like to maintain a margin of flexibility by either hiring workers informally (10% of their employment) or using temporary contractual forms (21%). Overall, only 45% of private sector-wage workers in Jordan are formal, and only 31% have permanent formal contractual arrangements.

The occupational structure also varies significantly by firm size. As shown in Figure 1.20, small firms hire very few professionals and managers. Professionals become significant only in firms of ten workers and above. This highlights the growing conundrum in the Jordanian labor market, which

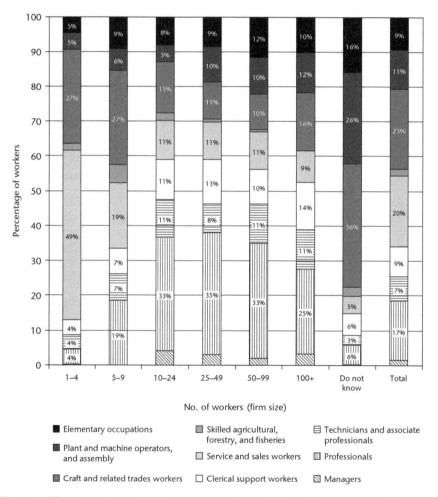

**Figure 1.20.** Proportions of different occupations within private-wage employment by firm size, 2010

*Source*: JLMPS (2010).

is the fact that the educational system is producing increasing numbers of university graduates, but the structure of labor demand in the private sector is still highly skewed towards semi-skilled and unskilled occupations. These occupations tend to be, for the most part, below the professional expectations of Jordanian university graduates.

### 1.4.2 Non-Wage Benefits in Private-Wage Work

Formal employment in Jordan is associated with a number of non-wage benefits that are likely to make it attractive to educated workers. Our definition of formal employment is based on the presence of social insurance coverage, but a question still remains whether it comes with other non-wage benefits, such as various types of paid leaves or medical insurance. We also distinguished between permanent formal work and other formal work, based on the availability of an indefinite duration contract. We maintain this distinction in the following analysis. As shown in Figure 1.21, most permanent

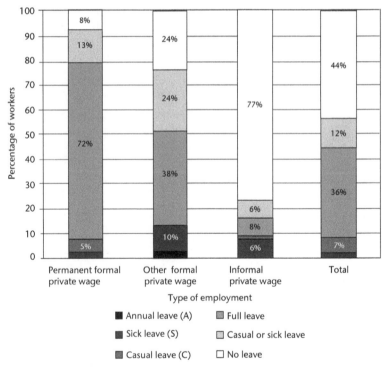

**Figure 1.21.** Proportions of the different types of vacations within private-wage employment by type of job, 2010

*Note:* PRWW = private-wage workers.

*Source:* JLMPS (2010).

formal jobs come with either full paid leave (72%) or some other kind of paid leave (20%). However, other formal employment, which tends to be more precarious, is much less likely to be accompanied by paid leave, with up to 24% of these jobs not having any kind of leave. As expected, informal jobs, which make up 55% of wage and salary jobs in the Jordanian private sector, are most typically not accompanied by paid leave. Overall, only 36% of Jordanian private-sector-wage workers get full paid leave, and up to 44% do not get any kind of paid leave.

The type of leave is also strongly associated with establishment size. As shown in Figure 1.22, establishments of one to four workers provide very little in paid leave, with only 4% of their workers having full leave and 20% having any paid leave. By the time we reach the 100+ category, 66% of workers have full paid leaves and 88% have some kind of paid leave.

Other non-wage benefits, such as the availability of medical insurance, are also strongly associated with firm size. As shown in Figure 1.23, the proportion with medical insurance increases steadily from 3% in enterprises of one

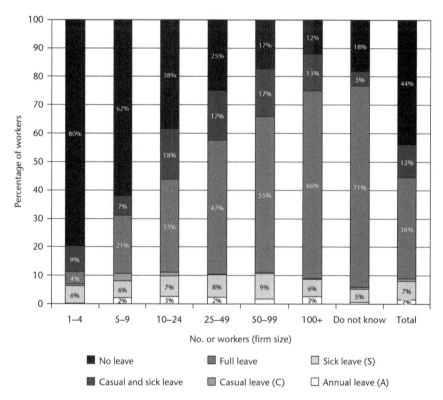

**Figure 1.22.** Proportions of the different type of vacations within the private-wage employment by establishment size, 2010
*Source*: JLMPS (2010).

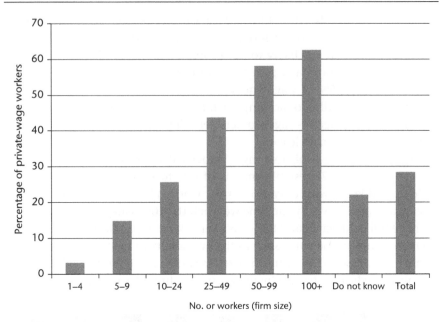

**Figure 1.23.** Proportion of private-wage workers with medical insurance by firm size, 2010

*Source*: JLMPS (2010).

to four workers to 62% in enterprises of 100+ workers, with the overall average being 28% of all private-sector-wage workers receiving such benefits.

### 1.4.3 The Role of Non-Jordanians in Jordan's Private Sector

Although the proportion of non-Jordanians is probably understated in the JLMPS 2010, we can still get some information about what type of work and activities they are concentrated in. The expected pattern is that non-Jordanians are recruited to occupy the kind of jobs that Jordanians are less willing to take. These would include informal jobs without benefits and jobs in smaller enterprises.

Both the JLMPS 2010 and the first two rounds of the EUS in 2010 estimate a proportion of non-Jordanians of about 8% of the working-age population and about 10% of employment. The fact that the two sources agree does not necessarily mean that the figure is accurate, but that they have the same sampling scheme, which leads to the same degree of underestimation. Both surveys only sample traditional households and not the collective places of residence, which many foreign workers occupy.

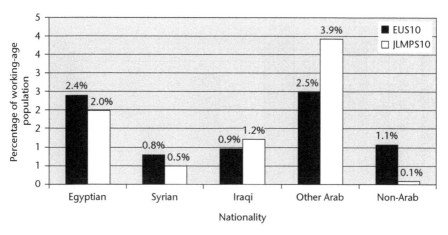

**Figure 1.24.** Distribution of the working-age population by nationality, EUS/ JLMPS 2010

*Note*: Proportion Jordanian 92.3% in both surveys.

*Source*: JLMPS (2010) and EUS (2010).

As shown in Figure 1.24, Egyptians are the largest single nationality group, but the group "other Arabs," which presumably includes Palestinians without Jordanian citizenship, is even larger. The percentages from the two surveys are fairly close with the exception of the "other Arabs" category and the "non-Arab" category. The discrepancy among the latter group is particularly large and probably involves some differences in the way that domestic workers were counted in the two surveys. It appears that in the JLMPS, foreign domestic workers were not counted as members of the Jordanian households in which they temporarily resided.

As shown in Figure 1.25, the proportion of non-Jordanians among private-wage and salary workers rises to 16%, since these workers are more likely to be concentrated in that sector. Comparing the different types of private-wage and salary jobs, the highest concentration of non-Jordanians (25%) is in informal jobs, the least desirable jobs for Jordanians.

It is not surprising that the highest proportion of non-Jordanians is in the two smallest firm size categories. As shown in Figure 1.26, the proportion of non-Jordanians is above average only for the one to four and five to nine categories and is below 10% in the other firm size categories. It is possible that the proportion is even more understated for larger firms if these firms are more likely than smaller firms to use collective residential arrangements for their foreign workers.

Combining the type of job and firm size, we see that non-Jordanians are more likely to be informal in all firm size categories, but the highest

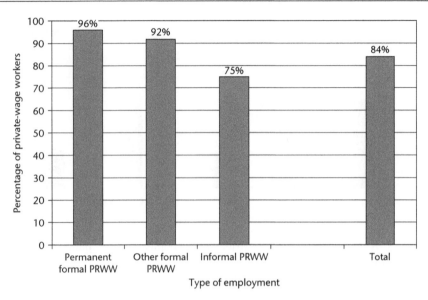

**Figure 1.25.** Proportion of Jordanian workers in private-wage employment by type of employment, 2010
*Source:* JLMPS (2010).

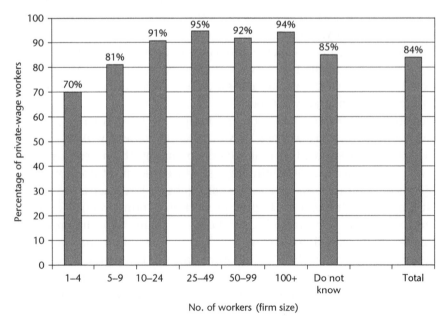

**Figure 1.26.** Proportion of Jordanians in private-wage employment by firm size, 2010
*Source:* JLMPS (2010).

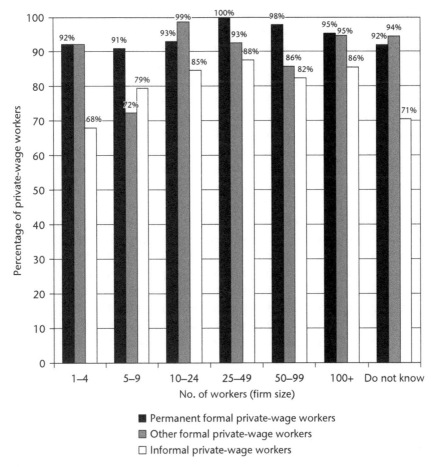

**Figure 1.27.** Proportion of Jordanians in private-wage employment by firm size and type of employment
*Source*: JLMPS (2010).

proportion is found among informal workers in the smallest firms. As shown in Figure 1.27, informal workers in the smallest firms are the most likely to be non-Jordanian (32%) and formal workers in the medium to large firms are almost entirely Jordanian.

## 1.5 Conclusion

The analysis of the JLMPS 2010 data has demonstrated clearly that the Jordanian labor market has gone through a period of rapid transformation as the Jordanian economy liberalized. The rate of government hiring has dropped precipitously since the mid- to late 1980s, only to recover somewhat in the 2000s. This was done partly by delaying the hiring of educated workers into the government and partly by reducing government hiring altogether. Formal private-sector employment appears to have picked up the slack, with its share in the hiring of new entrants tripling from 11% in 1985 to 33% in 1995 and then continuing to rise slowly to 38% in 2010 as the share of government stabilized and recovered. This experience is in sharp contrast to that of Egypt, where a similar restructuring away from government employment resulted in a significant informalization of employment among new entrants. Jordan was able to achieve this dramatic increase in the role of private formal employment by making such employment much more flexible through the use of temporary contracts, or in some case no contracts at all. New hires were being enrolled with the social insurance, but increasingly not being given indefinite duration contracts. While this meant a greater precariousness of private-sector employment, a majority of these new entrants in temporary employment managed to obtain permanent contracts within ten years of their entry into the labor market. Nevertheless, there appears to be an increasing reliance on temporary employment arrangements in recent years, even for workers with ten or more years of experience.

Despite Jordan's success at formalizing employment relations by providing social insurance coverage, private informal employment is still the second largest category of employment after government. This category makes up 55% of private-wage employment and is particularly concentrated in enterprises of fewer than five workers, a category that was until recently exempt from social insurance coverage. This category of employment is generally seen as undesirable by Jordan's increasingly educated workforce and, as such, attracts a large number of non-Jordanian workers. There also appear to be very few opportunities for workers with informal jobs to upgrade to formal employment by changing jobs. At best, informal-wage workers are able to upgrade to becoming self-employed.

The main problem facing the Jordanian labor market appears to be the mismatch between the kinds of jobs that are being created in the private sector and the expectations of the very rapidly growing supply of university graduates (Ministry of Labor and Ministry of Planning and International Cooperation 2012). Temporary and informal jobs in small, private-sector enterprises generally do not come with the kinds of non-wage benefits and stability that university graduates in Jordan have come to expect. This mismatch is currently being accommodated by continued high unemployment rates among graduates and the employment of large numbers of foreign workers to take the jobs that are shunned by the increasingly educated Jordanian workforce.

## APPENDIX

## Comparison of JLMPS 2010 with EUS (Q1 and Q2 2010)

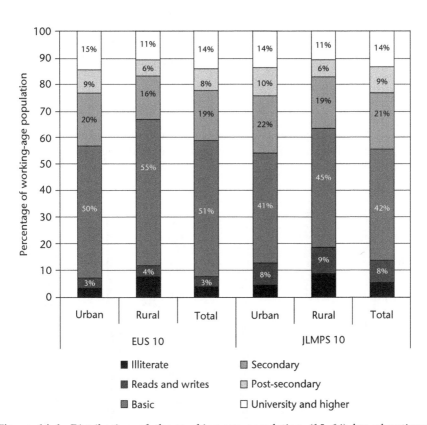

**Figure 1A.1.** Distribution of the working-age population (15–64) by educational attainment and urban/rural location, EUS/JLMPS 2010

*Source*: JLMPS (2010) and EUS (2010).

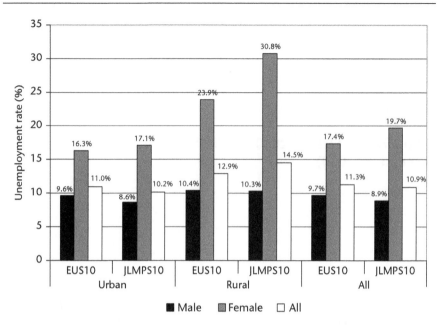

**Figure 1A.2.** Unemployment rate by gender and urban/rural location, ages 15–64 (standard unemployment definition and market labor definition) EUS/JLMPS 2010
*Source*: JLMPS (2010) and EUS (2010).

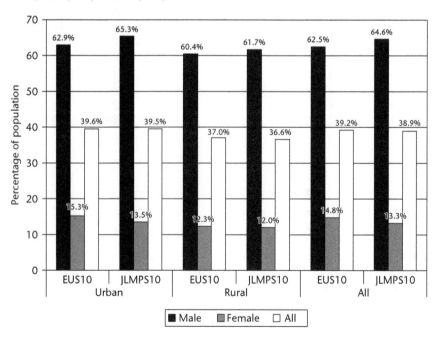

**Figure 1A.3.** Employment to population ratios by gender and urban/rural location, ages 15–64, and market definition of economic activity, EUS/JLMPS 2010
*Source*: JLMPS (2010) and EUS (2010).

36

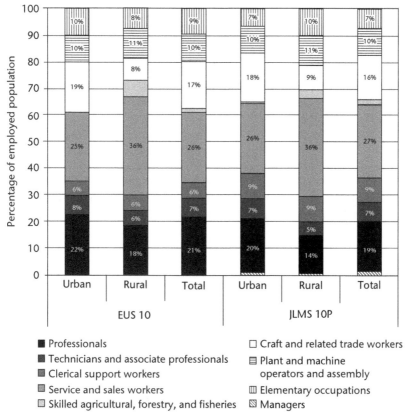

**Figure 1A.4.** Distribution of the employed population by occupation, ages 15–24, EUS/JLMPS 2010
*Source*: JLMPS (2010) and EUS (2010).

### References

Amer, M., 2014. The school-to-work transition of Jordanian youth. In *The Jordanian Labor Market in the New Millennium*, ed. Ragui Assaad. Oxford: Oxford University Press, pp. 64–104.

Assaad, R. and M. Amer, 2008. Labor market conditions in Jordan 1995–2006: An analysis of microdata sources. A report for Al-Manar Project. Amman, Jordan: National Center for Human Resource Development: <http://www.almanar.jo/AlManaren/Portals/0/PDF2/Jordanian%20Labor%20Demand.pdf> (accessed November 8, 2013)

Department of Statistics (Jordan), various years. *Employment and Unemployment Survey*. Amman, Jordan: Department of Statistics.

Department of Statistics (Jordan), various years. *Job Creation Survey*. Amman, Jordan: Department of Statistics.

The Economic Research Forum, 2006. *Egypt Labor Market Panel Survey of 2006 Dataset* (ELMPS 2006). Cairo, Egypt: The Economic Research Forum: <http://erfdataportal. com> (accessed November 8, 2013).

The Economic Research Forum, 2010. *Jordan Labor Market Panel Survey of 2010 Dataset* (JLMPS 2010). Cairo, Egypt: The Economic Research Forum: <http://erfdataportal. com> (accessed November 8, 2013).

Ministry of Labor and Ministry of Planning and International Cooperation, 2012. *Jordan's national employment strategy 2011–2020*. Amman, Jordan: http://esc.jo/ National_Employment_Strategy.aspx (accessed November 8, 2013).

The World Bank, 2007. Resolving Jordan's labor market paradox of concurrent economic growth and high unemployment. Report No. 39201-JO. Middle East and North Africa Region. Washington DC: The World Bank.

# 2

# Demographics, Labor Force Participation, and Unemployment in Jordan

*Nader Mryyan*

## 2.1 Introduction

To better understand the demographic trends in Jordan, it is useful to relate these trends to the historical population displacement in the region and the geostrategic location of Jordan. Established in 1921 as "Trans Jordan," the country was made of the East Bank of the Jordan River. The creation of Israel in 1947 and the 1948 war between the Arab states and Israel forced some Palestinians out of Palestine and into Jordan, among other Arab countries in the region. The population of Jordan was 1,330,021 in 1952, which included the East and West Banks of the Jordan River that were united under the Hashemite Kingdom of Jordan. Under the unity of both banks, Palestinian West Bankers became part of Jordan's population. In the 1967 war, Israel occupied the West Bank of Jordan and forced some Palestinians out of their homes; more refugees fled to Jordan and stayed there. Political instability in the region over the past sixty years has forced immigration into Jordan from Lebanon, Kuwait, and Iraq, in addition to Palestine, which led to the increase of Jordan's population to 3.9 million in 1995, 5.1 million in 2006, and 5.5 million in 2010. In other words, Jordan's population has increased by more than four times in less than 50 years.

Jordan's location in the middle of the Arab World influences labor mobility to and from the kingdom. On the one hand, Jordan is surrounded by Arab countries with large populations like Iraq, Syria, and Egypt; the citizens of these countries can enter Jordan without an entry visa, except for Iraq lately. Due to differences in the economic structure and management between Jordan and these countries, hundreds of thousands of workers from these countries have made Jordan their final destination. Some live and work there, and others commute monthly or bi-monthly, mainly between Jordan and Syria. On the other hand, Jordan is close to the rich Gulf countries (GCC), which have abundant natural resources and small populations. The availability and quality of jobs and the higher wages in the GCC have enticed hundreds of thousands of Jordanian workers to migrate to those countries.

This flow of people and workers to and from Jordan characterizes Jordan's labor market, giving it some distinctive features. In a way, Jordan is a safe haven for many Arab citizens living in troubled countries, which makes immigration to Jordan a key factor in contributing to the population growth and structure. Because the mobility of many Arab workers—between Jordan and their home countries—is easy and relatively unrestricted by the Jordanian government, Jordan ends up hosting hundreds of thousands of Arab workers, among other nationalities. The total number of legal foreign workers in Jordan reached 300,000 in 2010, which obviously reflects on the labor supply. Another characteristic of the Jordanian labor market is that skilled, highly educated Jordanian workers choose to work in the GCC. Accurate estimates about their number, qualifications, and working conditions are not available; some estimates put their number between 500,000 and 600,000 workers or about one-third of Jordan's total labor force (IOM, 2011). Due to this continuous brain drain from Jordan, it is hard to predict future labor supply, which inevitably leads to an unstable labor supply model, and complicates its forecast and development.

## 2.2 Demographic Analysis

The analysis rendered in the following sections is mainly based on the Jordan Panel Labor Market Survey of 2010 (JLMPS 2010).

JLMPS data confirms Jordan's main demographic indicators, which reveal that Jordan is a young society. Table 2.1 shows that 38% of Jordan's population is below the age of 15. The age brackets (15–24), (15–64), (65 and above) represent 20%, 58%, and 4% of the total population, respectively. Annex 1 shows that the total population has increased from approximately five million in 2006 to around 5.5 million in 2010, with an average annual growth rate of 2.5%. Table 2.2 shows that the majority of the population is concentrated around the capital city of Amman; 60% of the population lives in Amman and the three governorates adjacent to it. Approximately 81% of the population lives in urban centers, which makes Jordan a highly urbanized economy.

Figures 2.1 and 2.2 show the age distribution of the urban and rural population by gender; both distributions were uni-modal, and the mode was around the age of 3 for both males and females in urban areas, and

**Table 2.1.** Distribution of the population by location and selected age groups, 2010 (%)

| | Population below 15 | Working-age population (15–64) | Youth population (15–24) | Population over 65 |
|---|---|---|---|---|
| Urban | 38 | 58 | 20 | 4 |
| Rural | 38 | 58 | 20 | 4 |
| Total | 38 | 58 | 20 | 4 |

*Source*: DoS Statistical Annual Report (2010).

**Table 2.2.** Distribution of the Jordanian population by governorate (%)

| | 2010 | | |
|---|---|---|---|
| Governorate | Male | Female | Total |
| Amman | 36.7 | 37.3 | 37.0 |
| Balqa | 7.2 | 7.0 | 7.1 |
| Zarqa | 13.6 | 14.0 | 13.8 |
| Madaba | 2.5 | 2.3 | 2.4 |
| Irbid | 19.6 | 18.8 | 19.2 |
| Mafraq | 4.8 | 5.0 | 4.9 |
| Jarash | 2.9 | 3.0 | 2.9 |
| Ajloun | 2.5 | 2.5 | 2.5 |
| Karak | 4.4 | 4.3 | 4.4 |
| Tafileh | 1.7 | 1.7 | 1.7 |
| Ma'an | 1.8 | 1.9 | 1.9 |
| Aqaba | 2.3 | 2.0 | 2.2 |
| Total | 100.00 | 100.00 | 100.00 |

*Source*: DoS Statistical Annual Report (2010).

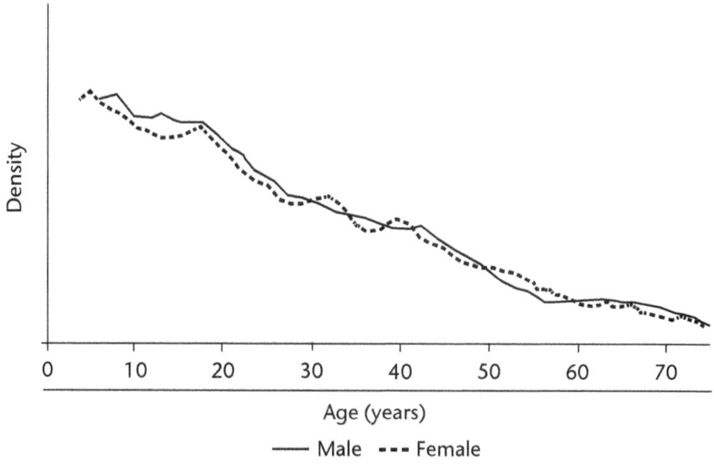

**Figure 2.1.** Age distribution of urban Jordanian population by gender
*Source*: DoS Statistical Annual Report (2010).

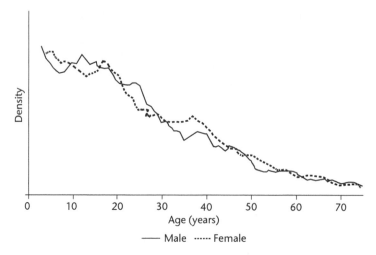

**Figure 2.2.** Age distribution of rural Jordanian population by gender
*Source*: DoS Statistical Annual Report (2010).

about 1 year for males and 2 years for females in rural areas. This distribution reflects that more babies are born every year. Thus, the number of children going through to the education system and the number of youth joining the labor market is expected to rise for the coming two decades at least.

The second feature of the working-age population is the education. School enrollment is almost universal for both males and females; this makes new entrants to the labor market not only younger but also more educated. Table 2.3 shows that the average number of school years rose from six for males born in 1930 to more than 11 for males born in 1960. The number of years spent in school for males born between 1960 and 1980 was around 11 years, but this number increased to 13 years for those born in 1987. The progress was faster for females. Their average years of schooling jumped from about 5 years for those born in 1930 to about 8 years for those born in 1960, and to more than 13 years for those born in 1987. Figures 2.3 and 2.4 indicate that the illiteracy rate is low in Jordan if compared with other countries in the region (about 3% for males and 8% for females) and, as expected, the illiteracy rates are higher in the rural areas than in the urban areas, and more than double for females. The percentage of the population with tertiary education was 22% for males and 24% for females, which indicates gender equality in the education system (DoS, 2010). Since basic education is compulsory in Jordan, it is not surprising that it makes up the largest segment of the population cohort.

**Table 2.3.** Average years of education by birth cohort and gender

| Year of birth | Male | Female |
|---|---|---|
| 1930 | 6.30 | 4.50 |
| 1960 | 11.20 | 7.74 |
| 1970 | 11.25 | 10.66 |
| 1980 | 11.40 | 12.01 |
| 1987 | 12.60 | 13.13 |

*Source:* JLMPS (2010).

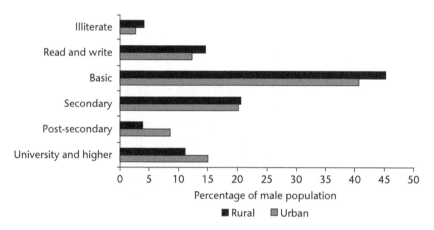

**Figure 2.3.** Distribution of male population by educational attainment and location
*Source*: DoS Statistical Annual Report (2010).

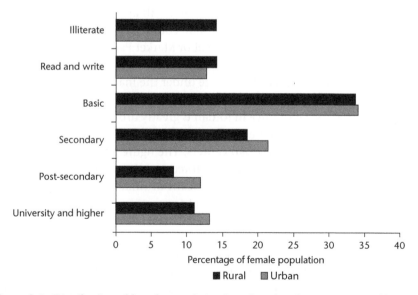

**Figure 2.4.** Distribution of female population by educational attainment and location
*Source*: DoS Statistical Annual Report (2010).

## 2.3 Labor Force Participation

Two definitions of the labor force are used in the analysis that follows, as per Assaad and Amer (2008).

The market labor force includes all those who are either engaged in an economic activity for purposes of market exchange or seeking such work.

The extended labor force includes those engaged in the production and processing of primary products, whether for the market, for barter, or for their own consumption.

The distinction between the two definitions becomes important in economies where many women are engaged in animal husbandry and in the processing of dairy products for household consumption and are thus counted as employed in the extended definition of the labor force.

It is expected that the differences between the two measures will not be significant in Jordan, mainly due to the small size of the agricultural sector, which in general employs a significant number of the informal workers—mainly females who spend some of their time and effort processing and storing their families' food and other basic commodities.

The dependency of Jordanian employers on foreign workers, particularly in the agricultural and service sectors, has made Jordanian job-seekers look to the formal private sector and the public sector to work for wages.

Using both definitions of the labor force will deepen our understanding of unemployment size, since there is a general feeling that the actual unemployment rates are higher than the official published rates. On the other hand, using these two definitions of the labor force will also allow us to compare the labor market indicators with other Arab countries that have already conducted or are expected to conduct the Labor Market Panel Survey.

Figure 2.5 confirms these expectations; the size of the labor force under the extended definition exceeded its size under the market definition by just 1.5%, while that difference was 20% for Egypt in 2006 (Assaad, 2009). The figure shows that the labor force in Jordan is greatly urbanized: almost 88% of the labor force according to the market definition and 79% according to the extended definition work in urban centers. The figure reveals that while the differences between the extended labor force and the market labor force are negligible in urban areas, they are significant in rural areas, indicating that most non-market work takes place in rural areas.

Figures 2.6 and 2.7 show the labor participation rates for males and females in urban and rural locations, respectively. Both figures indicate that Jordan suffers a large intellectual capital loss; if we take into consideration the high enrollment rates in all levels of education for males and females, the labor participation rates for males and females, at 50% and 14% respectively, seem rather low.

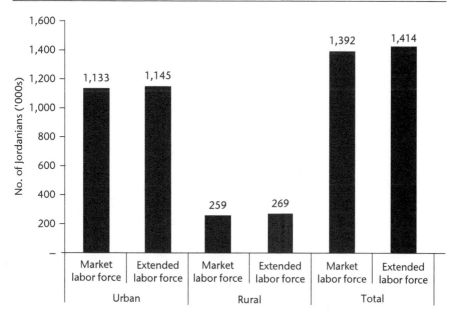

**Figure 2.5.** Market and extended labor force by location, Jordanians ('000)
*Source:* JLMPS (2010).

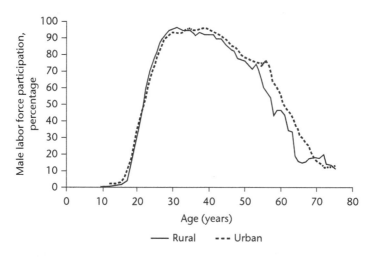

**Figure 2.6.** Male labor force participation rates by age and location (extended labor force definition)
*Source:* JLMPS (2010).

45

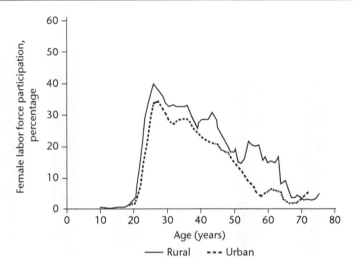

**Figure 2.7.** Female labor force participation rates by age and location (extended labor force definition)
*Source:* JLMPS (2010).

Male participation rates are modest under the age of 18 (Figure 2.6), which is expected since most are still attending school at that age. Eighteen is a critical age for Jordanian students—those who successfully complete the secondary education phase can proceed to tertiary education, and those who do not may enter the labor market. After this age we witness a gradual increase in the labor participation rate, which exceeds 50% at the age of 20 and reaches a peak at the age of 25 in both urban and rural areas. Male labor force participation rates remain high between 25 and 44 years of age (almost 90%) in both urban and rural areas, and then start to decline in urban and rural areas—but more rapidly in rural areas—down to 50% and beyond for ages 57 and above. Given the high life expectancy rate in Jordan (73 years for men in 2009), and that the official retirement age is at 60, it is difficult to understand why Jordanian men pull out of the labor force early.

The female labor force participation rate in Jordan is among the lowest worldwide, even in the region. Few women below the age of 20 join the work force, partially because some of them are still in school. Those who drop out of the education system at an early age and acquire only a low level of education find it difficult to join the work force for economic, social, and cultural reasons. Between the ages of 22 (the age at which most females graduate from university) and the age of 26 (the age at which they get married and start having children), the female labor participation rate reaches its peak and ranges between 28% at the age of 22 and 38% at the age of 26 in urban areas. In rural areas, it reaches 40% at the age of 22 and drops down to 33% at the age of 26. Figure 2.7 shows that female participation rate in rural areas is higher than the participation rate in urban areas for most ages, indicating that rural women work harder.

Figure 2.8 illustrates male labor participation rates by level of education. Since we are dealing with people of working age (15–64), and most of the people finish their basic education at the age of 16, it is therefore expected that the majority of the people with this level of education are already in the labor market, which to some extent explains the big jump in their labor participation rate to 75%. The labor participation rate for the secondary education group declined to the range of 45–50%. This is because a higher percentage of this group are still enrolled in education and are classified as inactive population. At the tertiary education stage, these are males with post-secondary, university, and postgraduate qualifications, which make them eligible for employment, and therefore their labor participation rates jump to the highest levels. One can say that male labor participation is influenced positively by the level of education.

Figure 2.9 illustrates female labor force participation rates by level of education. The figure reveals an interesting female attitude towards female employment, or more precisely a social attitude towards female employment. To explain this, let us take secondary education as a reference point, and if we ignore vocational education for the time being—because it is not a separate level of education in Jordan—it is possible to say that the female labor market participation has two distinct segments. The first segment concerns females with education below the secondary level, where their labor participation

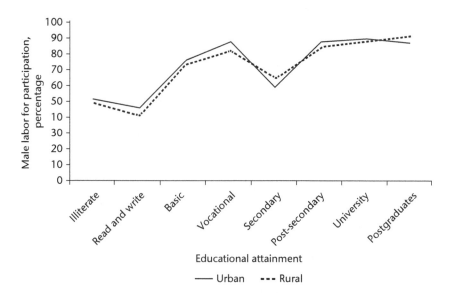

**Figure 2.8.** Male labor force participation rates by educational attainment and location (extended labor force definition)

*Source:* JLMPS (2010).

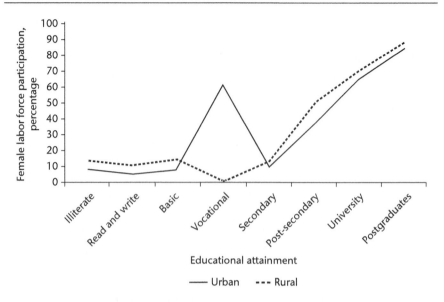

**Figure 2.9.** Female labor force participation rates by educational attainment and location (extended labor force definition)
*Source:* JLMPS (2010).

rates reach a ceiling of 10% in both urban and rural areas. The second segment concerns females with secondary education or higher; their labor force participation rates start at 37% and 51% for females with post-secondary education and jump to 84% and 87% for postgraduates in urban and rural areas, respectively. Educated women work more than uneducated women in Jordan, because women in the first group can easily find work in the public sector and in the formal private sector, as well as in economic activities, which are deemed fit for female employment by the society.

Figure 2.10 examines the trends in labor force participation rates by gender over ten years between 2000 and 2010, which indicate a decline in male participation rates from 69% to 67% and a rise in female participation rates from 13% to 16% from 2000 to 2010, respectively. As stated earlier, the decline in male participation rates is mainly due to early retirement among Jordanian males, and the increase in female participation rates is mainly due to the increase in the number of female university graduates and the delay in the age of marriage. The early withdrawal of males from the labor market is partially explained by legislation concerning the labor market, which make the early retirement from the military and the social security system least costly.

Figure 2.11 reveals an important trend in labor participation rates in Jordan over the last decade when measured across educational levels. The figure shows that labor participation rates are lower in 2010 than in 2005, and lower in 2005 than in 2000 for secondary levels of education and higher.

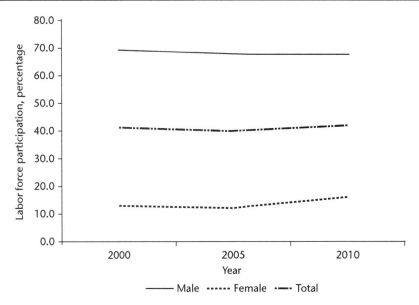

**Figure 2.10.** Labor force participation rate by gender, 2000, 2005, and 2010
*Source:* EUS, 2000, 2005, and 2010.

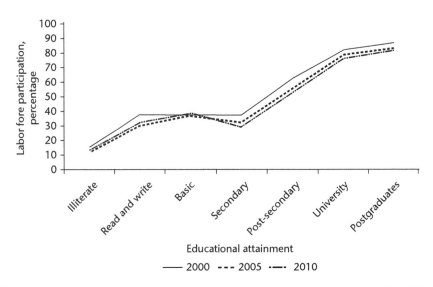

**Figure 2.11.** Labor force participation rate by educational attainment, 2000, 2005, and 2010
*Source:* EUS, 2000, 2005, and 2010.

## 2.4 The Economic Activity of the Labor Force

The working-age population is divided between the active population, which includes those participating in the labor force (employed and unemployed), and the non-active population, which includes groups of people who do not join the labor force, such as students, housewives, and property owners. The withdrawal of some productive human resources from the production process generates an opportunity loss to the economy; the value of such a loss depends on the quality and the productive life of the inactive resources.

Jordan stands out in terms of the low rate of the economic activity of its human resources: the total inactivity rate was at about 60% in 2010, which means that more than half of the working-age population are not contributing to the GDP (National Employment Strategy, IOM, 2011). Figure 2.12 shows that female inactivity is rather high in the age cohort 20–25. Approximately 92%, 86%, and 65% of females aged 20, 22, and 25, respectively are inactive. On the other hand, males between the ages of 26 and 40 are highly active. The inactivity rates start to rise after the age of 40, but they remain within internationally accepted ranges.

Figure 2.13 shows the inactivity rate with reference to educational attainment for males and females. Female inactivity rates are rather high at lower levels of education but decline radically for university graduates. Male inactivity rates follow a similar trend but with a lower inactivity rate across all levels of education.

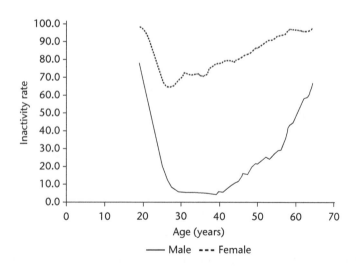

**Figure 2.12.** Inactivity rate by age (15–64) and gender
*Source:* JLMPS (2010).

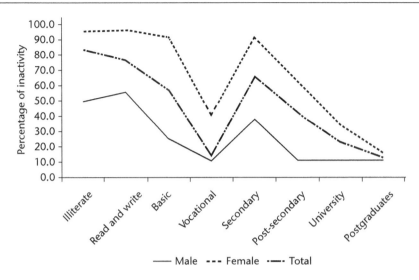

**Figure 2.13**. Distribution of inactive participation by gender and education
*Source:* JLMPS (2010).

However, the gap in activity rates between males and females narrows at higher education levels, and becomes practically insignificant among university graduates of both sexes. Figure 2.13 also shows that females with lower education levels (secondary and below) rarely join the labor force. The reason for this is most probably a combination of social, cultural, and work environment factors.

Figure 2.14 shows the trends in inactivity rates for males and females over the past decade, which indicate that the inactivity rates are not only high in general and extremely high for females, but that they are also long-term and structural. The drop in the activity rates between 2000 and 2010 is marginal for the whole population. However, male inactivity rates have slightly increased, which means that Jordanian men have been dropping out of the labor force at a faster rate over the past decade. To interpret this trend, other important factors such as labor legislation, labor immigration, and the reliability of statistics for those returning to employment after an early retirement should be examined more carefully. On the other hand, female inactivity rates have declined, as expected, during the time period. This is not surprising given the increased numbers of female university graduates and the rise in marriage age for females, which combined pushed more females to join the labor force. While this may sound like good news, the economy's ability to generate sufficient jobs for the new entrants to the labor market remains to be seen.

Figure 2.15 shows that the inactivity rates were higher in 2000 than in 2005, and were higher in 2005 than in 2010 for secondary-education level

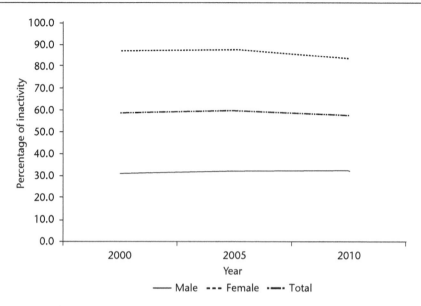

**Figure 2.14.** Inactivity rate by gender, 2000, 2005, and 2010
*Source:* EUS, 2000, 2005, and 2010.

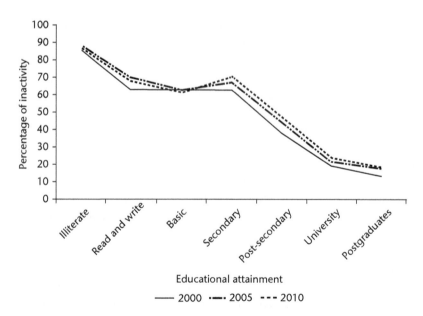

**Figure 2.15.** Inactivity rate by educational attainment, 2000, 2005, and 2010
*Source:* EUS, 2000, 2005, and 2010.

and higher. The structure of the curves does not change, indicating the same trends over time—high inactivity rates at the lower levels of education, and low inactivity rates at the higher levels of education. This figure again illustrates that these high inactivity rates in Jordan are structural and long-term, and therefore they generate a huge loss of resources, and should be carefully investigated.

## 2.5 Unemployment Evolution

Two definitions of unemployment are used in the following analysis, as per Assaad (2009).

The standard definition of unemployment: under this definition, only those individuals who match the following characteristics are counted as unemployed. He/she had not worked at all in the week prior to the interview, was not attached to a job but wanted to work and was available to do so, and had actively searched for work during the three months prior to the survey. Such individuals are called "active unemployed."

The broad definition for unemployment includes all the individuals counted under the standard definition, in addition to the discouraged unemployed among the unemployed.

Under the market labor force definition of economic activity discussed earlier, only market work counts as work; thus subsistence workers can be considered unemployed if the rest of the definition applies to them.

Under the extended labor force definition, any subsistence work counts as work and subsistence workers are not considered unemployed, even if they are searching for market work, which thus reduces the numerator of the unemployment rate. Moreover, the denominator now includes subsistence workers, most of whom are counted as out of the labor force in the market definition. As a result, the estimates of the unemployment rate under the extended definition are much lower than unemployment rates under the market definition.

Figure 2.16 illustrates unemployment rates using the market labor force definition and the standard unemployment definition. Generally speaking, unemployment has always been high in Jordan; its rate has been in double digits for decades and it is more concentrated among females and youth. JLMPS data confirms this fact. As shown in Figure 2.16 the unemployment rate was 11.5 % in 2010 (9% among males and 20% among females), and it was higher in rural areas. Male unemployment rates were 9% and 11% in urban and rural areas, respectively. Female rates were even higher, at 17% and 31% in urban and rural areas, respectively.

53

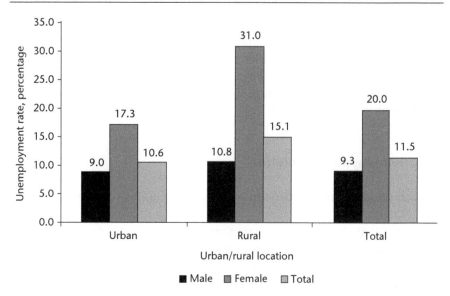

**Figure 2.16.** Unemployment rate by gender and location (standard unemployment definition and market labor force definition)
*Source:* JLMPS (2010).

Figure 2.17 illustrates unemployment rates using the extended labor force definition and again the standard unemployment definition. Since the differences between the market and the extended definitions for the labor force are marginal in Jordan, as presented earlier, nearly the same unemployment rates were rendered: an unemployment rate of 11.2 % in 2010 (9.3% among males and 18.3% among females). The situation was different when Egyptian data was subjected to the same analysis, where the difference in unemployment rates between the two definitions of the labor force was more than two percentage points in 2006 (Assaad, 2009).

As for the regional pattern for unemployment, Figures 2.18 and 2.19 clearly illustrate that unemployment is lowest in the middle region and highest in the southern region, whether using the market labor force definition (Figure 2.18) or the extended labor force definition (Figure 2.19). The middle region, which has the capital city and the highest percentage of the population and of national economic activity, scored the lowest unemployment rate. Unemployment in the northern region, which has a reasonable economic base and from which many workers commute daily to work in the middle region was three percentage points higher than the middle region. The southern region, despite its small population, ranked highest in terms of unemployment and exceeded the unemployment rate of the middle region

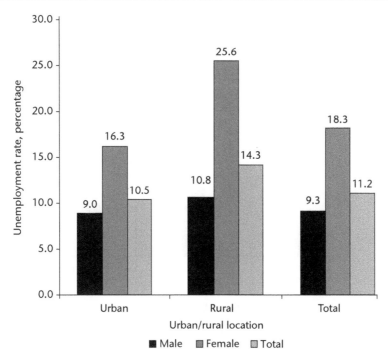

**Figure 2.17.** Unemployment rate by gender and location (standard unemployment definition and extended labor force definition)
*Source:* JLMPS (2010).

by 10 percentage points. The same differences in unemployment rates were observed for both males and females in the three regions.

Figure 2.20 introduces the broad definition of unemployment and illustrates the number of unemployed using the two definitions of unemployment as well as both labor force definitions. The figure reveals no significant differences when one unemployment definition is used with the market or the extended labor force definition. However, there are significant differences in numbers when using the standard unemployment definition or alternatively the broad unemployment definition. For example, when using the broad unemployment definition, the number of unemployed differs by only 246 persons between market and extended labor force definitions. Almost the same result is reached under the standard definition of unemployment with both definitions of the labor force. However, under the market labor force definitions, the number of unemployed was 174,097 when using the broad unemployment definition and159,568 when using the standard unemployment definition. The difference amounted to 14,500 individuals, or approximately 9%. The same held true when using the extended labor

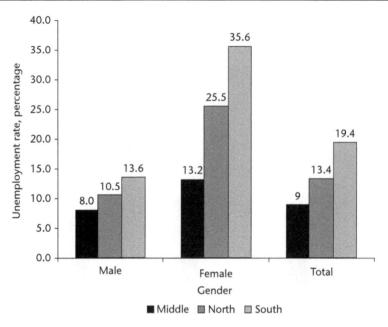

**Figure 2.18.** Unemployment rate by gender and region (standard unemployment definition and market labor force definition)
*Source:* JLMPS (2010).

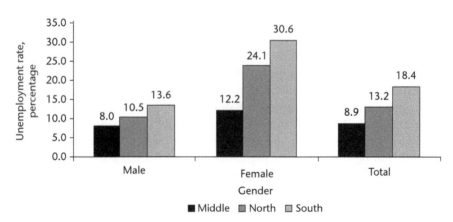

**Figure 2.19.** Unemployment rate by gender and region (standard unemployment definition and extended labor force definition)
*Source:* JLMPS (2010).

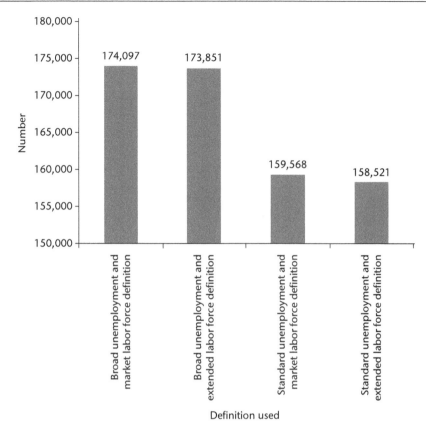

**Figure 2.20.** Number of unemployed (various definitions)
*Source:* JLMPS (2010).

force definition. The difference between the two measures came to 15,330, or 10%. The differences in the number of unemployed in both cases represent the number of discouraged workers.

It is worth noting that unemployment is very high among youth (15–24 years) in Jordan. Figure 2.21 shows that male unemployment rate exceeds 30% among the young new entrants to the labor market, with higher rates in rural areas than in urban areas. This rate is more than double the national average. The high unemployment rate for youth reflects the presence of some structural problems in the economy, mainly its inability to absorb the Jordanian newcomers to the labor market, the existence of a mismatch between education outputs and labor market requirements, in addition to the lack of programs that would facilitate the transition of youth from school to work. Unemployment declines sharply for males above the age of 25, reaching its

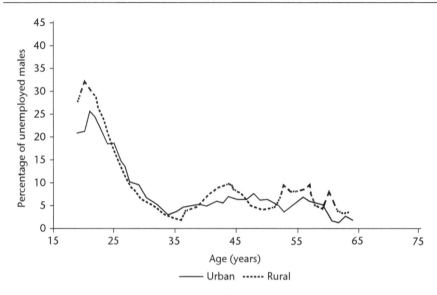

**Figure 2.21.** Male unemployment rates by age and location (standard unemployment definition and market labor force definition)
*Source:* JLMPS (2010).

lowest level for males around the age of 35. Unemployment again starts to rise for the ages of 35 and 45, to settle thereafter.

The picture is more gloomy for females, as illustrated in Figure 2.22. Unemployment among young females (15–24) exceeds 40%, with a big gap between the rural and urban areas, and remains high for females in the age range of 25–35, but drops to nearly zero around the age of 45, when Jordanian women decide to leave the labor force altogether.

Socio-economic and cultural factors, social perceptions, the economic structure, and employment legislation and regulations affect the decisions of Jordanian females on whether to join the labor market or not. One may ask what is special about Jordan in this regard because the same factors influence females' employment decisions anywhere in the world. The answer might come from the different weight that different factors have in different countries. In Jordan, and probably to a lesser extent in some Arab countries, the social and cultural factors have more weight than other economic factors. This leads to a situation where young, poor females with low levels of education cannot work because their families would not approve a job at a hotel or a factory for example. At the other end of the spectrum, educated women with a university degree cannot join the labor market because no jobs are available in the public sector or in the education sector, or because the job

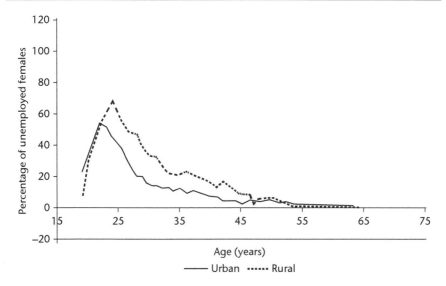

**Figure 2.22.** Female unemployment rates by age and location (standard unemployment definition and market labor force definition)
*Source:* JLMPS (2010).

requires working night shifts or commuting further than the psychologically accepted distance.

If we look at male unemployment in relation to levels of education we notice that male university graduates have the highest unemployment rate among all the unemployed (Figure 2.23). This rate was close to 10% and 15% in urban and rural areas, respectively in 2010. Males with vocational education show unemployment rates as high, but that is because vocational education is part of the secondary education in Jordan. The fact that university graduates have the highest unemployment rates is the result of two factors. First, the higher education system largely expanded in Jordan in the past two decades, when more public and private universities opened, and thus more university graduates are joining the labor market and will continue to do so in the coming years. Second, the demand for labor is oriented towards individuals with lower levels of education, which is suitable for almost 60% of the Jordanian workforce (those with secondary education or lower), but not for university graduates.

As for female unemployment, it seems that educated females search for jobs after they graduate, for a short period of time, and that uneducated females rarely join the labor force altogether (Figure 2.24). Therefore, the unemployment rate is low for females with low levels of education, but high

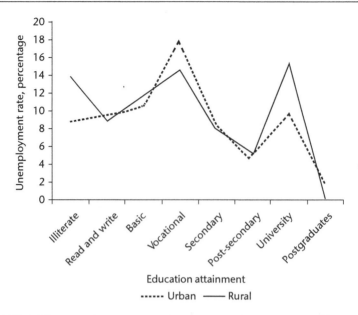

**Figure 2.23.** Male unemployment rates by educational attainment and location, ages 15–64 (standard unemployment definition and market labor force definition)
*Source:* JLMPS (2010).

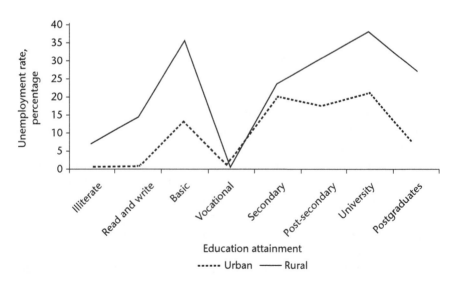

**Figure 2.24.** Female unemployment rates by educational attainment and location, ages 15–64 (standard unemployment definition and market labor force definition)
*Source:* JLMPS (2010).

for university graduates (24% in 2010). Female unemployment in rural areas is higher than in urban areas for all levels of education, not only because there are fewer jobs available, but also because there are more restrictions on women's employment in rural areas.

Finally, Figures 2.25 and 2.26 show the unemployment trend by gender and by educational attainment for the past decade (2000–2010). A double-digit unemployment rate prevailed throughout the decade.

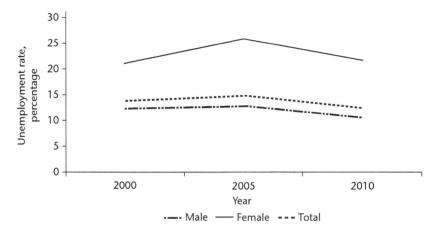

**Figure 2.25.** Unemployment rate by gender, 2000, 2005, and 2010
*Source:* EUS, 2000, 2005 and 2010.

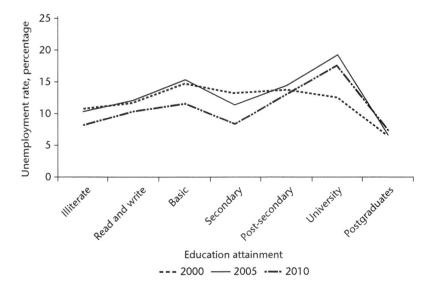

**Figure 2.26.** Unemployment rate by educational attainment, 2000, 2005, and 2010
*Source:* EUS, 2000, 2005, and 2010.

Unemployment was higher in 2005 than in 2000 and 2010. Female unemployment was double that of male unemployment. The high unemployment rate was structural and persistent, was more pronounced for youth and women, and was highest among university graduates, with the exception of the year 2000.

## APPENDIX

**Table 2A.1.** Distribution of the Jordanian population by location and age group, 2006 and 2010

| Age group | 2006 | | | 2010 | | |
|---|---|---|---|---|---|---|
| | Urban | Rural | Total | Urban | Rural | Total |
| 0–4 | 518,176 | 73,231 | 591,407 | 604,342 | 143,798 | 748,140 |
| 5–9 | 539,570 | 79,600 | 619,170 | 560,066 | 132,297 | 692,363 |
| 10–14 | 566,588 | 81,803 | 648,391 | 527,409 | 129,700 | 657,109 |
| 15–19 | 532,086 | 76,425 | 608,511 | 499,543 | 125,285 | 624,828 |
| 20–24 | 460,299 | 65,066 | 525,365 | 395,911 | 101,826 | 497,737 |
| 25–29 | 348,125 | 49,295 | 397,420 | 347,244 | 82,812 | 430,056 |
| 30–34 | 290,201 | 38,217 | 328,418 | 310,013 | 70,224 | 380,237 |
| 35–39 | 268,013 | 31,817 | 299,830 | 290,821 | 68,364 | 359,185 |
| 40–44 | 229,316 | 27,475 | 256,791 | 252,583 | 50,688 | 303,271 |
| 45–49 | 168,149 | 20,633 | 188,782 | 178,348 | 40,844 | 219,192 |
| 50–54 | 125,156 | 16,908 | 142,064 | 139,171 | 27,894 | 167,065 |
| 55–59 | 111,911 | 12,349 | 124,260 | 108,422 | 23,282 | 131,704 |
| 60–64 | 109,002 | 11,339 | 120,341 | 96,410 | 19,686 | 116,096 |
| 65 | 181,115 | 23,380 | 204,495 | 192,108 | 40,409 | 232,517 |
| Total | 4,447,707 | 607,538 | 5,055,245 | 4,502,391 | 1,057,109 | 5,559,500 |

*Source*: DoS Statistical Annual Report (2006/2010).

### References

Assaad, R., 2009. Labor supply, employment, and unemployment in the Egyptian economy, 1988–2006. In *The Egyptian Labor Market Revised*, ed. R. Assaad. Cairo, Egypt: The American University in Cairo Press.

Assaad, R. and M. Amer, 2008. *Labor Market Conditions in Jordan, 1995–2006: An Analysis of Micro Data Sources*. Amman, Jordan: Al Manar Project.

Department of Statistics (Jordan), 2010. *The Employment and Unemployment Survey (EUS), 2000, 2005, 2010*. Amman, Jordan: Department of Statistics.

Department of Statistics (Jordan). 2010, 2011. *Statistical Annual Reports, 2009, 2010*. Amman, Jordan: Department of Statistics.

Economic Research Forum (EFT), 2010. Jordan Panel Labor Market Survey, Cairo, Egypt, EFT.

International Organization for Migration (IOM), 2011. *Intra-regional Labor Mobility in the Arab World*. Cairo, Egypt: International Organization for Migration.

Ministry of Labor; Ministry of Planning and International Cooperation, 2011. *National Employment Strategy, 2011–2020*. Amman, Jordan: Ministry of Planning and International Cooperation.

# 3

# The School-to-Work Transition of Jordanian Youth

*Mona Amer**

## 3.1 Introduction

Youth (15–34 years) is a very important segment of the Jordanian population, which also suffers the most from difficult insertion into the labor market after leaving the education system. This chapter aims to understand the dynamics of school-to-work transition for youth using the rich data set of the recently implemented Jordan Labor Market Panel Survey of 2010 (JLMPS 2010). It pays particular attention to post-secondary and university graduates and to females, who have the highest unemployment rates and find it most difficult to enter the labor market.

The chapter uses the employment history of the Jordanian labor market provided by JLMPS to determine the trajectories of young people entering the labor market and to analyze their dynamics. It seeks to understand what the education outputs are and what happens to young Jordanians after completing their studies. Are they employed, unemployed, or out of the labor force? If they do work, what kind of jobs do they get, differentiated by gender and educational attainment? The chapter also looks at how old they are and how long they have to wait until they get their first job, and discusses the impact of gender and education on the time it takes to do so.

Assaad (2014) shows that the type of first job has changed significantly over the past fifty years. He indicates that between 1960 and 2010 the share of precarious and informal first jobs has risen significantly at the expense

* The author would like to thank Ragui Assaad for his valuable comments and suggestions for this chapter.

of permanent public jobs. He also notes that five and ten years after the date of obtaining the first job, the shares of both private formal permanent jobs and self-employment substantially rise.[1] From that springboard, this chapter attempts to understand whether the informalization of the initial insertion leads to a better status a few years later.

The chapter is divided into three main parts. The first one presents the socio-demographic characteristics of youth (size and share, geographical distribution, enrollment and educational attainment) and presents a brief overview of youth labor market performances, in particular labor force participation and unemployment rates in relation to gender, age, and educational attainment. The second part focuses on school-to-work transition by analyzing the characteristics of the first employment status after leaving school, age at first job, and the time it takes to get it. The last part presents a sequence analysis of the dynamics of labor market transitions from 1999 to 2010 for young males and females who had finished school before 1999.

## 3.2 Socio-demographic Characteristics of Youth and Labor Market Performances

In Jordan, one-third of the population is young. The educational attainment of youth has dramatically increased over the past decades, resulting in one of the highest levels of educational attainment and school enrollment in the Middle East and North Africa (MENA) region, with females obtaining higher educational levels than males. However, it seems that young people are facing difficulties in entering the labor market, as demonstrated by their high unemployment rates, particularly among the more educated, and specifically among females. This section presents the main socio-demographic characteristics of Jordanian youth in terms of enrollment, educational level, labor force participation, and unemployment.

As the objective of this chapter is to study not only the insertion of youth into the labor market (i.e. the school-to-work transition) but also their early labor market paths, it focuses on people aged 15 to 34. Moreover, as the JLMPS 2010 underestimates the foreign population in Jordan, this study is limited to the Jordanian population.[2]

---

[1] See also Assaad and Amer (2008) for a detailed discussion of the evolution of the employment structure in Jordan over the period 1995 to 2006.

[2] The JLMPS 2010 seems to underestimate the size and share of foreigners, as compared to other studies. In particular, the sample size of the Syrians is very small (only 85 observations).

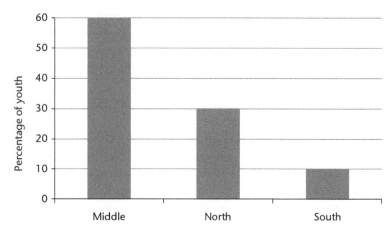

**Figure 3.1.** Distribution of youth (15–34) by region, 2010
*Source*: JLMPS (2010).

### 3.2.1 Youth: Size, Share, and Location of Residence

The Jordanian population is a very young population (Table 3A.1). Three-quarters of the population is under the age of 35 (72.6%). Out of six million inhabitants in Jordan in 2010, 1.7 million are aged 15–29 and 2.1 million are aged 15–34, representing 28.3% and 35.2% of the total population, respectively.

The youth population mostly lives in urban areas, predominantly in the Middle Region and in four governorates. Indeed, 81% live in urban areas and 19% are rural residents. Sixty percent reside in the Middle Region, 30% in the North, and only 10% in the South (Figure 3.1).

### 3.2.2 School Enrollment and Educational Attainment

Jordan has made remarkable progress in terms of school enrollment and educational attainment in recent decades.

School enrollment is high in Jordan. Almost two-thirds (63.5%) of young people aged 15–22 are enrolled in school. As expected, school enrollment declines with age, but remains relatively high at the ages of 18 to 22. While 83.8% of those aged 16–17 (age group corresponding to secondary school) are enrolled in school, 47% of those aged 18–22 are in university (Figure 3.2).

In addition, the gap between school enrollment for males and females has narrowed to the extent that enrollment rates for females in 2010 were higher than for males (Figure 3.2). This female advantage is particularly important among the youngest age group (16–17) in urban areas and among the 18–22 age group in rural areas. Indeed, in the 16–17 age group in urban areas 85.9%

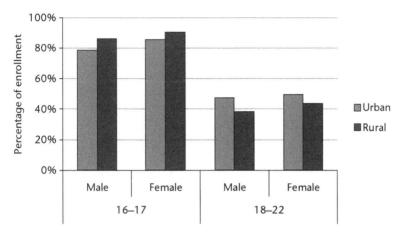

**Figure 3.2.** Enrollment ratio by gender, age group, and location, 2010
*Source:* JLMPS (2010).

of females versus 79% of males are enrolled. Among the 18–22 group in rural areas, 43.8% of females are studying, as compared to 38.1% of males. However, the urban enrollment rate for both genders is higher than the rural rate for the 18–22 group but lower for the 16–17 group.

Jordanian youth are relatively well educated. Nearly half (43.3%) of the young people in Jordan have a secondary level of education or higher, and illiteracy is almost negligible (1.6% in the 15–34 age group).

As shown in Table 3A.2, educational attainment has been substantially improving. The share of the less educated ('illiterate' and 'read and write' categories) increases with age and the share of the most educated decreases with age, showing a clear improvement in educational levels. Indeed, the proportion of illiterates is 2.2% in the 30–34 group but only 1.1% in the 15–19 group. Also the proportion of the 'read and write' category decreases from 3.5% in the 30–34 group to 1.2% in the 20–24 group. The numbers get even better at high levels of education, and particularly at the university level. For instance, the proportion of university graduates is much higher (25.8%) among the 25–29 group than among the 30–34 group (17.7%).

Females have now become better educated than males (Figure 3.3). Indeed, the proportion of females with secondary education and above is higher than males. The gender gap in favor of females is particularly important at the post-secondary and university levels. For instance, 7.6% of females have a post-secondary degree and 15% have a university degree, as compared to 4.7% and 11.6% of males, respectively.

These improvements could reflect on the labor market in many ways. A more qualified workforce could be more demanding in terms of working

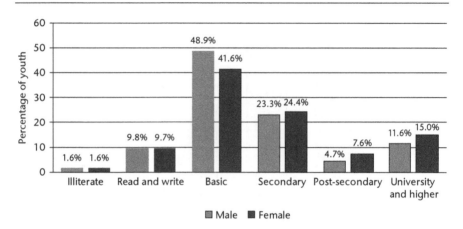

**Figure 3.3.** Educational attainment of youth (15–34) by gender, 2010
*Source:* JLMPS (2010).

conditions (work contract and job security) and therefore could remain temporarily unemployed in order to find good working conditions. Alternatively, females with higher education could increase their participation in the labor force.

### 3.2.3 Youth Labor Force Participation

Since the size of the labor force is not significantly affected by the definition of economic activity, the sections below use the extended definition of economic activity (which includes both market and subsistence activities).[3] The standard definition of unemployment is used, which requires that the unemployed individual be actively searching for a job (the search criterion).

Of the 2.1 million young people aged 15 to 34 years, the labor force comprises 900,000. The majority is male, with females representing only 22.2% of the total labor force.

Labor force participation varies greatly by gender (Figure 3.4). Female labor force participation is only 18.2%, while male labor force participation stands at 64.7% for the 15–34 group. Female labor force participation is lower than male participation across the board, regardless of the age group or the place of residence. Labor force participation increases for males and females with age. It is extremely low among the youngest age group (15–29)

---

[3] The size of the labor force within the 15–34 age bracket is 876,502 when the market definition is used along with the search criterion. When the extended definition of economic activity (including subsistence activities) is used along with relaxing the search for a job criterion, the labor force within the 15–34 age bracket becomes 898,974. The difference is small (only 2.6%) (see Table 3A.3).

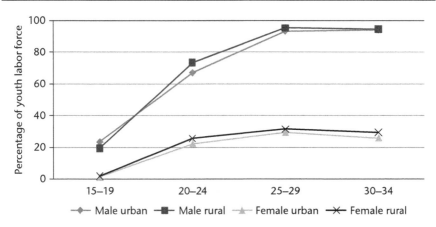

**Figure 3.4.** Youth labor force participation rate by gender, age group, and location, 2010
*Source:* JLMPS (2010).

as the majority is still enrolled in school. Then it increases significantly with age, reaching a peak for the 25–29 and 30–34 age groups for males (94.3%) and for the 25–29 age group for females (29.7%). Even though female labor force participation is very low, it decreases for the 30–34 group, revealing that females begin to withdraw from the labor market after the age of 29 (which most probably corresponds with marriage). Male and female participation is not affected by the place of residence; there are no significant differences in labor force participation rates in urban and rural areas for both young males and females.

Labor force participation by education (Figure 3.5 and Table 3A.4) also reveals major differences between genders. Male labor force participation oscillates according to the education level. Lower participation rates for young males who read and write and for secondary graduates could be explained by the fact that these educational levels are not the final levels and that young males are pursuing their education. Contrarily, female labor force participation is clearly related to educational attainment. Participation rates are higher for females with higher education. Female labor force participation is 3.2% to 9% for secondary graduates and lower. It then sharply increases for post-secondary (43.9%) and university graduates (62%). The secondary level of education is the dividing line. Females with pre-secondary education hardly participate in the labor market, while post-secondary graduates do so significantly. The gender gap in participation rates narrows significantly among university graduates and in particular among rural residents (68.5% for females and 90% for males).

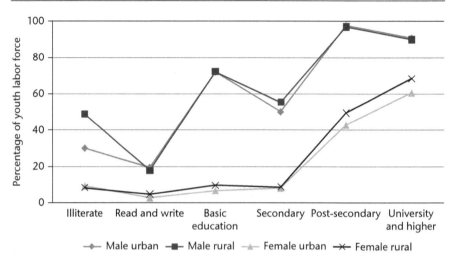

**Figure 3.5.** Labor force participation of youth (15–34) by gender, educational level, and location, 2010

*Source:* JLMPS (2010).

### 3.2.4 Youth Unemployment

The high unemployment rate among young people, and especially among young people without work experience, reflects the difficulty of transition from school to employment and therefore the difficulty of integration into the labor market.

Some 122,338 Jordanians aged 15–34 were unemployed in 2010: 74,169 males and 48,169 females. While young females represent only 22.2% of the total active population, they are overrepresented among the unemployed (39.4%). The young population represents the majority of the unemployed. The share of youth (15–34) in total unemployment is (76.9%) but those aged 20–24 are the most represented (36%), with the female share standing at 47.4% (Table 3.1).

The unemployment rate of young Jordanians (15–34) is relatively high at 15.4%. Female unemployment in that age bracket is twice as high as male unemployment (26.6% versus 12.1%). Female unemployment for all age brackets within the 15–34 age group is higher than male unemployment (see Figure 3.6). Youth unemployment rate decreases with age for both males and females. The unemployment rate for males decreases steadily with age. It declines from 27% for the 15–19 age bracket to 3% for the 30–34 age bracket. Female unemployment rate also decreases with age after increasing first between the 15–19 group and the 20–24 group, reaching a high of 45%. Then, like male unemployment, it declines sharply. However, even though

**Table 3.1.** Distribution of unemployed by age group and gender in 2010 (%)

|       | Male  | Female | Total |
|-------|-------|--------|-------|
| 0–14  | 0.5   | –      | 0.3   |
| 15–19 | 17.8  | 2.4    | 12.5  |
| 20–24 | 30.0  | 47.4   | 36.0  |
| 25–29 | 18.0  | 27.5   | 21.3  |
| 30–34 | 5.1   | 11.0   | 7.1   |
| 35–39 | 8.2   | 8.2    | 8.2   |
| 40–49 | 15.2  | 3.6    | 11.2  |
| 50–59 | 4.7   | –      | 3.1   |
| 60–65 | 0.4   | –      | 0.3   |
| 65+   | 0.1   | –      | 0.1   |
| 15–34 | 70.9  | 88.2   | 76.9  |
| Total | 100.0 | 100.0  | 100.0 |

*Source:* JLMPS (2010).

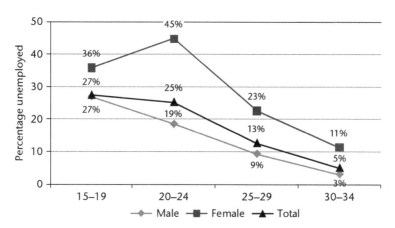

**Figure 3.6.** Unemployment rate by age group and gender
*Source:* JLMPS (2010).

the female unemployment rate decreases with age, it remains high (11%) among the 30–34 group.

Jordanian youth unemployment is strongly linked to educational level (Figure 3.7). Unemployment is zero for illiterate males, but rises sharply for those who read and write (14%). It then declines steadily with educational level to reach 6% among post-secondary graduates and goes back again to 14% among university graduates. Female unemployment rate, on the other hand, increases continuously with education. It goes from zero for illiterate females to 30% and 29% for post-secondary and university graduates, respectively.

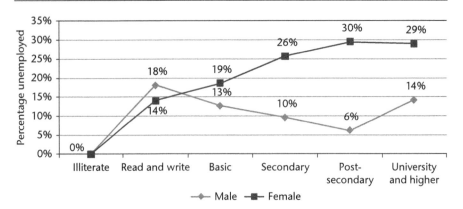

**Figure 3.7.** Unemployment rate of youth (15–34) by educational attainment and gender

*Source:* JLMPS (2010).

## 3.3 School-to-Work Transition

The high unemployment rates of the young population possibly reflect the difficulty in entering the labor market, and since unemployment is closely linked to the educational level as discussed in section 3.2.4, it is interesting to study the transition from school to work. This section presents the characteristics of the first employment status after the individual leaves school, the age at first job, and the time it takes to get the first job for each gender and educational level.

### 3.3.1 First Employment Status After School

In this section, we try to determine what young people do after leaving school. Do they work directly after graduation, and if so what type of job do they get? Are they looking for a job or are they inactive? We also try to analyze whether the first employment status differs by gender and educational level.

METHODOLOGY

The first employment status refers to the first employment status after the individual has left school. It is estimated using information on the current and previous employment statuses presented in the history of employment module of the JLMPS 2010. This information is crossed with the date at which the individual had left the educational system.[4] Seven employment statuses

---

[4] As the date of end of schooling is not included in the data, it is estimated using the number of years of education, assuming that the individual had entered school at the age of six. For

are distinguished: public employment, private formal employment (with social security or written contract); private informal employment (with no social security and no contract); non-wage work (self-employed or employer); unpaid work for family or other; unemployment; and inactivity.

The first employment status differs substantially by gender (Table 3.2). While 64.3% of males work, only 15.6% of females get a job after leaving school. Males work primarily in secure jobs (17.2% in the private sector and 15.6% in the public sector), but some settle for informal jobs (24.6%). Other types of employment (self-employment and unpaid work) are less common. Females also join the formal market (7.8% in the private sector and 4.1% in the public sector). Females hardly ever venture into informal employment or non-wage work as a first employment. Males who are not working after school are mainly unemployed (29.2%) and very few are inactive (6.5%). On the contrary, females who are not working after school are predominantly inactive (71.4%) and, to a lesser extent, unemployed (13.2%).

As shown in Table 3.2, the first employment status by educational level and gender reveals a real divide according to the educational levels for both males and females. The shares of formal employment and unemployment increase (more significantly among females) with the educational level of both males and females. This increase is offset by a decline in inactivity among both males and females and by informal employment among males. For example, the share of male formal employment (in both public and private sectors) nearly doubles (it goes from 24% among the least educated to 52% among university graduates), while the share of male informal employment drops by two-thirds. We find that the share of female formal employment increases even more sharply from 1.8% among the least educated to 29.4% among university graduates, while the share of inactive females is more than halved (it decreases from 90.7% to 36.5%).

The distribution of females' first employment status shows them to be inactive (almost exclusively among the less educated), unemployed, or in formal employment. Informal employment, self-employment, and unpaid family employment are more or less not options after graduation. When females work, they are employed formally. The substantial increase in the share of the unemployed with an educational level (from 4.4% for below secondary to 29.6% for university graduates) probably reflects the fact that the more educated females are very demanding in terms of working conditions and are looking for secure employment.

individuals who have never been to school or who dropped out from school before the age of 15, it is assumed that the start date of the first employment status corresponds to the date when the individual turns 15.

**Table 3.2.** Distribution of first employment status after school by educational level and gender (%)

| | Male | | | | Female | | | |
|---|---|---|---|---|---|---|---|---|
| | Less than secondary | Secondary | Post-secondary and university | Total | Less than secondary | Secondary | Post-secondary and university | Total |
| Public | 11.6 | 21.7 | 22.1 | 15.6 | 0.2 | 1.5 | 10.9 | 4.1 |
| Private formal | 12.4 | 16.2 | 29.9 | 17.2 | 1.6 | 3.9 | 18.5 | 7.8 |
| Private informal | 31.9 | 18.8 | 9.8 | 24.6 | 2.8 | 2.9 | 3.8 | 3.2 |
| Employer/ self- employed | 1.9 | 1.8 | 3.1 | 2.2 | 0.0 | 0.4 | 0.1 | 0.1 |
| Unpaid worker | 6.3 | 3.0 | 2.2 | 4.8 | 0.3 | 0.0 | 0.6 | 0.4 |
| Unemployed | 27.8 | 31.7 | 31.1 | 29.2 | 4.4 | 5.3 | 29.6 | 13.2 |
| Out of labor force | 8.2 | 6.8 | 1.9 | 6.5 | 90.7 | 86.0 | 36.5 | 71.4 |
| Total | 100.0 | 100.0 | 100.0 | 100.0 | 100.0 | 100.0 | 100.0 | 100.0 |

*Source:* JLMPS (2010).

### 3.3.2 Age at First Job and Time Duration to Get the First Job

The analysis given shows that many young people find themselves unemployed after leaving school. In this section, we try to explore the age of graduates when they enter the labor market and the time it takes them to find that first job.[5] We also investigate age and time to first job by gender and educational attainment.

AGE AT FIRST JOB

The Kaplan-Meier failure estimates are used to calculate the probability of obtaining the first job for various ages. Failure estimates calculate the probability of getting a job given a specific age; they calculate the probability of obtaining a first job given that the individual did not work until a specific age.[6]

As shown in Figure 3.8, the cumulative probability of getting that first job at a specified age is different for both genders. The wide gap between male and female failure curves reveals that the male probability of obtaining a first job is much higher than the female probability for all ages. While almost all males manage to get a first job by the age of 34, only one-third of females manage to do so. At the age of 25, almost 75% of males had obtained a first

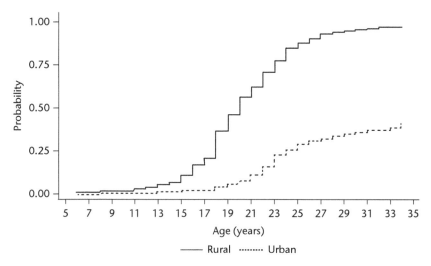

**Figure 3.8.** Cumulative probability of obtaining a first job conditional to age (15–34) by gender, 2010
*Source:* JLMPS (2010).

---

[5] The first job in this context refers to the first job ever obtained that lasted at least six months.
[6] For individuals who work while they are at school, age at first job has been set at the age of the end of schooling and therefore duration to get the first job has been set to zero.

job, but only 25% of females had done so. These result may also show that many females choose never to enter the labor market, and consequently they never get a first job; this group has different characteristics than females who actively search for work. Thus, to avoid selection problems we limit the following analysis to females who ever worked and we compare their age distribution at first job with all males.

Figure 3.9 presents the cumulative probability of getting the first job by age for people aged 15 to 49 years (restricting the analysis to females who ever entered the labor market). It shows that half the males get their first job by 18, while half the females get their first job by 22. Education could explain this age difference at first job. Most working females have post-secondary or university degrees; they are generally more educated than males and consequently enter into the labor market at an older age. The curves become flat at the age of 29–30 for males and 39 for females. This means that all males get their first job by 29–30 and females by 39. The analysis can therefore be limited to the age group 15–39 that includes all males and females who ever entered the labor market.

As Figure 3.10 illustrates, the longer people stay at school, the later they enter the labor market. Among males, age at first job increases steadily with the educational attainment. For example, half the males with less than secondary education obtain their first job by age 17, those with a secondary degree by age 19, those with a post-secondary degree by age 21, and finally the university graduates by age 23. Females with higher education enter

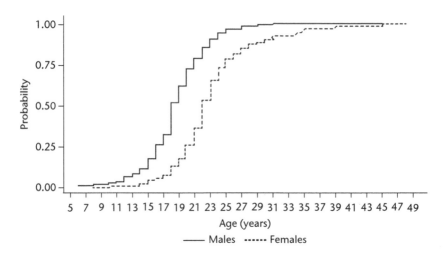

**Figure 3.9.** Cumulative probability of obtaining a first job conditional to age (15–34) by gender, 2010 in (females who ever worked)
*Source:* JLMPS (2010).

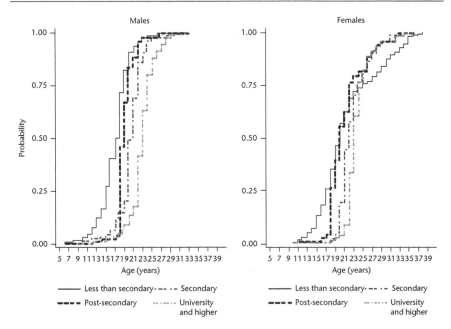

**Figure 3.10.** Cumulative probability of obtaining a first job conditional to age by gender and educational level, ages 15–39 in 2010 (females who ever worked)
*Source:* JLMPS (2010).

the labor market later but age differences are smaller between educational levels. They are also, at equivalent levels of education, generally older than males when they obtain their first job (with the exception of university graduates, who enter at the same age as males). We also find that from age 23 onwards, the less educated females enter the labor market less rapidly.

TIME TAKEN TO GET THE FIRST JOB
This section analyzes how long it takes for a young individual to find a job after leaving school. Failure estimates of the cumulative probability of transition from school to work in years are examined by gender and educational attainment. The time between end of schooling and obtaining the first job is estimated in years. In cases when young individuals find jobs before finishing school, the time to first job after school is set to zero (i.e. immediate entry).

Using the same methodology as for age at first job, we estimate the cumulative probability of getting the first job and the time between graduation and the date of first job by gender and educational level.

As shown in Figure 3.11, males generally get their first job more quickly than females. Half the males find their first job two years after they leave school, but half the females find their first job after three years. Also, three-quarters of

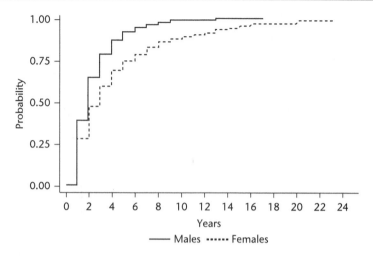

**Figure 3.11.** Conditional probability of obtaining a first job to years after school by gender, ages 15–39 in 2010 (females who ever worked)
*Source:* JLMPS (2010).

males are employed after three years from graduation, whereas three-quarters of females are employed after five years from graduation.

As shown in Figure 3.12, the educational level has minimal impact on the time it takes for males to get their first job after graduation, whereas it greatly affects the probability of females getting a first job. Half the males find a job within two years, regardless of their educational level. On the contrary, the more educated females are the faster they get their first job. Half the female university graduates get their first job within two years, while those with post-secondary education get theirs within three years, the secondary school graduates within four years, and finally those with less than secondary level education within five years. Also unlike males, gaps between females with different educational levels widen over time. For instance, 75% of female university graduates find a job within three years, which is comparable to males. But 75% of females with a post-secondary degree work only five years after graduation, those with a secondary diploma and the least educated work for seven and twelve years after finishing school, respectively. The curve of the least educated females is much flatter as they enter much more slowly into the labor market. Although the most highly educated females are more affected by unemployment and one could expect that they will be more demanding in terms of job security and work conditions, this does not prevent them from finding a job more quickly than other females.

More educated females are probably unemployed before finding their first job, given that their unemployment rates are very high. But why do less

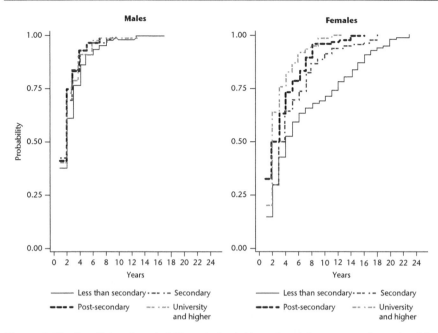

**Figure 3.12.** Conditional probability of obtaining a first job to years after school by gender and educational level, ages 15–39 in 2010 (females who ever worked)
*Source:* JLMPS (2010).

educated females take more time to work? Their unemployment and activity rates are lower and therefore we can assume that some of them are inactive before working. Sequence analysis of the transitions on the labor market may shed some light on this issue.

## 3.4 Sequence Analysis of Youth Labor Market Trajectories

This section describes youth labor market trajectories over time using a sequence analysis. It highlights the main labor market paths between 1999 and 2010 by sketching individuals' employment status year after year. More specifically, this analysis means to capture the degree of mobility or alternatively the persistency of particular employment statuses and the various sequences that follow each employment status in relation to gender and educational attainment. In brief, this section aims to answer the following questions: What were the main labor market paths in Jordan from 1999 to 2010? Which are the most persistent employment statuses and which are more mobile? To which employment status does one spell of unemployment lead? What are the trajectories that lead to public employment, private formal permanent employment, and self-employment? Are there any employment statuses that allow easier access to formal permanent employment in the public and private sectors?

METHODOLOGY

In order to illustrate the labor market dynamics over time we use a sequence analysis that generates a classification of all kinds of labor market paths by gathering together similar trajectories using a cluster analysis. First, we create a yearly calendar of labor market statuses over the period 1999–2010 using the employment history data that provides information of employment statuses for the current, previous, pre-previous, and 1999 situations. Eight employment statuses are distinguished: public job; private formal permanent job; private formal temporary job; private informal job; employer/self-employed; unpaid work; unemployment; and out of labor force. Second, the sequence analysis gathers together all identical trajectories. Since we are only interested in early career paths we restrict our analysis to those aged 15 to 29 in 1999, who finished school before 1999. This includes males and females who ever entered the labor market and reflects those aged 26 to 40 in 2010.

Since illustrations of sequential analysis are sometimes difficult to read (because of the multiple possibilities of transitions from one employment status to another), we also estimate the rate of transition from one employment status to another over alternate time periods. We calculate the transition rates between 1999 and 2000 (one-year period), 1999 and 2005 (six-year period) and between 1999 and 2010 (eleven-year period) from each employment status in 1999.

HOW TO READ THE SEQUENCE ANALYSIS FIGURES

The figures presenting the sequence analysis illustrate for each individual in the sample his/her employment status each year from 1999 to 2010 by grouping the similar trajectories beginning from the same employment status in 1999. The y-axis represents the number of observations in the sample. The x-axis represents the employment status sequence for each individual year after year from 1999 to 2010. Each date corresponds to an employment status, represented by a shade of gray. If the individual were not to change his or her employment status throughout the observation period, the succession of his employment status will be illustrated by a line of a single shade of gray. Instead, the grayscale line changes every time (here every year) that the individual changes his or her employment status.

Ordered sequences figures illustrate to where each employment status leads, not taking into account the length of each employment status. They show more clearly labor market paths for the most mobile individuals.

### 3.4.1 Young Jordanians Are not Mobile

One of the most obvious results of the dynamic analysis is the very high degree of immobility of Jordanian youth in the labor market. As shown in Table 3.3, very few change their employment status between 1999 and 2010. Indeed, the number of episodes show that 61.6% of young people aged 26–40 in 2010 have experienced a single episode during the eleven-year period and approximately one-third (34.5%) had two different employment statuses. Less than 4% changed their employment status twice.[7] Females changed their employment status more often than males (47.1% and 31% changed their employment once, respectively). However, this result also reflects the fact that females often change their employment status to withdraw from the labor market (Table 3.3).

Since the Jordanian labor market is highly differentiated by sex, the sequence analysis is presented separately for males and females.

### 3.4.2 Male Labor Market Sequences

Figure 3A.1 presents the twenty most frequent sequences and confirms the high degree of male immobility in the Jordanian labor market. These sequences represent around 70% of all sequences among males. It is clear that the majority of males aged between 26 and 40 in 2010 are not mobile. Indeed, almost two-thirds of the young males stay in the same employment status through the whole period of observation (Table 3.3).

Table 3.4 shows that most males (93%) are working at the beginning of the period of observation (1999), some are unemployed (6.1%), and only

**Table 3.3.** Distribution of the number of episodes by gender from 1999 to 2010, ages 26–40 in 2010 (%)

| Number of episodes | Male | Female | Total |
|---|---|---|---|
| 1 | 66.0 | 45.9 | 61.6 |
| 2 | 31.0 | 47.13 | 34.5 |
| 3 | 3.0 | 7.0 | 3.9 |
| Total | 100.0 | 100.0 | 100.0 |
| Sample size | 1,435 | 401 | 1,836 |

*Source:* JLMPS (2010).

[7] It has to be noted that the number of episodes that occurred is underestimated. By construction, the number of episodes cannot exceed four. Indeed, the estimation of the number of episodes is based on the history of employment module, which only gives information about four employment statuses (the current, previous, pre-previous ones, plus the employment status in 1999).

**Table 3.4.** Distribution of male employment status in 1999 by gender, ages 26–40 in 2010 (%)

| Employment status in 1999 | |
| --- | --- |
| Public | 35.9 |
| Private formal permanent | 8.4 |
| Private formal temporary | 3.4 |
| Private informal | 29.8 |
| Employer/self-employed | 11.1 |
| Unpaid worker | 4.4 |
| Unemployed | 6.1 |
| Out of labor force | 0.9 |
| Total | 100.0 |
| Sample size | 1,639 |

*Source:* JLMPS (2010).

**Table 3.5.** Male persistency rate by employment status over the period 1999–2010, ages 26–40 in 2010 (%)

| Employment status in 1999 | Persistency rate | Sample size |
| --- | --- | --- |
| Public | 82.8 | 594 |
| Private formal permanent | 86.3 | 90 |
| Private formal temporary | 44.0 | 36 |
| Private informal | 68.7 | 296 |
| Employer/self-employed | 76.3 | 121 |
| Unpaid worker | 0.0 | 42 |
| Unemployed | 2.4 | 65 |
| Out of labor force | 26.2 | 9 |

*Source:* JLMPS (2010).

0.9% are inactive. The majority of working males are employed in formal jobs (35.9% in the public sector and 11.8% in the private sector), 29.8% are in unprotected types of job, 11.1% are non-wage workers, and 4.4% are unpaid workers.

Table 3.5 shows male persistency rates for each employment status over the same period 1999–2010. It is possible to classify the different employment statuses according to their degree of persistency/mobility. Some employment statuses (public employment and private formal permanent employment) are highly stable, with persistency rates over 80%, some are very stable (self-employment and private informal employment), with persistency rates around 70%. Private formal temporary employment is somewhat unstable and susceptible to change, with persistency rates around 45%. Finally, unemployment and unpaid family work are very mobile statuses, with persistency

rates below 5%. The out-of-the-labor-force status is not statistically significant because of the very few observations (only nine).

Figure 3A.2 provides complementary information to the male labor market
sequences. It presents the sequences' order of male labor market paths from
1999 to 2010, not taking into account the length of each employment status,
and clearly illustrates the labor market paths for the most mobile individuals.
It also confirms the fact that young males rarely change their employment
statuses and that it is very rare that they change more than once.

Figure 3.13 presents male employment statuses in 2000, 2005, and 2010,
according to the employment status in 1999. It estimates transition rates
over one year (1999–2000), over six years (1999–2005), and over eleven years
(1999–2010).

First, Table 3.5 shows that some employment statuses are very persistent: public, private formal permanent, informal, and independent. The majority of
males in these statuses do not change statuses over the whole period of observation. Table 3.5 demonstrates that 83–86%, 76.3%, and 70.9% of males with
permanent jobs, who were self-employed or employers, and who were unprotected workers, respectively remain in the same employment status during the
eleven-year period of observation. Although these statuses are very persistent,
it is interesting to follow what happens when individuals do exit from these
persistent statuses. Figure 3.13 and Figure 3A.2 show that a significant proportion of civil servants do change their employment status. Some 4% become
self-employed or employers, 3.7% become private formal-wage workers and
3.1% become informal-wage workers. Few become unemployed (3.4%) or inactive (3%), which truly reflects the phenomenon of early retirement in Jordan.
The few young males who leave their private formal permanent job do so
mainly to work in the public sector (10.6%), thus maintaining their job stability, and very few get a private formal temporary job (3%). A small proportion of
the non-wage workers (self-employed or employers) in 1999 go into the formal
market (mainly in the public sector, 8.1%) or become informal-wage workers
(7.1%). Young males initially employed without a contract change their status
only to non-wage work (23% become self-employed or employers).

Second, over half (56%) the private-sector workers with a temporary contract change their employment status. In most cases, it is to get a permanent
contract in the public sector (29.6%) or in the private sector (26.4%). Thus
young people in the formal type of employment remain employed formally
and strive to improve their situation.

Finally, the unemployed or unpaid family workers in 1999 are very mobile.
Unsurprisingly, young males who were initially unemployed do not stay
in this state for a long time. Over a one-year period (from 1999–2000) only
45.3% are still unemployed and over a six-year period (1999–2005) only 7%
are still unemployed. We can identify the main exits from unemployment

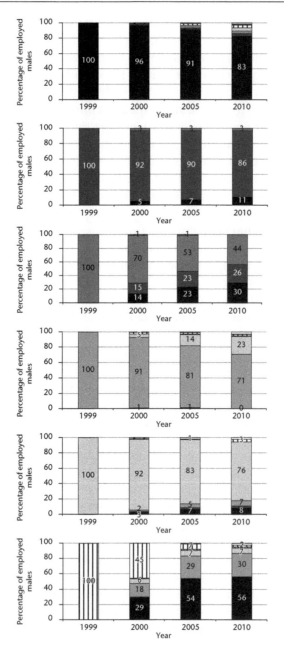

**Figure 3.13.** Distribution of male employment status in 2000, 2005, and 2010 according to employment status in 1999, ages 26–40 in 2010 (%)
*Source:* JLMPS (2010).

from Figure 3.13 and Figure 3A.2. They show that an unemployment episode leads to two very different types of status: mainly to public-sector employment (55.8%) and, to a lesser extent, to informal employment (30.3%).

Because young males are rarely mobile in the labor market, the initial employment status mostly persists. The main changes are observed among those who were initially in a private formal temporary job (who will find a permanent job either in the public sector or in the private sector) or who were working informally (and who will become non-wage workers), and finally the unemployed males (who will find a public job or a private informal job). The analysis of the dynamics of the male labor market also shows that there is a clear line between formal and informal sectors. Indeed, young males who were initially in a formal type of employment maintain their situation, or improve it by getting a permanent contract. We do not observe any transition from informal employment to formal employment. The fact that we do not observe such a transition over the 1999–2010 period probably indicates that the history of employment module does not capture the formalization that occurs when new entrants are first hired informally and then acquire formal status within the same job. It only captures transitions between informal and formal employment when a job change is involved, that is, from the informal sector to the formal sector. Therefore we can conclude that males in formal types of employment remain formally employed but that males who were employed informally either remain informal wage workers or become self-employed or employers because they cannot find a job in the formal sector.

EDUCATION AND MALE TRANSITIONS
The distribution of young males by their employment status in 1999 clearly differs depending on their educational attainment, as shown in Table 3.6. Those with secondary education or higher are mostly employed in formal jobs (public or private), while those with lower than secondary education are employed in informal jobs (informal private and unpaid work). While 57.7% of males with high education get secure jobs, only 41.6% of males with lower education had a formal employment in 1999. Education makes a big difference in the private sector (for both permanent and temporary employment). The share of males with higher education is almost double that of males with lower education. The opposite is true for informal work; in informal employment and unpaid family work, it is the less educated that get the lion's share. Educational attainment does not make that big a difference for unemployed or inactive males.

Figures 3.14 and 3A.3 illustrate the influence of education on males' sequences, distinguishing males with low levels of education (less than secondary) and higher levels of education (secondary and above). We will try to answer a number of questions. Does the segmentation observed in general

85

**Table 3.6.** Distribution of male employment status in 1999 by educational attainment, ages 26–40 in 2010 (%)

| Employment status in 1999 | Below secondary | Secondary and above | Total |
|---|---|---|---|
| Public | 32.4 | 41.8 | 35.9 |
| Private formal permanent | 6.5 | 11.5 | 8.4 |
| Private formal temporary | 2.8 | 4.4 | 3.4 |
| Private informal | 35.7 | 20.0 | 29.8 |
| Employer/self-employed | 10.2 | 12.7 | 11.1 |
| Unpaid worker | 5.4 | 2.9 | 4.4 |
| Unemployed | 5.8 | 6.5 | 6.1 |
| Out of labor force | 1.3 | 0.3 | 0.9 |
| Total | 100.0 | 100.0 | 100.0 |
| Sample Size | 1,069 | 570 | 1,639 |

*Source:* JLMPS (2010).

between formal and informal sectors persist according to educational levels? Do the more educated have greater opportunities to transit from informal to formal jobs? Are the transitions from temporary contracts to permanent contracts easier among the better educated?

Figure 3.14 presents the distribution of male employment status in 2000, 2005, and 2010 according to their educational level and their employment status in 1999.[8] We find that the more educated males stay longer in public employment. Their persistency rate is 87.9% compared to 78.4% for the less educated, who are more likely to leave the public sector to get a private informal or a private temporary job or to become inactive.

Persistency rates in permanent employment over the period 1999–2010 are relatively similar regardless of the educational level (88% among the less educated and 85% among the more educated). The only noticeable difference is the fact that the more educated leave private permanent employment only to go to the public sector (15%), while the less educated go to either public employment (7%) or to private temporary employment (6%).

Although less educated males are more likely to hold informal jobs, education does not seem to influence their transition from informal employment. Around 70–71% remain in informal employment from 1999 to 2010, regardless of their education level. Only some of those who were initially informally employed in 1999 transition to self-employment or employer (28.8% of the more educated and 21.2% of the less educated).

---

[8] We study here the transitions from only four employment statuses in 1999 (public employment, permanent private employment, informal employment, and unemployment) due to the small number of observations for other employment statuses.

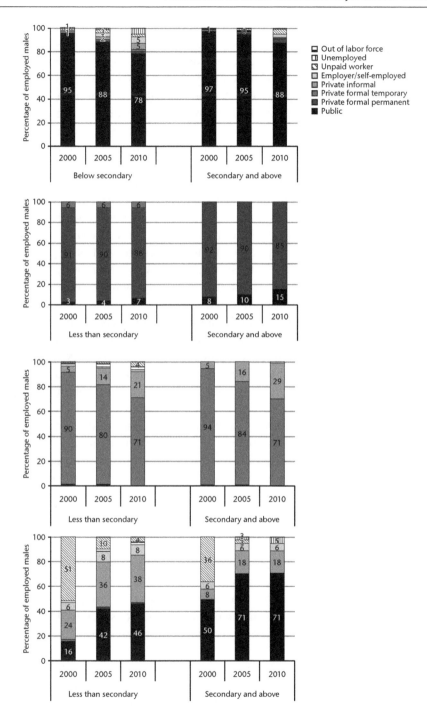

**Figure 3.14.** Distribution of male employment status in 2000, 2005, and 2010 by educational level according to employment status in 1999, ages 26–40 in 2010
*Source:* JLMPS (2010).

87

Young males who were non-wage workers in 1999 have almost the same chances of holding their status over the 1999–2010 period by educational level (75% for below secondary graduates and 78% for above secondary graduates). Yet their transitions to other employment statuses differ by educational level. Exit to public employment is more probable for the more educated than the less educated (12.8% to 4.4%, respectively) and likewise to private formal permanent employment (6.5% to 0%, respectively). Meanwhile, exit to informal employment is less likely for the more educated (1.9% to 11.2%), and this hold true for exits to unemployment or inactivity.

Finally, although the transition from unemployment leads to two statuses—public employment or informal employment—the education level greatly affects the final destination. Those with higher education have a higher probability of getting public employment than those with lower education (70.8% to 45.8%, respectively) and a lower probability of going into informal employment (18.2% to 38.4%, respectively). Moreover, it is quite remarkable that the rate of persistency in unemployment decreases much more rapidly among the more educated.

In summary, the most educated males are more likely to improve their employment status than the less educated. When they do change their employment status, it is usually to secure their job or to go to a better or more stable employment status (transition from a private temporary job to a private permanent job; or transition from self-employment or unemployment to public job).

The observed divide between formal and informal sectors remains very strong at every level of education. On all levels, informal jobs are not a temporary step to secure employment. The only way of transition out of informal employment is to self-employment, for both the highly educated and the lower educated.

### 3.4.3 Female Labor Market Sequences

Unlike males, the majority of females are either inactive (44.7%) or unemployed (14.3%) in 1999 (see Table 3.7). Only 41% of females aged 26–40 in 2010 are working in 1999. Most of them are in secure jobs (16.8% in the public sector and 10.8% in the private formal jobs). Only 9.8% are in private informal wage work and very few are non-wage workers or unpaid workers.

Because the number of observations is very low for certain statuses (private temporary employment, non-wage work, and unpaid family work), the sequence and transitions analyses between 1999 and 2010 are restricted to five employment statuses: public employment; private formal employment; informal employment; unemployment; and inactivity.

**Table 3.7.** Distribution of female employment status in 1999 by gender, ages 26–40 in 2010 (%)

| Employment status in 1999 | |
| --- | --- |
| Public | 16.8 |
| Private formal permanent | 5.4 |
| Private formal temporary | 5.4 |
| Private informal | 9.8 |
| Employer/self-employed | 2.0 |
| Unpaid worker | 1.7 |
| Unemployed | 14.3 |
| Out of labor force | 44.7 |
| Total | 100.0 |
| Sample size | 473 |

*Source:* JLMPS (2010).

Table 3.3 shows that many females stay in the same employment status between 1999 to 2010. Even though females seem more mobile than males, when they do change their status it is generally to withdraw from the labor market. Figure 3A.4 illustrates the twenty most frequent female sequences, which represent a little more than two-thirds of all female sequences. It confirms that females either stay in the same employment status or become inactive (except for those who were initially unemployed and who end up working in the public sector).

As illustrated in Table 3.8, the persistency rates vary greatly from one employment status to another. Only females working in the public sector in 1999 largely (84.8%) maintain their status over the eleven-year period of observation. Almost half the females employed in the formal private sector and who were inactive in 1999 stay in the same employment status. However, most of those who were employed informally or were unemployed will change their employment status.

Figure 3.15 presents the distribution of female employment status in 2000, 2005, and 2010, according to various employment statuses in 1999. It provides transition rates over one year (1999–2000), six years (1999–2005), and eleven years (1999–2010). Table 3.8, Figures 3.15 and 3A.5 (female ordered sequences) confirm that public employment and formal private employment are the two most stable statuses. The vast majority (85%) of females who were working in the public sector in 1999 remain in that employment status during the whole period. Very few become inactive (9%) or employed in formal private work (6%). It is interesting to note that the majority of changes occur during the first year (between 1999–2000) and that six years and eleven years later we observe very little mobility.

**Table 3.8.** Female employment status persistency rate over the period 1999–2010, ages 26–40 in 2010 (%)

| Employment status in 1999 | Persistency rate | Sample size |
| --- | --- | --- |
| Public | 84.8 | 83 |
| Private formal | 52.1 | 60 |
| Private informal | 20.6 | 31 |
| Employer/self-employed | 48.0 | 9 |
| Unpaid worker | 28.7 | 7 |
| Unemployed | 1.3 | 51 |
| Out of labor force | 50.9 | 135 |

*Source:* JLMPS (2010).

Half the females who are working in 1999 in formal private employment keep their secure job until 2010. Those who change their status mainly withdraw from the labor market (31%) and, to a lesser extent, get a public job (12%).

Contrary to what one might expect, a significant proportion (51%) of females who were initially inactive in 1999 change their employment status over the 1999–2010 period (see Table 3.8). The majority find a secure job (18% in the public sector and 12% in the private sector), 11% are employed informally and 8% become self-employed or employers. Thus, for almost half the females who were initially out of the labor force, inactivity is not an end in itself; it can lead to different types of employment.

The vast majority (79%) of females who were in informal private jobs in 1999 change their employment status in 2010, but when they do, it is only to exit from the labor force (76%).

Almost all females who were unemployed in 1999 changed their employment status in 2010. Three-quarters of those who were initially unemployed get a secure job (54% in the public sector and 21% in the formal private sector), some become informal wage workers (10%) and a small proportion is discouraged and withdraws from the labor market (10%). In this light, unemployment could be considered a temporary status leading to a secure job later on.

Finally, females who are employed in secure jobs are less likely to withdraw from the labor market. Indeed the exit rates decrease substantially with the degree of employment stability (from 76% for the informally employed, to 31% for the formally employed in the private sector and to only 9% for public sector employees).

EDUCATION AND FEMALE TRANSITIONS

Education plays a crucial role in female labor market transitions. Table 3.9 shows that in 1999 some 72% of females with low levels of education are either inactive (61%) or unemployed (10%). Very few are employed in private

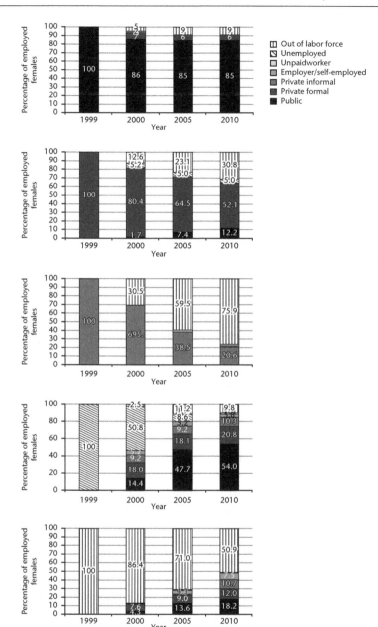

**Figure 3.15.** Distribution of female employment status in 2000, 2005, and 2010 according to employment status in 1999, ages 26–40 in 2010

*Source:* JLMPS (2010).

**Table 3.9.** Distribution of female employment status in 1999 by educational attainment, ages 26–40 in 2010 (%)

|  | Below secondary | Secondary and above | Total |
|---|---|---|---|
| Public | 4.3 | 24.9 | 16.8 |
| Private formal permanent | 1.4 | 8.0 | 5.4 |
| Private formal temporary | 0.8 | 8.4 | 5.4 |
| Private informal | 15.6 | 6.0 | 9.8 |
| Employer/self-employed | 1.8 | 2.1 | 2.0 |
| Unpaid worker | 4.4 | 0.0 | 1.7 |
| Unemployed | 10.4 | 16.8 | 14.3 |
| Out of labor force | 61.3 | 33.8 | 44.7 |
| Total | 100.0 | 100.0 | 100.0 |

*Source:* JLMPS (2010).

unprotected types of jobs (16%) and more rarely (4%) in the public sector. Contrarily, the majority of those with high levels of education are working (49%), and in most cases they are employed in secure jobs (25% in the public sector and 16.4% in the formal private sector), and rarely in informal jobs (6%). But the proportion of unemployed highly educated females is relatively high (17%) as compared to the less educated ones (10%). Finally, the most educated females are nearly half as inactive as the less educated (34% against 61%).

Given the very low number of observations for certain employment statuses, Figure 3.16 presents the female transition rates by educational level only from public employment and inactivity in 1999. Figure 3A.6 presents complementary information, with the ordered female sequences by educational level.

The persistency rate in public employment is the same regardless of the educational level (84–85%) throughout the period 1999–2010. However, education levels influence exits from public employment to other employment statuses. A large portion of females with low levels of education leave public employment to withdraw from the market (16%), while only 8% of females with high levels of education do so. Alternatively, 7% of the latter group may move to a formal job.

Among females who were inactive in 1999, a higher proportion of the more educated eventually enter the labor market one year, six years, and eleven years later. Moreover, when they do enter the labor market they get more formal jobs (in both public and private sectors) than the less educated females (41% versus 21%).

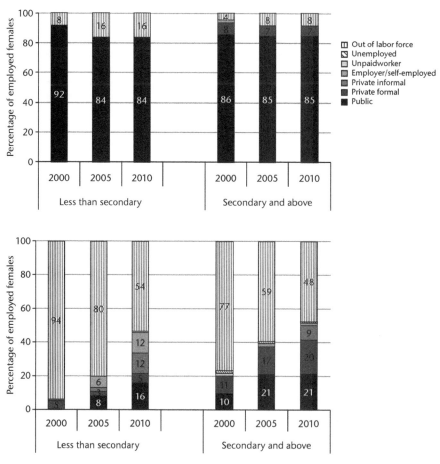

**Figure 3.16.** Distribution of female employment status in 2000, 2005, and 2010 by educational level according to employment status in 1999, ages 26–40 in 2010
*Source:* JLMPS (2010).

### 3.4.4 How to Get a Permanent Job or to Be a Self-employed/Employer?

We now try to understand whether there are specific paths that allow access to protected permanent jobs in the public and private sectors or alternatively to non-wage work by looking at sequences that lead to one of these employment statuses in 2010.

Figure 3.17 presents the distribution of male employment statuses in 1999, 2000, and 2010 according to the employment status in 2010. We consider in particular transitions to public employment, private formal permanent employment, and self-employment in order to see whether there are specific statuses that lead to formal wage work or non-wage work. For females, Figure 3.18 illustrates the distribution of employment statuses in 1999, 2000,

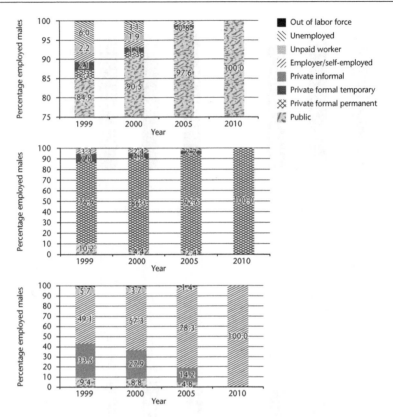

**Figure 3.17.** Distribution of male employment status in 1999, 2000, and 2010 according to employment status in 2010
*Source:* JLMPS (2010).

and 2010 according to public employment, formal employment, or inactivity in 2010.[9]

Figures 3.17 and 3.18 show that only formal employment, inactivity, or unemployment lead to stable formal-wage work. We never observe transitions from informal employment to formal employment (whether public or private).

For instance, the vast majority of males (85%) who hold a public job in 2010 were already working in that same job in 1999. If not, they were either unemployed (6%) or in another form of formal job (2% in private permanent job and 2% in private temporary job). We find similar results for females. Only formal employment, unemployment, and inactivity lead to public

---

[9] The number of females in non-wage work in 2010 is too small to be examined. We also give particular attention to inactive females in 2010, as they represent an important share of the distribution of all females in 2010.

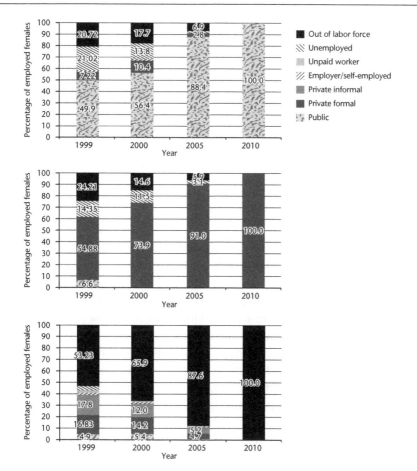

**Figure 3.18.** Distribution of female employment status in 1999, 2000, and 2010 according to employment status in 2010
*Source:* JLMPS (2010).

employment. However, the proportions are different to the male proportions: 50% were already in a public job, 21% were unemployed, and 21% were inactive in 1999.

Some 77% of males who are in private formal permanent employment in 2010 were already in the same status in 1999. For the rest, the statuses that preceded private formal permanent employment were either in public employment (10%) or formal temporary employment (8%). Females follow a more or less similar path. Half the females who are in formal employment in 2010 were already in formal employment, 24% were inactive, and 14% were unemployed in 1999.

Instead, the statuses that lead to male self-employment in 2010 are very different. Self-employment is less stable; half of those who are non-wage workers in 2010 were not so in 1999. In 34% of the cases, informal employment preceded self-employment, and more rarely public employment (9%) or unpaid family work (6%).

Finally, we note that half the inactive females in 2010 were also inactive in 1999. The other half was employed mainly in the private sector (18% informally and 17% formally), and more rarely in the public sector (5%). This result confirms the fact that females withdraw from the labor market more often when they were working in the private sector (especially informal), rather than in the public sector.

## 3.5 Conclusion

The Jordanian labor market has experienced major changes in recent decades. On the one hand, young Jordanians have become more educated, and a significant proportion hold a university degree. The educational level of young females has exceeded that of young males. Despite the improvement in their level of education young Jordanians, especially those with a university degree—and particularly females, are experiencing very high unemployment rates. Meanwhile, although the most highly qualified females are also more unemployed, they also participate at relatively high rates in the Jordanian economic activity. On the other hand, the share of unprotected jobs (with no written contract)—and in particular the share of informal jobs in total first jobs—rose sharply in recent decades, compensating the decline of the share of public employment in total first employment. The wealth of the JLMPS 2010 data allows for the first time a dynamic analysis to be made of the Jordanian labor market and especially to follow year after year the different employment statuses of individuals. It thus allows us to better understand the school-to-work transition. Five main results can be concluded from this study.

First, young Jordanians are relatively immobile; they rarely change their employment status during the observation period 1999–2010.

Second, the more educated males (especially those with a university degree) get protected jobs in both the public and private sectors. The formal jobs they obtain are relatively stable; they rarely change their employment status. But when they do change, it is usually to get another formal employment (transition from a private protected job to public employment or transition from temporary employment to permanent employment). On the other hand, less educated males have more difficulty obtaining a stable employment and/or a formal employment. They more often work informally.

Third, the observation of female transitions from one employment status to another shows that females are either inactive, unemployed, or working in formal employment (public or private). Informal employment is almost non-existent among females, even among the less educated. Females with more education are more active and much less likely than the least educated females to withdraw from the labor market (whatever the type of job they obtain). Although the least educated females do not participate much in economic activity, around half of those who were initially inactive will eventually work. The behavior of females with a university degree is relatively similar to that of males. Their participation rate is very high and they find their first job as quickly as males. However, they are much more affected by unemployment than males.

Fourth, there is a clear segmentation between formal and informal sectors. Young people who at one time worked informally are not able to get another job that is protected by a contract and social security. Informal and non-wage work seem to be related, as informal-wage work often leads to self-employment. The informalization of employment is not a temporary status for accessing a stable protected employment a few years later.

Finally, very few initial employment statuses lead to a formal permanent employment (public or private) eleven years later. Only initial formal employment or unemployment (and inactivity for females) lead to the two best types of wage work (public and private formal employment).

## APPENDIX

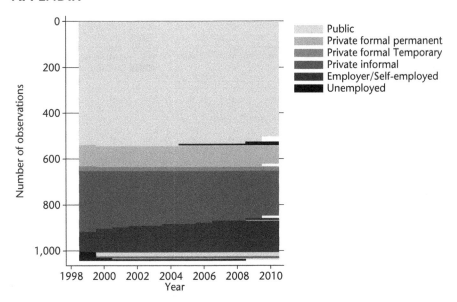

**Figure 3A.1.** The 20 most frequent male sequences over the period 1999–2010, ages 26–40 in 2010

*Source:* JLMPS (2010).

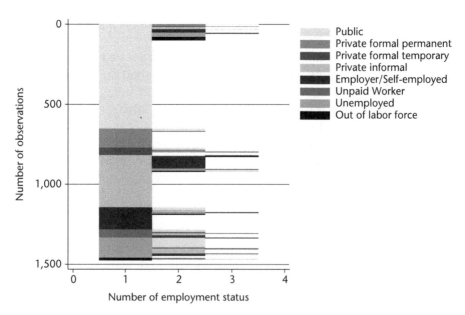

**Figure 3A.2.** Male ordered sequences over the period 1999–2010, ages 26–40 in 2010
*Source:* JLMPS (2010).

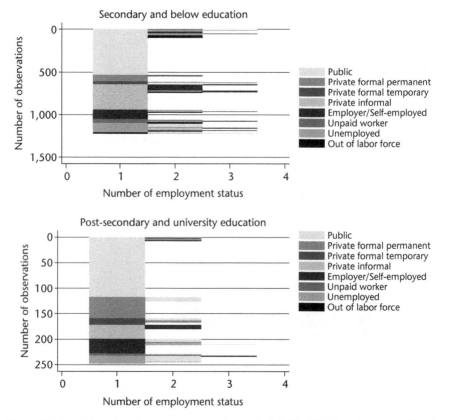

**Figure 3A.3.** Male ordered sequences over the period 1999–2010 by educational level, ages 26–40 in 2010
*Source:* JLMPS (2010).

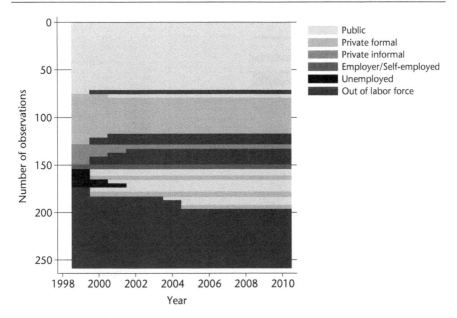

**Figure 3A.4.** The 20 most frequent female sequences over the period 1999–2010, ages 26–40 in 2010

*Source:* JLMPS (2010).

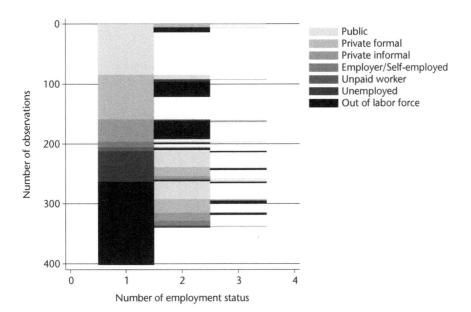

**Figure 3A.5.** Female ordered sequences over the period 1999–2010, ages 26–40 in 2010

*Source:* JLMPS (2010).

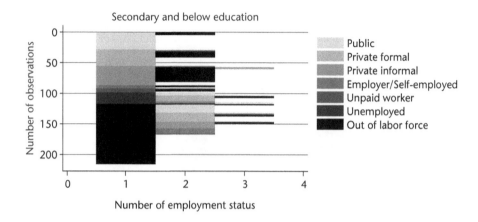

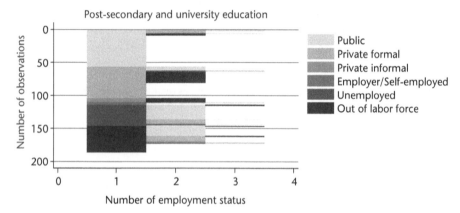

**Figure 3A.6.** Female ordered sequences by educational level over the period 1999–2010, ages 26–40 in 2010

*Source:* JLMPS (2010).

**Table 3A.1.** Distribution of the population by age group, 2010

| | Male | | Female | | Total | | |
|---|---|---|---|---|---|---|---|
| | Frequency | Percentage | Frequency | Percentage | Frequency | Percentage | Cumulated Percentage |
| 0–14 | 1137491 | 37.7 | 1106925 | 37.0 | 2244416 | 37.3 | 37.3 |
| 15–19 | 336610 | 11.1 | 336918 | 11.3 | 673528 | 11.2 | 48.6 |
| 20–24 | 285875 | 9.5 | 271338 | 9.1 | 557213 | 9.3 | 57.8 |
| 25–29 | 241097 | 8.0 | 230983 | 7.7 | 472080 | 7.9 | 65.7 |
| 30–34 | 205704 | 6.8 | 208531 | 7.0 | 414235 | 6.9 | 72.6 |
| 35–39 | 186967 | 6.2 | 194727 | 6.5 | 381694 | 6.4 | 78.9 |
| 40–49 | 293098 | 9.7 | 279580 | 9.4 | 572678 | 9.5 | 88.4 |
| 50–59 | 146081 | 4.8 | 174365 | 5.8 | 320446 | 5.3 | 93.8 |
| 60–64 | 64311 | 2.1 | 62465 | 2.1 | 126776 | 2.1 | 95.9 |
| 65+ | 123346 | 4.1 | 124124 | 4.2 | 247470 | 4.1 | 100.0 |
| 15–29 | 863582 | 28.6 | 839239 | 28.1 | 1702821 | 28.3 | |
| 15–34 | 1069286 | 35.4 | 1047770 | 35.0 | 2117056 | 35.2 | |
| Total | 3020580 | 100.0 | 2989956 | 100.0 | 6010536 | 100.0 | |
| Sample size | 13027 | | 12942 | | 25969 | | |

*Source:* JLMPS (2010).

**Table 3A.2.** Distribution of youth by gender, urban/rural location, age group, and educational level, 2010 (%)

| | Urban | | | Rural | | | Total | | |
|---|---|---|---|---|---|---|---|---|---|
| | Male | Female | Total | Male | Female | Total | Male | Female | Total |
| **15–19** | | | | | | | | | |
| Illiterate | 1.6 | 0.8 | 1.2 | 0.5 | 0.6 | 0.6 | 1.4 | 0.7 | 1.1 |
| Read and write | 26.1 | 24.7 | 25.4 | 27.7 | 28.9 | 28.3 | 26.4 | 25.5 | 26.0 |
| Basic | 55.4 | 52.8 | 54.1 | 57.7 | 53.3 | 55.5 | 55.8 | 52.9 | 54.3 |
| Secondary | 16.6 | 21.8 | 19.1 | 14.0 | 17.2 | 15.6 | 16.1 | 20.9 | 18.5 |
| Post-secondary | 0.0 | 0.0 | 0.0 | 0.0 | 0.0 | 0.0 | 0.0 | 0.0 | 0.0 |
| University and higher | 0.4 | 0.0 | 0.2 | 0.0 | 0.0 | 0.0 | 0.3 | 0.0 | 0.2 |
| **20–24** | | | | | | | | | |
| Illiterate | 1.2 | 0.5 | 0.9 | 0.5 | 3.2 | 1.8 | 1.1 | 1.0 | 1.0 |
| Read and write | 1.6 | 0.9 | 1.3 | 1.1 | 1.0 | 1.0 | 1.5 | 0.9 | 1.2 |
| Basic | 38.9 | 34.4 | 36.7 | 48.3 | 31.6 | 40.5 | 40.8 | 33.9 | 37.5 |
| Secondary | 41.8 | 36.4 | 39.1 | 32.9 | 37.5 | 35.0 | 40.0 | 36.6 | 38.3 |
| Post-secondary | 5.4 | 8.6 | 7.0 | 2.4 | 7.2 | 4.6 | 4.8 | 8.4 | 6.5 |
| University and higher | 11.0 | 19.1 | 15.0 | 14.7 | 19.5 | 17.0 | 11.8 | 19.2 | 15.4 |
| **25–29** | | | | | | | | | |
| Illiterate | 2.3 | 2.4 | 2.3 | 2.2 | 5.7 | 3.8 | 2.3 | 3.0 | 2.6 |
| Read and write | 1.2 | 3.1 | 2.2 | 3.2 | 1.9 | 2.6 | 1.6 | 2.9 | 2.2 |
| Basic | 45.4 | 33.6 | 39.6 | 49.1 | 34.9 | 42.5 | 46.2 | 33.8 | 40.1 |
| Secondary | 18.2 | 21.5 | 19.9 | 17.6 | 17.8 | 17.7 | 18.1 | 20.9 | 19.4 |
| Post-secondary | 9.1 | 11.6 | 10.4 | 2.8 | 12.5 | 7.3 | 7.9 | 11.8 | 9.8 |
| University and higher | 23.7 | 27.7 | 25.7 | 25.0 | 27.3 | 26.1 | 24.0 | 27.7 | 25.8 |
| **30–34** | | | | | | | | | |
| Illiterate | 2.1 | 1.9 | 2.0 | 1.3 | 4.8 | 3.2 | 2.0 | 2.4 | 2.2 |
| Read and write | 3.5 | 2.6 | 3.1 | 6.3 | 5.5 | 5.8 | 4.0 | 3.1 | 3.5 |
| Basic | 50.3 | 40.3 | 45.4 | 60.3 | 48.9 | 54.1 | 52.0 | 41.9 | 46.9 |
| Secondary | 17.8 | 18.9 | 18.4 | 19.2 | 15.0 | 16.9 | 18.0 | 18.2 | 18.1 |
| Post-Secondary | 9.7 | 16.0 | 12.8 | 2.4 | 7.8 | 5.3 | 8.5 | 14.4 | 11.5 |
| University and Higher | 16.5 | 20.3 | 18.4 | 10.5 | 18.0 | 14.6 | 15.5 | 19.9 | 17.7 |
| **Total 15–34** | | | | | | | | | |
| Illiterate | 1.8 | 1.3 | 1.5 | 1.1 | 3.2 | 2.1 | 1.6 | 1.6 | 1.6 |
| Read and write | 9.6 | 9.3 | 9.5 | 10.8 | 11.4 | 11.1 | 9.8 | 9.7 | 9.8 |
| Basic | 47.8 | 41.3 | 44.6 | 53.4 | 43.1 | 48.3 | 48.9 | 41.6 | 45.3 |
| Secondary | 23.8 | 25.0 | 24.4 | 21.1 | 21.9 | 21.5 | 23.3 | 24.4 | 23.8 |
| Post-secondary | 5.4 | 8.0 | 6.7 | 1.8 | 6.0 | 3.9 | 4.7 | 7.6 | 6.2 |
| University and higher | 11.6 | 15.2 | 13.4 | 11.9 | 14.3 | 13.1 | 11.6 | 15.0 | 13.3 |

*Source:* JLMPS (2010).

**Table 3A.3.** Labor force size by gender, urban/rural residency, age group, and economic activity definition, 2010

| | Urban | | | Rural | | | Total | | |
|---|---|---|---|---|---|---|---|---|---|
| | Male | Female | Total | Male | Female | Total | Male | Female | Total |
| **15–29** | | | | | | | | | |
| Market and search | 397,358 | 107,149 | 504,507 | 99,891 | 25,193 | 125,084 | 497,248 | 132,343 | 629,591 |
| Extended and search | 398,534 | 108,384 | 506,919 | 100,112 | 27,049 | 127,160 | 498,646 | 135,433 | 634,079 |
| Market no search | 401,866 | 112,167 | 514,033 | 100,822 | 27,226 | 128,049 | 502,688 | 139,393 | 642,082 |
| Extended no search | 403,351 | 114,004 | 517,354 | 101,043 | 29,082 | 130,125 | 504,394 | 143,085 | 647,479 |
| **15–34** | | | | | | | | | |
| Market and search | 559,886 | 149,276 | 709,161 | 131,687 | 35,653 | 167,340 | 691,573 | 184,929 | 876,502 |
| Extended and search | 561,063 | 151,942 | 713,005 | 131,908 | 38,788 | 170,696 | 692,970 | 190,731 | 883,701 |
| Market no search | 564,650 | 155,111 | 719,762 | 133,115 | 37,989 | 171,104 | 697,765 | 193,100 | 890,865 |
| Extended no search | 566,135 | 158,380 | 724,514 | 133,336 | 41,123 | 174,459 | 699,471 | 199,503 | 898,974 |

Source: JLMPS (2010).

**Table 3A.4.** Labor force participation by gender, educational level, urban/rural residency, and economic activity definition, 2010

|  | Male | | | Female | | | Total | | |
|---|---|---|---|---|---|---|---|---|---|
|  | Urban | Rural | Total | Urban | Rural | Total | Urban | Rural | Total |
| Illiterate | 0.300 | 0.488 | 0.323 | 0.094 | 0.083 | 0.090 | 0.214 | 0.186 | 0.207 |
| Read and write | 0.194 | 0.178 | 0.190 | 0.027 | 0.047 | 0.032 | 0.112 | 0.112 | 0.112 |
| Basic education | 0.721 | 0.722 | 0.721 | 0.067 | 0.097 | 0.073 | 0.421 | 0.447 | 0.426 |
| Secondary | 0.501 | 0.555 | 0.510 | 0.081 | 0.087 | 0.082 | 0.288 | 0.319 | 0.294 |
| Post-secondary | 0.976 | 0.970 | 0.975 | 0.429 | 0.495 | 0.439 | 0.652 | 0.604 | 0.646 |
| University and higher | 0.908 | 0.900 | 0.906 | 0.606 | 0.685 | 0.620 | 0.738 | 0.783 | 0.746 |
| Total | 0.646 | 0.651 | 0.647 | 0.178 | 0.197 | 0.182 | 0.414 | 0.427 | 0.417 |

*Source:* JLMPS (2010).

### References

Assaad, R., 2014. The structure and evolution of employment in Jordan. In *The Jordanian Labor Market in the New Millennium*, ed. Ragui Assaad. Oxford: Oxford University Press, pp. 1–38.

Assaad, R. and M. Amer, 2008. Labor market conditions in Jordan 1995–2006: An analysis of microdata sources. A report for Al-Manar Project. Amman, Jordan: National Center for Human Resource Development: <http://www.almanar.jo/AlManaren/Portals/0/PDF2/Jordanian%20Labor%20Demand.pdf> (accessed November 8, 2013).

# 4

# Gender and the Jordanian Labor Market

*Ragui Assaad, Rana Hendy, and Chaimaa Yassine*

## 4.1 Introduction

It is by now well established that Jordan has one of the lowest female labor force participation rates (LFPR) in the world (Kalimat and Al-Talafha, 2011; Mryyan, 2012). According to the World Bank, Jordan, with a LFPR of 16.3% in 2010, has the sixth lowest female participation rate among 183 countries and territories that report such data (World Bank, 2013). The countries with lower reported LFPR are Syria, Iraq, West Bank and Gaza, Algeria, and Afghanistan. Not only is female LFPR in Jordan very low, but it also appears to have been relatively stagnant over the past decade. This is a seemingly paradoxical finding given the rapid rise in female educational attainment in Jordan and the strong gradient of participation with rising educational attainment, especially above the secondary level (Mryyan, 2012). The only way to resolve this paradox is to have dropping participation rates among educated women over time, which are counteracted by an improving educational composition to produce flat participation rates over time. It is argued in this chapter that this is in fact what is happening in Jordan and that the decline in participation among educated women is due to a deteriorating opportunity structure in the Jordanian labor market for these women. Educated women in Jordan are employed primarily in the education and health fields, two areas in which public-sector employment is dominant. With the curtailment of public-sector employment in Jordan since the mid-1980s, opportunities for educated women are becoming scarce. Although private sector employment has been growing fairly rapidly, this employment is increasingly temporary and precarious in nature and is generally perceived to be inhospitable to women, especially married women. In fact, women working in the private sector tend to leave the labor force at marriage, whereas those working in the government are much more likely to stay on, as government employment is viewed as more family-friendly. Our primary argument is therefore that female labor supply in Jordan is being constrained by changes that are occurring on the demand side of the Jordanian labor market. Faced with an inhospitable labor market, women in Jordan are opting to stay out of the labor market altogether or to leave at marriage.

Much of the literature on female participation in Jordan is concerned with the barriers Jordanian women face in the labor market, either from prevailing social norms about women's mobility and the sorts of jobs deemed acceptable for them or from the discrimination they face in the private sector (Miles, 2002; Peebles et al., 2007; Kalimat and Al-Talafha, 2011). Miles (2002) attributes the constraints to women's participation in employment in Jordan to the "gender system," by which she means the interplay between cultural and family-level factors and those associated with the state and employers to shape women's job search and employment strategies. Miles cites the rapid increase that occurred in women's labor force participation from the mid-1970s to the early 1990s, supported by state policies to increase employment for educated women in the public sector. These policies were intended to reduce the conflict between reproductive and productive responsibilities by providing a generous maternity leave and requiring institutions that hired a certain number of women to provide day care. With the introduction of economic adjustment policies in the mid-1980s, the expansion of public-sector employment, came to an abrupt halt, as we will see, leading to a significant narrowing of employment opportunities for educated women. A more recent study done under the auspices of the Al-Manar Project of the National Center for Human Resources Development in Jordan (NCHRD) explored in more detail the barriers facing women in the private sector (Peebles et al., 2007). The study concludes that some of the barriers facing women in the private sector are related to a number of factors. First, there is the highly protective legislation on women's working conditions and maternity leave, which lead employers to avoid hiring married women. Second, employers discriminate against married women out of a conviction that their marital responsibilities would prevent them from being as committed to their jobs as men or young, unmarried women. Third, social insurance legislation treats women as dependents rather than independent workers, even when they work. Fourth, practices confine women to occupations that are closely associated with their more traditional roles in the household, such as education and health care. Another more recent study sponsored by Al-Manar explored barriers to women pursuing self-employment through small and micro enterprises (Kalimat and Al-Talafha, 2011). Based on focus group discussions, the study concludes that women were neither aware of opportunities to set up their own enterprises nor enthusiastic about the prospect. This is supported by the very low levels of self-employment observed among Jordanian women in labor force data.

This chapter agrees with the general thrust of literature that it is the interplay between conservative social and cultural norms about gender roles in the household and in society, on the one hand, and economic and policy-related factors, on the other, which shapes the prospects for female employment in Jordan. In particular, the shift away from public-sector employment in recent decades has severely restricted the employment prospects of educated married women, which had expanded significantly in the previous era. Our main contribution is to document these trends with recent survey data and to show through careful analysis the way in which women's employment prospects are shaped by education and marriage and the way in which these prospects have narrowed dramatically in recent years.

The outline of the chapter is as follows: section 4.2 presents the data we use; section 4.3 discusses the structure of opportunity for women in the Jordanian labor market and the way it has changed in recent years; section 4.4 examines the determinants of female participation in the labor force and in different kinds of employment in Jordan; and section 4.5 concludes.

## 4.2 Data

This chapter relies for the most part on data from the JLMPS 2010, which is supplemented with quarterly data from the Employment and Unemployment Survey (EUS) of the Jordanian Department of Statistics (DoS) for the years 2000 to 2010. The JLMPS 2010 is the first wave of a panel survey carried out by the Economic Research Forum (ERF) in cooperation with the National Center for Human Resource Development (NCHRD) and the DoS. The survey was carried out on a nationally representative sample of 5,102 households containing 25,969 individuals of all ages. The JLMPS 2010 contains a wealth of data on individuals aged six and above, including full job histories based on retrospective questions, which we use to conduct our dynamic analyses.

The EUS is the official labor force survey of Jordan collected quarterly by the Jordanian DoS. We use a harmonized dataset containing quarterly data from the first quarter of 2000 to the fourth quarter of 2010. The EUS was carried out on a nationally representative sample of about 9,000 households per quarter from 2000 to 2006, and about 12,000 households per quarter from 2007 to 2010. The sampling and stratification scheme of the EUS was modified in the first quarter of 2007, when the sample frame from the 2004 census was used for the first time.

## 4.3 The Structure and Evolution of Female Participation in the Jordanian Labor Market

### 4.3.1 Issues in the Measurement of Female Labor Force Participation in Jordan

Although Jordan has one of the lowest rates of female labor force participation in the world, a quick look at the data would suggest that participation has increased rapidly over the past two decades from 8.9% in 1990 to 12.5% in 2000 and to 15.3% in 2010—a rate of increase of 40% per decade in the 1990s and of 22% per decade in the 2000s. However a more careful look at the data in the 2000s belies the notion that female LFPR in Jordan has been rising, at least in the past decade. Figure 4.1 shows the quarterly LFPR as estimated by the EUS. The figure also shows the annual estimates from the World Development Indicators (2013). As is clear from the figure, there is a major break in the data just before the first quarter of 2007, where LFPR suddenly jumps from around 12% to 15%. This break happens to correspond to the round of the survey in which there was a switch in the sampling frame of the EUS to the 2004 population census data and the introduction of a new stratification system. It is therefore highly probable that this break is due to

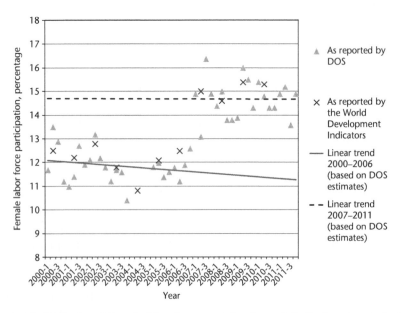

**Figure 4.1.** Evolution of female labor force participation rate in Jordan, quarterly data 2000–2011, ages 15+

*Source:* EUS (various years).

differences in sampling strategy. The data from before and after the break clearly suggest that female LFPR was stable in Jordan throughout the decade. On the assumption that the new sample frame is a more accurate representation of the Jordanian population, we can assume that the more correct estimate is closer to 15%.

## 4.3.2 The Structure of Employment by Gender in Jordan: A Static Analysis

As stated in the introduction, Jordan not only has relatively low female labor participation, but this participation is strongly shaped by both educational attainment and marital status. It is also characterized by high levels of occupational and job segregation, with women being generally concentrated in very specific segments of the labor market. Our main objective in this section is to describe the structure of employment in Jordan by gender in terms of these powerful structural factors as a way to set the stage for the subsequent dynamic analysis.

We begin our analysis by examining the way education shapes women's participation in employment in Jordan as compared to men's (see Tables 4.1 and 4.2). We first note that while male participation in employment rises somewhat with education, the association between participation in employment and education for women is much stronger. While male participation rises from about 61% for those with below secondary education to 80% for those with university education and higher, it rises from 5% to 46% for women—more than a nine-fold increase. The biggest increase occurs as education rises from the secondary to the university level. Unemployment as a reflection of the readiness for work also rises strongly with education for women, going from 1% of the working-age population at the below secondary level to 14% at the university and above level. In contrast, the association between education and unemployment is almost non-existent for men (see also Mryyan, 2012).

The pattern of employment is also more strongly associated with education for women than for men. While the more educated groups are more likely to be employed in government for both genders, the increase in the share of government in employment by education is much sharper for women than for men. Going from below secondary to university and higher, the share of employment in government rises from 21% to 57% for women, that is, nearly tripling, whereas it goes up only from 28% to 41% for men. Employment in the formal private sector also increases with education, but in a fairly similar manner for both women and men. Informal wage employment declines significantly with education for both women and men, but the decline is somewhat steeper for women. Self-employment and unpaid family labor

**Table 4.1.** Distribution of female working-age population by employment status, education, and marital status, 2010 (%)

| | Below secondary | | | Secondary and above | | | University and higher | | | Total | | |
|---|---|---|---|---|---|---|---|---|---|---|---|---|
| | Never married | Ever married | Total | Never married | Ever married | Total | Never married | Ever married | Total | Never married | Ever married | Total |
| Government-wage worker | 11 | 29 | 21 | 28 | 49 | 40 | 35 | 71 | 57 | 27 | 55 | 43 |
| Formal private-wage worker | 36 | 12 | 23 | 38 | 27 | 32 | 51 | 20 | 33 | 43 | 20 | 30 |
| Informal private-wage worker | 38 | 32 | 35 | 28 | 8 | 17 | 10 | 6 | 8 | 23 | 12 | 17 |
| Employer/Self-employed | 7 | 18 | 13 | 1 | 15 | 9 | 2 | 3 | 2 | 3 | 10 | 7 |
| Unpaid worker | 8 | 9 | 8 | 4 | 1 | 2 | 1 | 1 | 1 | 4 | 3 | 3 |
| Total Employment | 100 | 100 | 100 | 100 | 100 | 100 | 100 | 100 | 100 | 100 | 100 | 100 |
| Employed | 7 | 5 | 5 | 15 | 12 | 13 | 53 | 43 | 46 | 15 | 12 | 13 |
| Unemployed | 2 | 1 | 1 | 7 | 2 | 4 | 26 | 8 | 14 | 6 | 2 | 4 |
| Out of labor force | 92 | 95 | 94 | 78 | 85 | 82 | 21 | 50 | 40 | 78 | 86 | 83 |
| Total | 100 | 100 | 100 | 100 | 100 | 100 | 100 | 100 | 100 | 100 | 100 | 100 |

*Source:* Constructed by the authors using JLMPS (2010).

**Table 4.2.** Distribution of male working-age population by employment status, education, and marital status, 2010 (%)

| | Below secondary | | | Secondary and intermediate | | | University and higher | | | Total | | |
|---|---|---|---|---|---|---|---|---|---|---|---|---|
| | Never married | Ever married | Total | Never married | Ever married | Total | Never married | Ever married | Total | Never married | Ever married | Total |
| Government-wage worker | 30 | 27 | 28 | 37 | 34 | 35 | 38 | 42 | 41 | 33 | 31 | 32 |
| Formal private-wage worker | 14 | 16 | 15 | 22 | 20 | 21 | 38 | 28 | 32 | 21 | 20 | 20 |
| Informal private-wage worker | 47 | 30 | 36 | 35 | 19 | 24 | 14 | 10 | 11 | 38 | 23 | 28 |
| Employer/Self-employed | 7 | 27 | 20 | 4 | 27 | 20 | 7 | 19 | 15 | 6 | 26 | 19 |
| Unpaid worker | 2 | 0 | 1 | 2 | 0 | 1 | 3 | 0 | 1 | 2 | 0 | 1 |
| Total Employment | 100 | 100 | 100 | 100 | 100 | 100 | 100 | 100 | 100 | 100 | 100 | 100 |
| Employed | 42 | 80 | 61 | 41 | 84 | 64 | 72 | 85 | 80 | 45 | 82 | 65 |
| Unemployed | 10 | 5 | 7 | 6 | 4 | 5 | 16 | 3 | 8 | 10 | 4 | 7 |
| Out of labor force | 48 | 15 | 32 | 53 | 13 | 31 | 12 | 12 | 12 | 45 | 14 | 29 |
| Total | 100 | 100 | 100 | 100 | 100 | 100 | 100 | 100 | 100 | 100 | 100 | 100 |

*Source:* Constructed by the authors using JLMPS (2010).

are relatively rare statuses among Jordanian women, and their prevalence declines sharply with education. Thus the fundamental reason educated women have a higher employment rate than their less educated counterparts is their differential ability to obtain work in the government and to a lesser extent in the formal private sector.

We now move to the impact of marriage on employment for women and its interaction with education. Table 4.1 shows that generally, and for all levels of educational attainment, there is a drop in female participation in employment once they get married. In contrast, as shown in Table 4.2, male employment rates rise significantly with marriage, in accordance with the predominant gender roles in Jordanian society of men as breadwinners and women as homemakers. The decline in employment with marriage is larger in relative terms for less educated women, but is larger in absolute terms (from 53% to 43%) for females with a university degree, who have higher participation rates to start with. Married women, like married men, are much less likely to be unemployed than their unmarried counterparts, but in the case of women, it is not necessarily because they eventually find work, but because they tend to stop seeking work after marriage and withdraw from the labor force altogether.

The pattern of employment also differs strongly by marital status for women, in sharp contrast to men, whose patterns of employment are not strongly associated with marital status. Employed married women at all education levels tend to be more concentrated in government work and in self-employment, two employment statuses that are more compatible with their marital responsibilities than private-sector-wage work. This pattern may result in part from migration to these employment statuses with age, but is more likely to be due to the higher persistence in the workforce of women employed in these statuses after marriage relative to those employed in private-sector-wage work. For instance, 61% of never married university graduates were employed in the private sector in 2010, as compared to only 26% of their ever married counterparts.

We finally deduce from these tables that unmarried university graduates have the highest participation rates among females in the Jordanian labor market (79%). They have both the highest participation in employment (53%) and in unemployment (26%) of the working-age population, which translates into an unemployment rate of 33%. When employed, this group tends to be concentrated in formal private-wage employment (51%). They are not too different in this regard from unmarried male university graduates, who also have similar levels of concentration in private-wage work (52%). Marriage is what tends to drive a wedge between the labor market experiences of educated males and females. Married female university graduates not only have much lower overall participation rates than their male counterparts, but also have very different patterns of employment when employed. Married female university graduates are predominantly concentrated in government employment (71%), while less than half of their married male counterparts are (42%). The increasing concentration of university-educated married women could either be due to the fact that educated women increasingly move to that family-friendly sector over time or to the fact that women in that sector are less likely to leave the labor force after marriage than women in other types of jobs. We will explore these two pathways further in the dynamic analysis. As for the less educated women who work (i.e., with an education below secondary), it seems easier for them to access informal private jobs (38% for the never married and 35% for the ever married).

To further investigate the constraints and barriers that the Jordanian labor market imposes on women's wage and salary employment, we examine the distribution of such employment by sector of economic activity and occupation. We can immediately see from Table 4.3 the dominant role that the education and health services sectors play in the wage and salary employment

**Table 4.3.** Percentage of females in employment by industry group and major occupational class, 2010

| | Managers and professionals | White-collar and services | Blue-collar | Total | Distribution of female employment |
|---|---|---|---|---|---|
| | | | | | (column %) |
| Agriculture, forestry, fishing, mining | – | – | 22.3* | 19.0* | 4.5 |
| Manufacturing | 17.8 | – | 12.5 | 13.2 | 9.7 |
| Utilities | – | 11.7 | 0.0 | 4.4 | 0.3 |
| Construction | – | – | 0.0 | 2.0 | 0.7 |
| Wholesale and retail trade | 18.5 | 6.3 | 1.0 | 5.8 | 5.2 |
| Transportation and storage | – | 21.5* | 0.0 | 3.7 | 1.7 |
| Restaurants and hotels | – | 5.5 | 5.8 | 5.0 | 0.7 |
| Information, finance, insurance | 23.2* | 10.8 | 19.6* | 16.3 | 7.9 |
| Public admin and defense | 24.4* | 7.3 | 5.8 | 9.0 | 11.6 |
| Education | 59.8* | 42.6* | 27.0* | 54.2* | 38.5 |
| Human health and social work | 45.1* | 57.8* | – | 52.3* | 12.6 |
| Other | 30.8* | 33.2* | 16.9* | 28.2* | 6.5 |
| Total | 39.9 | 13.7* | 8.1 | 17.0* | 100 |

*Source:* Constructed by the authors using JLMPS (2010).

*Notes:* * represents cells that have more than 20 observations in the unexpanded sample and above average female percentages.

of Jordanian women, with 51% of female employment concentrated in these two industries. Similarly, more than half of the employment in these sectors is female. The next highest industry group in terms of prevalence of female employment is the "other" category with 28% female employment, followed by the agriculture industry with 19%.[1] All other industry groups have a female prevalence that is lower than the average prevalence of 17%, with the highest among them being information, finance, and insurance services at 16%.

When industry groups are further broken up in three broad occupational categories, we note that the category "managers and professionals" has the highest female prevalence (39.9%), especially in education and health. It is followed by "white-collar and service occupations" (13.7%) and then by "blue-collar occupations." The greatest concentration of females in blue-collar work is in educational services and agriculture.

To abstract away from the higher female prevalence in government employment, we limit the analysis in Table 4.4 to the private sector. Although the overall female prevalence in the private sector at 14.7% is lower than that for the economy as a whole at 17%, roughly the same patterns are observed. Education and health services continue to be the top two industries in terms of female prevalence, with 63% and 59% female prevalence in the private-sector employment, respectively. Similarly, these two sectors together make up 37.5% of total female employment in the private sector. They are followed in importance by the manufacturing sector (16.6%), which has higher than average female prevalence and by the information, finance, and insurance sector (12.6%), which has lower than average female prevalence in all sectors. Similar conclusions apply to the concentration of female employment by occupation in the private sector as for the economy as a whole.

The main conclusions of the static analysis on the structure of the Jordanian labor market along gender lines is that the market appears relatively closed to less educated women and that married women, even if educated, find it hard to reconcile working for wages in the private sector with their family responsibilities. Moreover, employed women tend to be highly segregated in a few industries and occupations. Education and health are the two most feminized industry groups, which together account for over half of female employment. Within the private sector, education and health continue to be the most important sectors for women, followed by manufacturing and information, finance and insurance. The high level of gender segregation is most probably due to prevalent norms about what kind of employment is socially acceptable for women rather than simply to discrimination on the part of employers. If female participation in employment is to rise significantly in

---

[1] The category "Other" is mostly made up of personal services and probably dominated by foreign women in domestic services.

**Table 4.4.** Percentage of females in private employment by industry group and major occupational class, 2010

| Private sector only | Managers and professionals | White-collar and services | Blue-collar | Total | Distribution of female employemnt |
|---|---|---|---|---|---|
| | | | | | (column %) |
| Agriculture, forestry, fishing, mining | – | 0.0 | 22.4* | 19.1* | 7.9 |
| Manufacturing | 17.0* | 13.4 | 12.3 | 13.0 | 16.6 |
| Utilities | – | 7.7 | 0.0 | 3.3 | 0.3 |
| Construction | – | 11.5 | 0.0 | 1.6 | 1.0 |
| Wholesale and retail trade | 19.1* | 6.1 | 0.8 | 5.6 | 8.8 |
| Transportation and storage | – | 7.4 | 0.0 | 0.8 | 0.5 |
| Restaurants and hotels | – | 5.5 | 5.8 | 5.0 | 1.3 |
| Information, finance, insurance | 22.8* | 9.4 | 21.0* | 15.4 | 12.6 |
| Public admin and defense | – | 9.6 | – | 21.4* | 2.0 |
| Education | 67.8* | 61.7* | 20.6* | 62.8* | 26.8 |
| Human health and social work activities | 53.0* | 70.5* | 27.8* | 58.9* | 10.7 |
| Other | – | 40.5* | – | 33.3* | 11.3 |
| Total | 36.0* | 14.0 | 7.8 | 14.7 | 100 |

*Notes:* * represents cells that have more than 20 observations in the unexpanded sample and above average female percentages.

*Source:* Constructed by the authors using JLMPS (2010).

Jordan, other segments of the labor market will have to gradually open up to them.

### 4.3.3 The Structure of Employment by Gender in Jordan: A Dynamic Analysis

This section analyzes the differences between female and male workers in Jordan in terms of their progression through the labor market over time. The adopted method portrays the new flows of workers into the labor market and then follows these new entrants several years into their careers. Such a dynamic analysis allows us to highlight the evolution of the Jordanian labor market more precisely than when just dealing with stocks and cross-sectional data. As discussed in Assaad (2012), the JLMPS dataset provides a detailed characterization of jobs, which allows us to distinguish between five types of employment, namely: (i) government employment; (ii) permanent formal private-wage work, which includes all wage and salary work in the private sector or state-owned enterprises with indefinite-duration contracts and social insurance coverage; (iii) temporary formal private-wage work, which includes all wage and salary work in the private sector or state-owned enterprises with either definite-duration contracts or no contracts but with social insurance coverage; (iv) informal private-wage work, which is made up of wage and salary work in the private sector or state-owned enterprises with neither a contract nor social insurance coverage; and (v) non-wage work, which includes employers, self-employed individuals, and unpaid family workers.

We use these categories to look at the distribution of jobs obtained by new entrants into the Jordanian labor market every year since the early 1970s. This allows us to trace the change in the structure of the labor market facing new entrants of each gender over time. As shown in Figure 4.2, new female entrants were much more reliant on government jobs in the 1970s and 1980s than their male counterparts, with over 60% of new female entrants going into the government until 1985. The share of government jobs among new female entrants fell dramatically after the mid-1980s going from 60% to 25% in the late 1990s, only to recover slightly to 30% in the 2000s. Not only were new female entrants more affected by the slowdown in government hiring, they were affected earlier than their male counterparts, who continued to be hired by the government at relatively higher rates until the early 1990s. The recovery in government hiring in the 2000s is also more pronounced for new male entrants than for new female entrants.

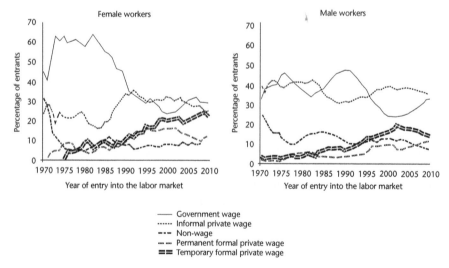

**Figure 4.2.** Distribution of employment of female and male new entrants by type in first job and year of entry into the labor market, 1970–2010, ages 15–64
*Source:* JLMPS (2010).

The decline in government hiring for women appears to have initially been counteracted by a sharp increase in informal-wage employment, which increased significantly from the mid-1980s to the mid-1990s. Subsequent declines in government employment were counteracted by formal but temporary-wage employment, which increased from 10% of first jobs for new female entrants to 20% from 1990 to 2000. Permanent formal employment increased as well in the early 1990s, but slowed down considerably in the 2000s. Trends for males were similar, with one main exception. While temporary formal-wage employment continued to rise in importance for women in the second half of 2000, its share fell for men during that period, when government employment recovered. We can conclude from this discussion that as government curbed its hiring of new female entrants, their employment became much more precarious, first in the form of informal-wage employment and later in the form of temporary-wage employment in the private sector. Together, these two categories constituted nearly 50% of new jobs for women in 2010. The share of formal permanent private-wage employment remains relatively low for both men and women, at about 10–12% of first jobs in 2010, after having risen to over 15% for women in the early 2000s. Non-wage employment, which is mostly made up of unpaid family labor, remains a fairly small and somewhat stable share of first jobs for both women and men.

Limiting this analysis to new entrants with secondary education and above provides a better comparison of labor market prospects along gender lines because a much larger proportion of female employment is made up of such educated workers. In fact, workers with secondary education or above made up 70% and 83% of the total female entrants and 40% and 56% of the total male entrants in 1970 and 2010, respectively. As shown in Figure 4.3, the observed decline in the share of government employment appears to be larger and more accentuated for these educated workers, but the pattern for females is very similar to those discussed in Figure 4.2; however, it is worth noting that the recovery in government employment observed in the early 2000s (Figure 4.2) is no longer apparent for the educated workers. The share of new entrants in government employment tends to stabilize after 1995 at around 30% for both female and male new entrants.

In Figure 4.4, we replicate this analysis for new entrants with below secondary education, showing that the share of government employment for this category rises rapidly in the 2000s to make up for its earlier decline. The incline is especially apparent for less educated new male entrants. Going back to the data to investigate this trend, we find that this "recovery" mainly involves higher levels of recruitment in the military after the sharp reductions of the 1990s.

To further understand the changing structure of the Jordanian labor market along gender lines, we follow new female and male entrants up to ten

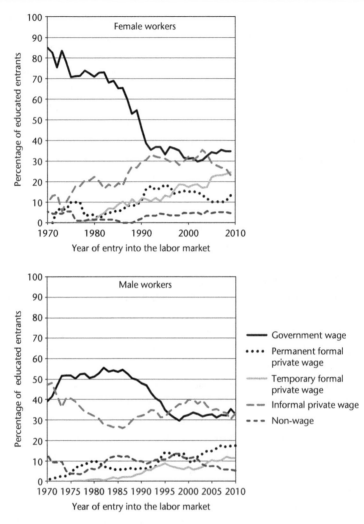

**Figure 4.3.** Distribution of employment of educated (i.e. secondary and above) female and male new entrants by type in first job and year of entry into the labor market, 1970–2010, ages 15–64

*Source:* JLMPS (2010).

years into their careers to see whether the changes in employment prospects at entry are attenuated by subsequent job mobility. In this analysis, we observe how the share of employment in each sector at entry, and five and ten years after entry, changes according to year of entry into the labor market. The idea is to examine changes over a person's life cycle and over time for the same point in the person's life cycle. In the leftmost panel of Figure 4.5, we show the evolution of these employment shares for all female new entrants,

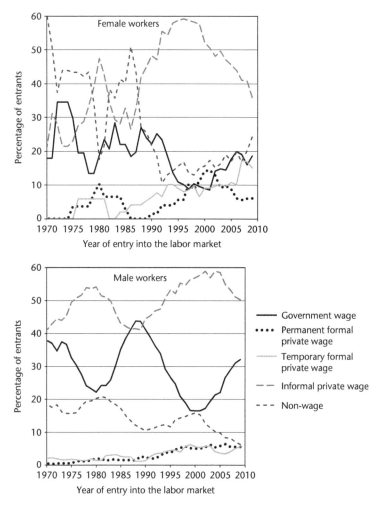

**Figure 4.4.** Distribution of employment of less educated (i.e below secondary) female and male entrants by type in first job and year of entry into the labor market, 1970–2010, ages 15–64

*Source:* JLMPS (2010).

that is, including those who exited the labor market within five and ten years. In the middle panel, we show the shares for only those who stayed in the labor market at least ten years, who constitute about 63% of those who entered between 1995 and 2000. The rightmost panel shows the shares for the new male entrants who stay for at least ten years, but since exit is not as much of an issue for males, there is no need to repeat them for all new entrants.

We begin by examining in Figure 4.5 the evolution of the share of new entrants employed in government at entry, after five and ten years of entry

119

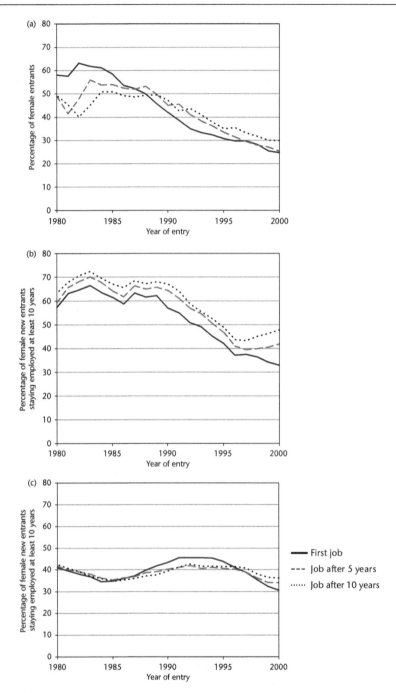

**Figure 4.5.** Evolution of the share of female new entrants employed in government in their first job, five years, and ten years after entry by year of entry into the labor market

*Source:* JLMPS (2010).

by year of entry. We first note the sharper decline in the government share of employment for new female entrants than for new male entrants that we observed earlier. Comparing the leftmost and middle panels shows that before 1985 female employees in government used to withdraw from the labor force after a short period of employment, but this does not seem to happen anymore after 1985. In fact, from the late 1980s onward the government share among new entrants tends to increase somewhat over the life cycle at the same time as it declined over time. This suggests that women tend to move out of other sorts of employment and into government as they advance in their careers. This appears to be the case for men as well, but only since 1995. Prior to that, the tendency for men was to move from the government to the private sector.

Next, we shift our focus to formal private-wage employment. As shown in Figure 4.6, although the fraction of women who enter formal private-wage employment over time in Jordan rose much faster than that of men, this tended to be a temporary employment state for most women. Comparing the leftmost panel to the center panel shows that most women who leave this state within ten years of entry leave the workforce altogether. For instance, among women who entered the labor market in 2000, over 35% got formal private-sector jobs, but only 25% were still in these jobs after five years, and only 20% were still in them after ten years. Of those who stayed in the workforce at least ten years, those who moved out of formal private-sector-wage work in the first ten years after entry appear to be heading primarily to the more family-friendly government sector, as there appears to be very little movement into the other two states, namely informal-wage work and non-wage work (Figures 4.9 and 4.10). For male workers, mobility into and out of formal private-sector work appears to be more limited than for female workers and exhibits variable patterns over time. From 1985 to 1995, the tendency was for males to join the formal private sector from other sectors, mostly government, but from 1995 onwards, the mobility was in the opposite direction.

In Figures 4.7 and 4.8, we decompose formal private-sector-wage work into permanent and temporary components to better understand the observed trends. We first note the trend towards slower growth of permanent formal work starting in the 1990s, with the continued rapid growth of temporary formal work. Nonetheless, both rise much more rapidly for women than for men. Next, we see that exit from temporary formal work is much more pronounced than exit from permanent formal work, and much of this exit is to leave the workforce altogether (by comparing the leftmost panel in Figure 4.8 with the center panel). Since 1995, there appears to be more chance of transitioning from temporary to permanent private-sector work over the life course for both male and female workers. This suggests that

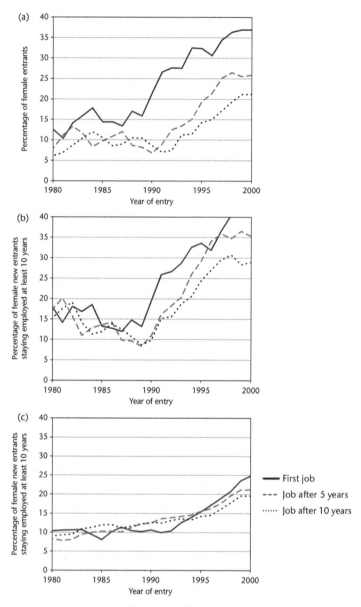

**Figure 4.6.** Evolution of the share of female new entrants employed in formal private-wage employment in their first job, five years, and ten years after entry by year of entry into the labor market

*Source:* JLMPS (2010).

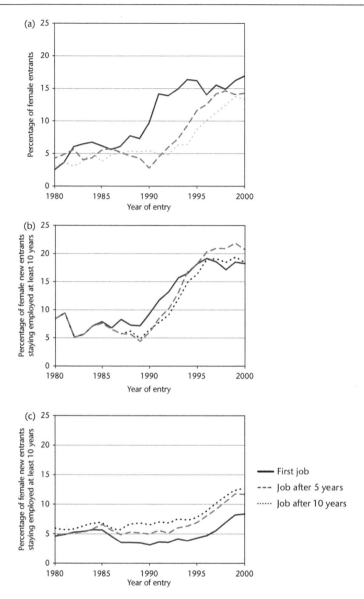

**Figure 4.7.** Evolution of the share of female new entrants employed in permanent formal-wage employment in their first job, five years, and ten years after entry by year of entry into the labor market

*Source:* JLMPS (2010).

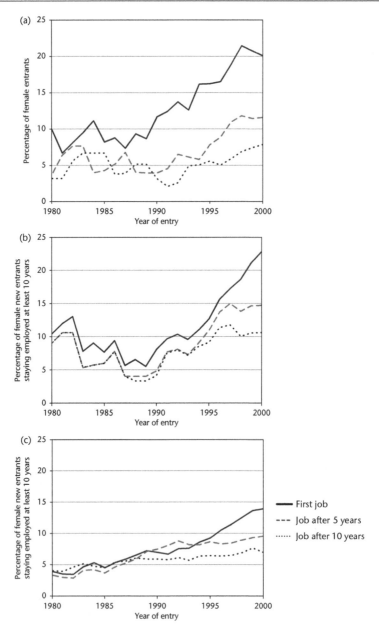

**Figure 4.8.** Evolution of the share of female new entrants employed in temporary formal wage employment in their first job, five years and ten years after entry by year of entry into the labor market

*Source:* JLMPS (2010).

employers are hiring workers in temporary positions first and then switching them to permanent positions as time goes on. Using the same data, Amer (2012) shows that there is very little mobility between formal and informal jobs in Jordan, so that most transitions are between temporary and permanent formal jobs in the private sector and between these and the government sector.

We now move to examine the remaining segments of employment of the female new entrants: informal private-wage employment and non-wage employment (Figures 4.9 and 4.10). As shown in the figures, there is an increase in the female share in informal wage employment from 1985 to 1993 or so, a time characterized by sharp declines in government employment. Non-wage employment, on the other hand, does not exhibit any clear trends over time. We also observe that women in informal wage employment tend to exit the labor market at high rates during the first ten years of employment. For the cohort entering form 1995 to 2000, 30% were informal-wage workers at entry, but only 15% remained so employed after ten years, with much of the dropout occurring within five years of entry. Among those who remain in the labor market for ten or more years, there is very little mobility from informal-wage employment. In contrast, for males, there has been some mobility out of the sector in recent years, mostly to self-employment.

The life-cycle patterns of non-wage employment for women are similar to those of informal-wage employment, but more attenuated. The degree of exit over the life cycle is lower. Most of these women are probably working as unpaid workers in family farms and enterprises, an employment state that is more compatible with starting a family and child-bearing than wage employment. Unlike males though, women are less likely to move into this state over time, since they are less likely to start their own businesses.

To sum up, this section shows that even though female workers enter the Jordanian labor market in different segments of employment, a significant group fails to remain in employment and exits the labor force in the first ten years after entry. This phenomenon is more important within formal and informal private-wage employment, where jobs tend not to be flexible and family-friendly enough. As for those who stay in the labor force, their employment tends to exhibit greater rigidity and lack of mobility, relative to what is observed for their male counterparts, especially within the informal private-wage sector and the non-wage segment. There is some mobility for women who remain employed from formal private-wage employment to government employment, which is deemed more family-friendly, but little mobility in other directions.

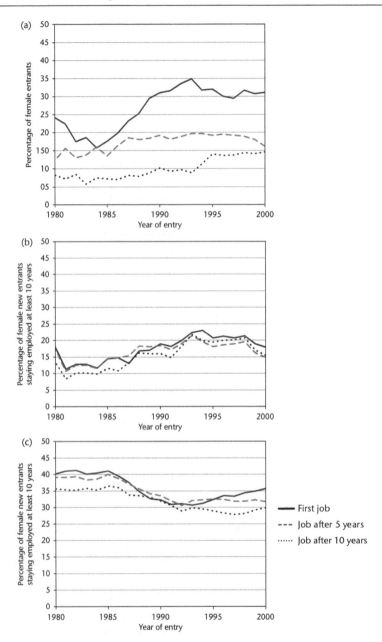

**Figure 4.9.** Evolution of the share of female new entrants employed in informal private-wage employment in their first job, five years, and ten years after entry by year of entry into the labor market

*Source:* JLMPS (2010).

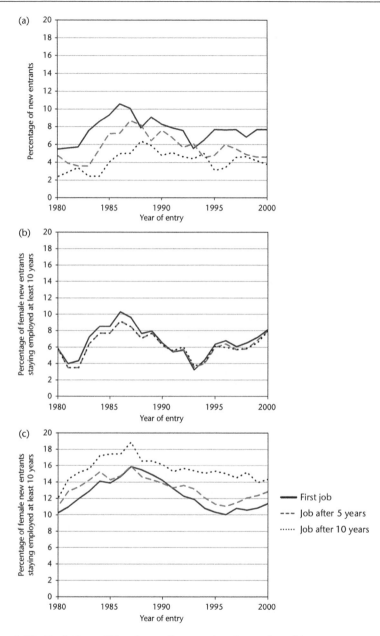

**Figure 4.10.** Evolution of the share of new entrants employed in non-wage employment in their first job, five years, and ten years after entry by year of entry into the labor market

*Source:* JLMPS (2010).

## 4.4 The Determinants of Females Participation: An Empirical Analysis

As discussed in section 4.2.1, female participation in the labor force in Jordan is quite low by international standards and has not been increasing in the past decade, despite significant increases in female educational attainment. We determined in section 4.2.2 that female participation in employment depends strongly on educational attainment and marital status. We would therefore expect that as both educational attainment and age at marriage rise, we should see increases in female labor force participation. However, we also saw that educated women tend to be concentrated in the public sector, and, in particular, in the education and health sectors. The curtailment of public-sector hiring that accompanied structural adjustment in Jordan contributed to limiting the employment possibilities for educated women. These two opposing trends may account for the stability of female participation in Jordan. In this section, we examine in more detail the determinants of female and male participation in the Jordanian labor market in an effort to ascertain the other forces that determine participation. We first begin by estimating a simple probit model for a binary participation variable (working or not) and then move to a multinomial logit model that distinguishes between working in the public sector, working for wages in the private sector, self-employment (which includes employers and unpaid family workers) and not working.[2]

Tables 4.5 and 4.6 show the marginal effects from the dichotomous model determining the probability of working versus not working. We first estimate a model on the pooled male and female sample with a female dummy variable to detect the effect of gender on participation, and then estimate separate models for females and males. We control for a number of characteristics such as age, marital status, the level of education, urban/rural residence, parental level of education, parental work status, and whether the household owns or cultivates agricultural land. The reference probability and marginal effects shown are for a reference individual whose continuous variables are set at the mean and whose dummy variables are set to zero. Thus the reference individual in Table 4.5 is a never married 32-year-old male with above secondary education living in a rural area. His father and mother both have above secondary education and were not working when he was 15. His household neither owns nor cultivates agricultural land. In Table 4.6 the reference individual is defined similarly in the male and female samples.

As shown in Table 4.5, Jordanian women have a significantly lower probability of employment compared to their male counterparts. A reference

---

[2] See also Spierings et al. (2008) for a similar analysis for Jordan and Egypt.

**Table 4.5.** Results of the probit model of labor market participation (population aged 15–64)

| Reference: not working state | dy/dx |
|---|---|
| *Probability for the reference individual:* | *0.878* |
| Age | 0.062*** |
| | (0.003) |
| Age squared/100 | −0.079*** |
| | (0.004) |
| Currently married | −0.030** |
| | (0.014) |
| Divorced/widowed | −0.009 |
| | (0.020) |
| Below secondary education | −0.227*** |
| | (0.011) |
| Secondary education | −0.280*** |
| | (0.014) |
| Female | −0.662*** |
| | (0.009) |
| Urban location | 0.008 |
| | (0.006) |
| Father's education, below secondary | 0.015 |
| | (0.010) |
| Father's education, secondary | 0.006 |
| | (0.014) |
| Mother's education, below secondary | −0.011 |
| | (0.012) |
| Mother's education, secondary | 0.016 |
| | (0.018) |
| Mother working when 15 | 0.028** |
| | (0.014) |
| Father working when 15 | −0.006 |
| | (0.010) |
| HH cultivates land | 0.01 |
| | (0.010) |
| HH owns but does not cultivate land | −0.011 |
| | (0.010) |
| Number of observations | 15,170 |

*Notes:* (i) Calculations are for a reference individual with means for the continuous variables and zeros for dummy variables. (ii) Age and age squared are continuous variables. (iii) The reference for the educational level is above secondary education. (iv) Rural is the reference for regions. (v) The reference level for parental level of education is below secondary. (vi) The reference for the land-holding variable is not having land. (vii) Standard errors in parentheses. (viii) *** p<0.01, ** p<0.05, * p<0.1.

female's probability of working is 66.2 percentage points (p.p.) below that of a reference male, giving her an estimated probability of 21.6% based on the coefficients for the pooled sample. The probability of employment for the reference female is significantly higher at 46.9% when the estimation is run separately for females and males, because the reference individual has

**Table 4.6.** Results of the probit model of labor market participation by gender

| | Females | Males |
|---|---|---|
| | dy/dx | dy/dx |
| Reference: not working state | | |
| *Probability for the reference individual:* | *0.469* | *0.670* |
| Age | 0.094*** | 0.110*** |
| | (0.006) | (0.004) |
| Age squared/100 | −0.117*** | −0.147*** |
| | (0.007) | (0.005) |
| Currently married | −0.236*** | 0.103*** |
| | (0.032) | (0.025) |
| Divorced/widowed | −0.100** | −0.107 |
| | (0.043) | (0.083) |
| Education below secondary | −0.363*** | −0.109*** |
| | (0.020) | (0.019) |
| Education secondary | −0.347*** | −0.207*** |
| | (0.020) | (0.021) |
| Urban location | 0.006 | 0.030** |
| | (0.019) | (0.014) |
| Father education, below secondary | 0.041 | 0.008 |
| | (0.031) | (0.028) |
| Father education, secondary | 0.048 | −0.022 |
| | (0.041) | (0.041) |
| Mother education, below secondary | −0.083** | 0.057** |
| | (0.036) | (0.024) |
| Mother education, secondary | −0.019 | 0.068 |
| | (0.053) | (0.053) |
| Mother working when 15 | 0.075* | 0.048 |
| | (0.042) | (0.050) |
| Father working when 15 | −0.025 | 0.003 |
| | (0.031) | (0.025) |
| HH cultivates land | 0.017 | 0.032 |
| | (0.033) | (0.023) |
| HH owns but does not cultivate land | −0.005 | −0.009 |
| | (0.030) | (0.021) |
| Husband education, below secondary | −0.038 | |
| | (0.026) | |
| Husband education, secondary | −0.042 | |
| | (0.032) | |
| Husband working in government | 0.137*** | |
| | (0.024) | |
| Husband employer/self-employed | −0.069** | |
| | (0.032) | |
| Number of observations | 7,636 | 7,534 |

Notes: (i) Calculations are for a reference individual with means for the continuous variables and zeros for dummy variables. (ii) Age and age squared are continuous variables. (iii) The reference for the educational level is above secondary education. (iv) Rural is the reference for region. (v) The reference level for parental level of education is below secondary. (vi) The reference for the land-holding variable is not having land. (vii) Standard errors in parentheses. (viii) *** p<0.01, ** p<0.05, * p<0.1.

above secondary education, and education has a much larger effect in the female regression than in the pooled regression. In fact, the marginal effect of going from above secondary to secondary education in the pooled sample is a 28 p.p. reduction in the probability of working, whereas it is a 35 p.p. reduction in the female sample (compare results in Table 4.5 with results in the first column of Table 4.6).

Age has the expected inverse U-shaped effect on participation, which is shown in Figure 4.11. Interestingly, the dichotomous model shows a slightly higher peak age for female employment than for male employment, which is reached at about age 41. Again, as a reflection of the consolidation of gender roles at marriage, being married has a positive and significant effect on participation for men and an even larger negative and significant effect on women's participation. Marriage is associated with a 13 p.p. increase in participation for men and a 27 p.p. decline for women. If widowed or divorced, women's participation rises by 14 p.p., but is still 13 p.p. lower than that of never married women.

The education of either parent does not have a significant effect on participation in either the pooled sample or for each sex separately. On the other

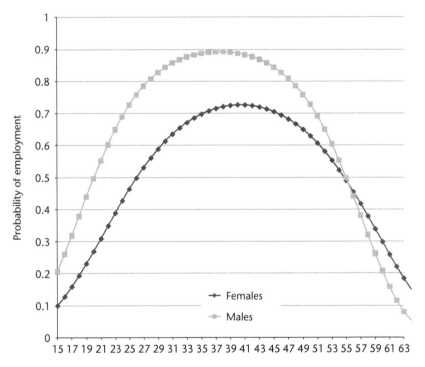

**Figure 4.11.** Predicted probability of working by age and gender
*Source:* Simulations based on probit model results using data from JLMPS (2010).

hand, if the mother was working when the individual was 15, there is a small positive effect on participation in the pooled sample, which turns out to be exclusively due to its effect on women's participation. Women whose mothers were working when they were 15 are 13.5 p.p. more likely to work than those with similar characteristics whose mothers were not working. This probably proxies for the cultural norms of the family and its degree of acceptance of women's work. Finally, ownership and cultivation of agricultural land has no significant effect on participation.

Because participation in employment takes different forms that can be differentially compatible with women's domestic and reproductive responsibilities, we move next to a model that breaks down participation into four states: employment in the public sector; employment for wages in the private sector; self-employment or unpaid family labor; and non-employment. We use a multinomial logit equation to model these polychotmous dependent variables. The marginal effects from this model for a reference female and male are shown in Tables 4.7 and 4.8, respectively, controlling for the same explanatory variables used in Tables 4.5 and 4.6.

The probability of working for wages in the public and private sectors by age has the same inverse U-shape detected in the dichotomous model. However, the peak for private-sector work is reached at close to age 36 and that for public-sector work at age 40 (see Figure 4.12), pointing to the lower compatibility of private-sector-wage work with women's marital responsibilities.

**Table 4.7.** Results of the multinomial logit model for females

| | Not working | Government/ public–wage work | Private–wage work | Employers/ self–employed/ unpaid work |
| --- | --- | --- | --- | --- |
| | dy/dx | dy/dx | dy/dx | dy/dx |
| Reference individual | 0.609 | 0.247 | 0.136 | 0.009 |
| Age | −0.136*** | 0.093*** | 0.041*** | 0.001 |
| | (0.009) | (0.011) | (0.007) | (0.001) |
| Age squared | 0.178*** | −0.122*** | −0.055*** | −0.001 |
| | (0.012) | (0.014) | (0.009) | (0.001) |
| Currently married (d) | 0.211*** | −0.100*** | −0.107*** | −0.004 |
| | (0.036) | (0.034) | (0.018) | (0.003) |
| Divorced/widowed (d) | 0.028 | 0.027 | −0.052** | −0.003 |
| | (0.057) | (0.058) | (0.023) | (0.003) |
| Education below secondary (d) | 0.321*** | −0.227*** | −0.094*** | −0.001 |
| | (0.026) | (0.027) | (0.017) | (0.002) |
| Education secondary (d) | 0.311*** | −0.208*** | −0.104*** | 0.002 |
| | (0.026) | (0.025) | (0.018) | (0.003) |

**Table 4.7** (Continued)

| | Not working | Government/ public–wage work | Private–wage work | Employers/ self–employed/ unpaid work |
|---|---|---|---|---|
| | dy/dx | dy/dx | dy/dx | dy/dx |
| Urban location (d) | −0.037 | −0.102*** | 0.138*** | 0.002 |
| | (0.026) | (0.021) | (0.023) | (0.002) |
| Father education, below secondary (d) | −0.026 | 0.007 | 0.016 | 0.002 |
| | (0.035) | (0.033) | (0.026) | (0.005) |
| Father education, secondary (d) | −0.035 | 0.016 | 0.019 | 0.001 |
| | (0.047) | (0.044) | (0.036) | (0.006) |
| Mother education, below secondary (d) | 0.069* | −0.019 | −0.049** | −0.002 |
| | (0.042) | (0.041) | (0.019) | (0.003) |
| Mother education, secondary (d) | 0.022 | −0.035 | 0.011 | 0.002 |
| | (0.058) | (0.052) | (0.040) | (0.007) |
| Mother working when 15 (d) | −0.064 | −0.032 | 0.090* | 0.007 |
| | (0.051) | (0.046) | (0.047) | (0.007) |
| Father working when 15 (d) | 0.014 | −0.005 | −0.01 | 0.001 |
| | (0.036) | (0.035) | (0.023) | (0.004) |
| HH cultivates land (d) | 0.016 | 0.016 | −0.046* | 0.013* |
| | (0.040) | (0.039) | (0.024) | (0.007) |
| HH owns but does not cultivate land (d) | −0.012 | 0.031 | −0.017 | −0.002 |
| | (0.035) | (0.034) | (0.022) | (0.003) |
| Husband education, below secondary | 0.043 | −0.039 | −0.004 | 0 |
| | (0.030) | (0.026) | (0.026) | (0.002) |
| Husband education, secondary | 0.028 | −0.038 | 0.012 | −0.002 |
| | (0.038) | (0.030) | (0.035) | (0.003) |
| Husband working in government | −0.160*** | 0.185*** | −0.028 | 0.003 |
| | (0.032) | (0.036) | (0.021) | (0.004) |
| Husband employer/ self–employed | 0.115*** | −0.062* | −0.064*** | 0.011 |
| | (0.037) | (0.034) | (0.024) | (0.007) |
| Number of observations | 7591 | 7591 | 7591 | 7591 |

Notes: (i) *** p<0.01; ** p<0.05; * p<0.1. (ii) Calculations are for a reference individual with means for the continuous variables and zeros for dummy variables. (iii) Age and age squared are continuous variables. (iv) The reference for the educational level is above secondary education. (v) Rural is the reference for region. (vi) The reference for the land-holding variable is not having land.

**Table 4.8.** Results of the multinomial logit model for males

| | Not working | Government/ public-wage work | Private-wage work | Employers/ self-employed/ unpaid work |
|---|---|---|---|---|
| | dy/dx | dy/dx | dy/dx | dy/dx |
| Reference individual | 0.324 | 0.466 | 0.167 | 0.043 |
| Age | −0.127*** | 0.102*** | 0.018*** | 0.008*** |
| | (0.006) | (0.006) | (0.004) | (0.002) |
| Age squared | 0.175*** | −0.145*** | −0.024*** | −0.007*** |
| | (0.008) | (0.008) | (0.005) | (0.002) |
| Currently married (d) | −0.124*** | 0.115*** | −0.029* | 0.038*** |
| | (0.026) | (0.032) | (0.016) | (0.014) |
| Divorced/widowed (d) | 0.099 | −0.001 | −0.098*** | 0.001 |
| | (0.100) | (0.102) | (0.030) | (0.022) |
| Education below secondary (d) | 0.144*** | −0.196*** | 0.030** | 0.022*** |
| | (0.022) | (0.019) | (0.012) | (0.005) |
| Education secondary (d) | 0.247*** | −0.206*** | −0.051*** | 0.010* |
| | (0.024) | (0.021) | (0.012) | (0.006) |
| Urban location (d) | −0.007 | −0.181*** | 0.165*** | 0.022*** |
| | (0.016) | (0.016) | (0.013) | (0.005) |
| Father education, below secondary (d) | −0.016 | 0.022 | 0.001 | −0.007 |
| | (0.030) | (0.032) | (0.017) | (0.006) |
| Father education, secondary (d) | 0.041 | −0.05 | 0.003 | 0.006 |
| | (0.047) | (0.045) | (0.024) | (0.011) |
| Mother education, below secondary (d) | −0.066** | 0.049 | 0.027 | −0.010* |
| | (0.026) | (0.030) | (0.018) | (0.005) |
| Mother education, secondary (d) | −0.078 | 0.06 | 0.003 | 0.015 |
| | (0.057) | (0.061) | (0.033) | (0.016) |
| Mother working when 15 (d) | −0.027 | −0.039 | 0.046 | 0.02 |
| | (0.060) | (0.058) | (0.035) | (0.014) |
| Father working when 15 (d) | 0.017 | −0.045 | 0.028 | 0 |
| | (0.029) | (0.029) | (0.018) | (0.006) |
| HH cultivates land (d) | −0.062*** | 0.134*** | −0.092*** | 0.020** |
| | (0.024) | (0.027) | (0.014) | (0.008) |
| HH owns but does not cultivate land (d) | −0.033 | 0.122*** | −0.087*** | −0.002 |
| | (0.023) | (0.025) | (0.012) | (0.006) |
| Number of observations | 7,419 | 7,419 | 7,419 | 7,419 |

Notes: (i) *** p<0.01; ** p<0.05; * p<0.1. (ii) Calculations are for a reference individual with means for the continuous variables and zeros for dummy variables. (iii) Age and age squared are continuous variables. (iv) The reference for the educational level is above secondary. (v) Rural is the reference for region. (vi) The reference for the land-holding variable is not having land.

Participation in self-employment also has an inverted U-shape, but the predicted probabilities of such work for the reference university-educated female is very low indeed.

We can also see from the marginal effects shown in Table 4.7 that being currently married increases the probability of not working for the reference

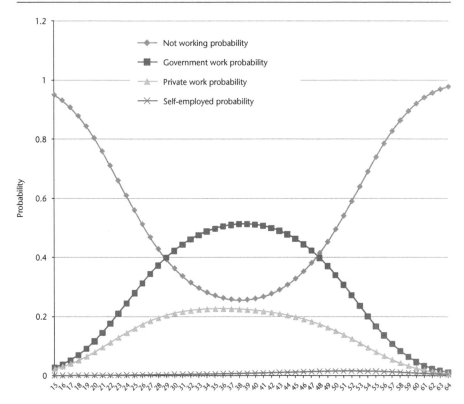

**Figure 4.12.** Predicted probability of female employment by employment state by age
*Source:* Simulations based on multinomial logit model results using data from JLMPS (2010).

woman by about one-third, from 61% to 82%. Currently, married women have a 10 p.p. lower probability of not working in government and for wages in the private sector than never married women, but these translate in very different relative effects because the base probabilities are different. In relative terms, marriage results in a 40% decline in the probability of working in government, but a 79% decline in the probability of working for wages in the private sector. In contrast, there is an insignificant difference in the probability of working between divorced or widowed women and never married women, except in the private sector, where it is lower by 5.3 p.p. These results are illustrated in Figure 4.13, which clearly shows how the probability of work in both the private and public sectors recovers upon divorce or widowhood. In contrast, being currently married for males reduces the probability of not working by 12 p.p., which results from an increased probability of public-sector employment (by 11.5 p.p.) and of self-employment/unpaid work (by 3.8 p.p.) and a reduced probability

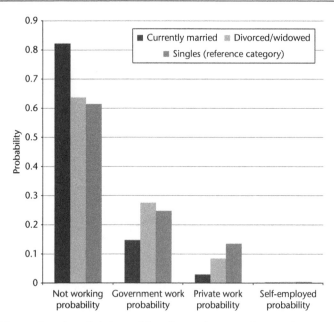

**Figure 4.13.** Predicted probability of female employment by employment state and marital status

*Source:* Simulations based on multinomial logit model results using data from JLMPS (2010).

of working for wages in the private sector (by 2.9 p.p.). The only predicted probability of work for males to be significantly affected by divorce or widowhood is a reduction in the probability of working for wages in the private sector by 10 p.p. (see Table 4.8).

As discussed, educational attainment is one of the strongest determinants of women's employment and the kind of work they perform. As shown in Table 4.7 and in Figure 4.14, the probability of not working is reduced by 31 p.p., or nearly one-third, as women move from the secondary to the above secondary level. The probability of working for wages in the private sector increases by 10 p.p., or more than quadruples, and the probability of working in government increases by 21 p.p., virtually increasing six-fold. The difference between secondary and below secondary is not very large, suggesting that it is the acquisition of higher education that is important for women's employment status in Jordan. Men's employment patterns are also affected by education, but to a lesser extent. Going from secondary to above secondary raises men's predicted probability of employment in government by 20.6 p.p., which is less than double, and raises the probability of being employed for wages in the private sector by 1.4 p.p.

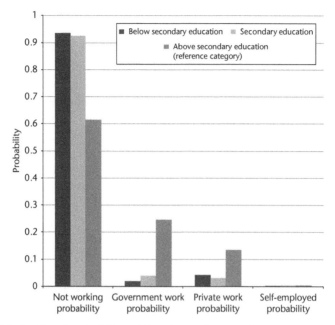

**Figure 4.14.** Predicted probability of female employment by employment state and level of education

*Source:* Simulations based on multinomial logit model results using data from JLMPS (2010).

Once own education is controlled for, parents' education does not have much of an additional effect on women's probability of employment. The main exception is when the mother has below secondary education, the daughter is less likely to work by 7 p.p. and, in particular, is less likely to work for wages in the private sector. Interestingly, having a mother with below secondary education has the opposite effect for men. It raises their probability of working, but this increased probability is spread over both the government and the private sector. Similar to education, parental work status when the woman was 15 does not have a strong influence on her employment probability, again with one exception. If the mother was working, the woman's probability of working for wages in the private sector rises by about 9 p.p. In contrast, men's employment patterns are not affected by their parents' employment status when they were 15. These results suggest that the impact of mother's work is a proxy for the cultural norms of the family and its view about women's work. When there is a history of women working in the family, it is easier for the daughter to do so.

Living in an urban area slightly reduces the probability of not working compared to residing in a rural area, but has contradictory effects on the probability of government and private-sector employment for women. It tends to reduce the probability of working in government by about 10 p.p., but increases the probability of working for wages in the private sector by 14 p.p. (see Figure 4.15). There appears to be similar effects for males. Residing in an urban area reduces the probability of working in the government for males by 18 p.p. and increases the probability of working in the private sector by 16.5 p.p., compared to a male residing in rural areas. Urban males are also 2.2 p.p. more likely to be self-employed compared to rural males.

We turn next to the effect of the household owning and cultivating agricultural land on women's and men's work status and type of employment. Simply owning agricultural land does not affect the probability or pattern of employment for women, but cultivating land does. It reduces the probability that a woman will be employed for wages in the private sector by 4.6 p.p. and increases the probability that she will be self-employed or an unpaid family worker by 1.3 p.p., which is a very significant relative increase for this low-prevalence activity for women. In contrast, ownership and cultivation of land has a much stronger effect on men's work

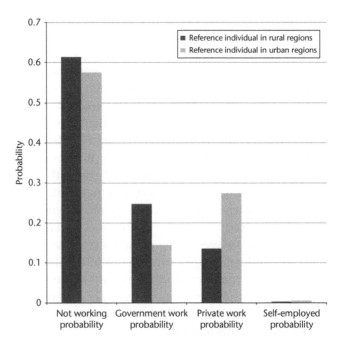

**Figure 4.15.** Predicted probability of employment by employment state and urban/rural region for the female reference individual

*Source:* Simulations based on multinomial logit model results using data from JLMPS (2010).

patterns. Surprisingly, merely owning but not cultivating land raises men's probability of employment in government, by 12 p.p. and reduces the probability of employment for wages in the private sector by nearly 9 p.p., without a significant effect on the overall probability of employment. Owning and cultivating land has an even larger positive effect on the probability of employment in government and a larger negative effect on the probability of private-sector employment, but an additional positive effect on being self-employed. The net effect is an increase in the probability of working by 6.2 p.p.

We turn finally to the effect of husband's education and employment status on women's probability of employment. Correcting for own education, husband's education has no significant effect on women's probability and pattern of employment. However, husband's employment status does. Women whose husbands work for the public sector have an 18.5 p.p. increase in their probability of working in the public sector themselves, and therefore a similar increase in the probability of working. This could either be because government employees tend to meet other government employees at work and get married to them or because husbands help provide opportunities for their wives in the public sector. When husbands are either employers or self-employed, women's probability of employment declines by 11.5 p.p., with the decline distributed equally over the probability of employment in the public and private sectors.

To illustrate the combined effect of the different determinants of employment for women, we carry out a simulation to estimate the employment probabilities of the woman that is least likely to work in both urban and rural areas and one that is most likely to work also in each of the two settings. Based on the signs and sizes of the coefficients in the multinomial logit equation, we define the least likely woman to work as a woman who is 18 years old, currently married, has a below secondary education, has parents who have below secondary education and who were not working when she was 15. Her household does not own or cultivate land and her husband has below secondary education and is an employer or self-employed. The most likely woman to work is 32 years old, with above secondary education, never married. Her parents have above secondary education and were both working when she was 15. The predicted probabilities of not working, working in the government, working for wages in the private sector and being self-employed are shown in Figure 4.16. The first result here is that the woman with the least-likely-to-work profile has a probability of not working of virtually one, and this is the same for urban and rural areas. The woman with the most-likely-to-work profile, on the other hand, has a probability of not working of 21% in urban areas and 27% in rural areas. If she lives in rural areas she has a higher probability of working in the government than in the

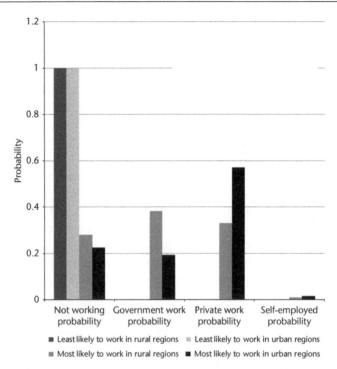

**Figure 4.16.** Predicted probability of employment by employment state and urban/rural region for the female profile that is least and most likely to work

*Source:* Simulations based on multinomial logit model results using data from JLMPS (2010).

*Notes:* (i) The least-likely-to-work female profile is an 18-year-old woman who is currently married, has below secondary education, has parents who have below secondary education, lives in a household that does not own or cultivate land, and has a husband who has a below secondary education and is an employer or self-employed. (ii) The most-likely-to-work female profile is a 30-year-old woman who was never married. Her parents have above secondary education and were both working when she was 15.

private sector, but if she lives in an urban area, her probability of working in the private sector is more than two-and-a-half times as high as her probability of working in the government. Her probability of being self-employed is still very low.

So far, we have analyzed the determinants of work by gender in a static fashion using data from the JLMPS 2010. To get a more dynamic picture of how the probability of work has changed for women over time in Jordan keeping key characteristics constant, we ran a series of models on the quarterly EUS data. The explanatory variables used in these models were age, age squared, own education specified in the same way as mentioned earlier, marital status specified as earlier, and urban dummy variable. We estimated a separate model for each quarter, from the first quarter in 2000 to the last quarter in 2010.[3] We then used these models to predict the employment probability of a reference woman in each quarter—the reference woman being a 32-year-old never married woman with above secondary education, living in an urban area. These predicted probabilities are plotted in Figure 4.17, together with trend lines for the 2000–2006 period and the 2007–2010 period.[4]

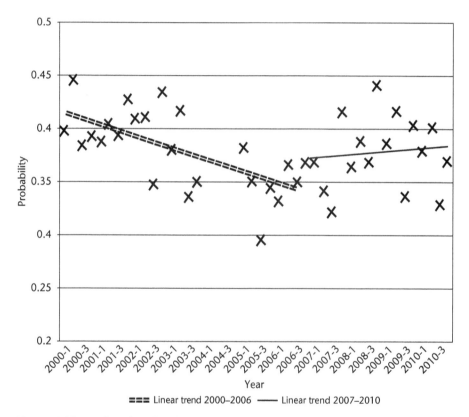

**Figure 4.17.** Predicted probability of female employment in Jordan for a reference woman by quarter from first quarter 2000 to fourth quarter 2010

*Source:* EUS (various years).

*Note:* The reference woman is 32 years old, she has above secondary education, has never been married, and lives in an urban area.

---

[3] EUS quarterly data was not available for 2004.

[4] As noted in section 4.3.1, there is a break in the data between the last quarter of 2006 and the first quarter of 2007 due to a change in the sampling methodology.

As is clear from Figure 4.17, there is a declining trend in the female rate of participation in employment from 2000 to 2006 once compositional issues have been controlled for. This is in contrast to the much shallower declining trend seen in Figure 4.2, when no characteristics were held constant. This suggests an explanation for the apparent paradox of participation rising with educational attainment, increasing educational attainment over time for Jordanian women, but flat overall female participation levels. This figure suggests that participation for educated women has actually been falling between 2000 and 2006, a period that corresponds—as we have seen—to a sharp curtailment of government employment opportunities. The stability in participation for educated women after 2007 corresponds to the most recent period of stabilization in government employment shown in Figure 4.2.

## 4.5 Conclusion

Much of the literature on women's participation in Jordan is concerned with why female participation in paid employment in Jordan remains so low despite rising educational attainment among Jordanian women to levels that now exceed those of men (Mryyan, 2012), the delay in age at first marriage (Salem, 2012) and the falling fertility rates. In fact, we argue that participation rates are not only low but are actually declining once we correct for educational attainment, suggesting that the labor market opportunity structure for educated women is deteriorating over time. As we clearly demonstrate, this deterioration can be directly attributable to the diminishing role of the family-friendly public sector in the Jordanian labor market in general. Although formal private-sector employment has risen significantly in Jordan during the period of shrinking public-sector opportunities, the private sector has not provided a hospitable environment for women in general and for married women in particular. Much of the recent increase in private-sector employment for women has been in temporary positions that women either leave of their own accord or are induced to leave by their employers upon marriage. Further restraining employment opportunities for women lie in their high levels of concentration in education and health jobs, and to a lesser extent in insurance and finance, and their inability to expand their presence in other segments of the labor market. Given that a return to an expansionary public sector in Jordan is unlikely due to the fiscal unsustainability of such a strategy, Jordan must find a way to reduce the cost to private employers to hire women and to support married women with child care and other interventions to allow them to better reconcile their marital responsibilities with work in the private sector. Recent changes in social insurance laws to socialize the cost of maternity leave go some way in achieving this, but much more is needed. Over the long run, gender norms about the division of labor within the household will have to shift to accommodate women's growing professional roles. Jordan risks wasting a significant portion of the considerable investment it has made in women's education if the participation rates remain so low and continue to decline for educated women as has been happening in the recent past.

### References

Amer, M., 2014. The school-to-work transition of Jordanian youth. In *The Jordanian Labor Market in the New Millennium*, ed. Ragui Assaad. Oxford: Oxford University Press, pp. 64–104.

Assaad, R., 2014. The structure and evolution of employment in Jordan. In *The Jordanian Labor Market in the New Millennium*, ed. Ragui Assaad. Oxford: Oxford University Press, pp. 1–38.

Department of Statistics (Jordan), 2000–2011. *Employment and Unemployment Surveys*. Amman, Jordan: Department of Statistics.

The Economic Research Forum, 2010. *Jordan Labor Market Panel Survey 2010 (JLMPS 2010)*. Cairo, Egypt: The Economic Research Forum.

Kalimat, H. and H. Al-Talafha, 2011. Obstacles hindering women's labor force participation in Jordan. A report for Al-Manar Project. Amman, Jordan: National Center for Human Resource Development.

Miles, R., 2002. Employment and unemployment in Jordan: The importance of the gender system. *World Development* 30(3): 413–27.

Mryyan, N., 2012. Demographics, labor force participation and unemployment. ERF Working Paper No. 670. Cairo, Egypt: The Economic Research Forum.

Peebles, D., N. Darwazeh, H. Ghosheh, and A. Sabbagh, 2007. Factors affecting women's participation in the private sector in Jordan. A report for Al-Manar Project. Amman, Jordan: National Center for Human Resource Development: <http://www.almanar.jo/AlManaren/Portals/0/PDF2/Mayssa%20Gender%20report.pdf> (accessed June 2012).

Salem, R., 2012. Trends and differentials in Jordanian marriage behavior: Marriage timing, spousal characteristics, household structure and matrimonial expenditures. ERF Working Paper No. 668. Cairo, Egypt: The Economic Research Forum.

Spierings, N., J. Smits, and M. Verloo, 2008. Arab women's employment in a globalized world. A multilevel analysis of changing participation rates and shifting influences in Egypt and Jordan. Institute for Management Research, RU, Nijmegen, the Netherlands: <http://www.ru.nl/publish/pages/529479/spieringssmitsverloo-workingpaper-amman2008.pdf> (accessed June 2012).

The World Bank, 2013. *World Development Indicators*: <http://data.worldbank.org/data-catalog/world-development-indicators> (accessed March 31, 2013).

# 5

# Wage Formation and Earnings Inequality in the Jordanian Labor Market

*Mona Said*

## 5.1 Introduction

This chapter uses data provided by the Jordan Labor Market Panel Survey of 2010 (JLMPS 2010) to analyze the evolution of wage formation and differentials in the Jordanian labor market. The JLMPS's individual and household questionnaires contain a wealth of information ideal for investigating distributional issues in wages and this chapter is one of the first studies to base its analysis on the reported data.

Four key questions are addressed in this analysis. First, what are the main distributional features of the Jordanian wage structure in 2010? The analysis differentiates for gender, sector of ownership, occupation, industry, and level of education. Second, what do different wage measures tell us about the dispersion for these different groups? And is most of the observed inequality of the "between-group" or "within-group" variety? Third, what is the size of public–private and gender-based wage differentials and how do these compare to the recent past in Jordan and other countries in the region? Finally, how robust are these wage differentials to changes in the underlying estimation strategy, and to assumptions regarding the allocation mechanism across employment states?

This chapter is organized in six sections. Section 5.2 presents the data sources and documents some stylized facts of the Jordanian labor market, especially in the aftermath of the world financial crisis. It also presents an investigation of developments in raw sectors and gender wage differentials across socio-economic groups (gender, occupations, industries, levels of education). Section 5.3 discusses methodological concerns and introduces the empirical models and the definitions of indicators used in the wage differentials analyses. Section 5.4 then applies this model to estimate a joint model of sector selection and wage determination, and uses the estimates to calculate selectivity-corrected wage equations. Section 5.5 examines trends in overall wage inequality in Jordan, decomposing it into "within-group" and "between-group" components. Section 5.6 concludes, and suggests further related research.

## 5.2 Data and Stylized Facts of the Jordanian Labor Market

### 5.2.1 Data Sources

The paper primarily uses wage data from JLMPS 2010. This survey is the result of the collaborative efforts of the Economic Research Forum (ERF), the National Center for Human Resource Development (NCHRD), and the Jordanian Department of Statistics (DoS). The JLMPS 2010 contains a wealth of information on household composition and socio-economic characteristics such as income, parental background, access to the labor market, education history, ownership of assets, migration histories, and activity statuses. The survey is nationally representative, covering approximately 5,000 households. It is the first round of a planned longitudinal panel survey.

Wages across gender and sector groups, for 2000–2008, are also calculated and reported by the DoS and average wage data based on establishment surveys published on the DoS's website (<http://www.dos.gov.jo>). In addition, the Jordanian Employment and Unemployment Surveys (EUS) carried out on a sample of 12,000 households per quarter from 2006 to 2009 are used to examine developments in employment ratios and hours of work before and after the crisis. The EUS report information on demographic characteristics, education, labor force participation, unemployment, and the characteristics of employment, including employment status, occupation, economic activity, and sector. Unfortunately, EUS's wage data, which is collected as ranges of wages, is not suitable for detailed empirical analysis.

### 5.2.2 The Jordanian Labor Market: Adjustment After the International Financial Crisis

It is important to note that the year 2010 represents the Jordanian labor market two years after the international financial crisis, and thus reflects the adjustments that took place in response to the economic shock. On the firm front, there are three main channels through which firms adjust labor demand in response to an economic shock: working hours, employment, and wages. Firms often start by adjusting working hours, rather than number of workers, particularly for those workers of rare skills. Some firms may also reduce wage levels to minimize production costs (Cazes et al., 2009; Verick, 2010).

Figure 5.1 shows the growth rates of GDP and employment before and after the crisis, and Figure 5.2 plots GDP growth against inflation growth as measured by the consumer price index (CPI). GDP grew at a rate that exceeded 8% before the crisis and then growth dropped to 4% in the fourth quarter of 2008, and continued to decline thereafter. In terms of the employment-to-population ratio (proportion of employed to population aged 15 to 64), the figure shows

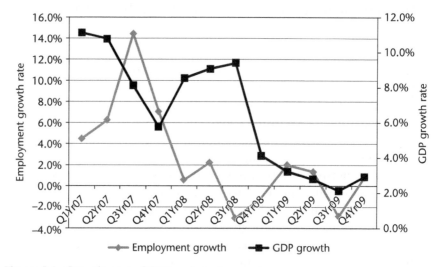

**Figure 5.1.** Growth rates of GDP and employment
*Source:* Population Council (2010), as calculated from Department of Statistics, Jordan (2009).

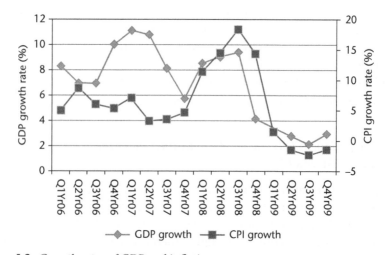

**Figure 5.2.** Growth rates of GDP and inflation
*Source:* Population Council (2010), as calculated from Department of Statistics, Jordan (2009).

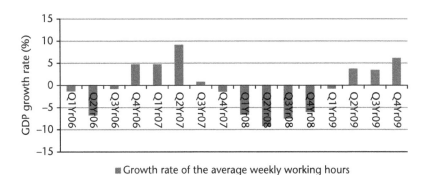

**Figure 5.3.** Growth rate of average weekly working hours
*Source:* Population Council (2010), as calculated from EUS (2006–2009).

an irregular pattern, with fluctuations from one quarter to the next. The inflation rate was considerably low in 2006 and 2007 but spiked to unprecedented rates in 2008, fueled by the increase in food prices. However, in the period following the crisis the inflation rate declined and continued to do so through the fourth quarter of 2009. The combined drop in GDP growth and the price levels indicate that 2009 was a year of recession for the Jordanian economy (Population Council, 2010).

Figure 5.3 shows quarterly growth rate of average working hours per week as reported in Jordan's Employment and Unemployment surveys. The pattern is consistent with the rapid adjustment to hours of work reported in European countries during the financial crisis, as reported by Cazes et al. (2009). As shown in Figure 5.3, there was a decline in hours of work that continued from the beginning of the crisis to the first quarter of 2009. Later, the hours of work increased during the last three quarters of 2009. This confirms that during periods of high inflation (in 2008), the hours of work declined. These movements in hours of work are relevant to the wage trends in Jordan reported later because they would moderate the impact of inflation on erosion of real hourly wages.

### 5.2.3 Sector and Gender Wage Differentials during the Crisis in Jordan

Previous studies have reported that wages have been fairly stable over 2000–2004 in the private sector but have fallen in the public sector (Assaad and Amer, 2008), and females have fared worse compared to males in terms of wage growth. Figure 5.4 shows a stability of wages in both sectors up to 2008, with a caveat that these cannot be easily compared to JLMPS data in 2010 (the former is restricted to wages within establishment).

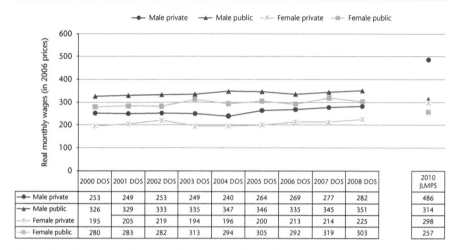

**Figure 5.4.** Real monthly wages by sector and gender (in 2006 prices)

*Source:* Author's calculations based on DoS wage data (2000–2008).

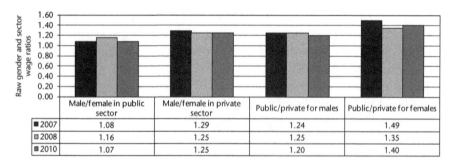

**Figure 5.5.** Raw gender and sector wage ratios (2007–2010)

*Source:* Author's calculations based on EUS (2007–2008) and JLMPS (2010).

Figure 5.5 illustrates gender and sector wage ratios for Jordan (2007–2010). The raw gender gap slightly widened in both the public and private sectors over the crisis period. In 2010, it was 20% in the public sector and 32% in the private sector. The decline in public-sector real wages only resulted in a moderate decline in the public–private median wage ratio for males, whereas the public–private wage ratio for women slightly increased.

### 5.2.4 Gender and Sector Crude Wage Differentials by Occupations, Sectors of Economic Activity and Educational Level

We now move to a more detailed analysis of raw wage differentials based on JLMPS. Figures 5.6 to 5.8 and Tables 5A.1 to 5A.3 in the appendix provide

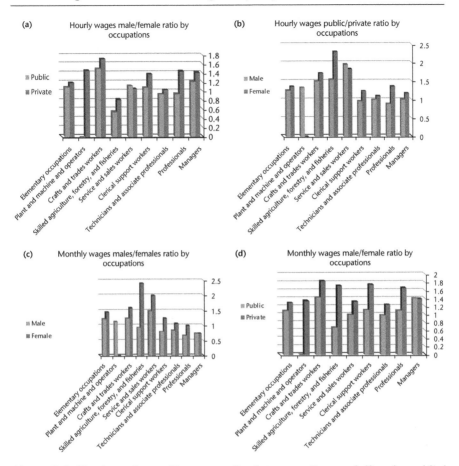

**Figure 5.6.** Hourly and monthly wage ratios by occupation, male/female, public/private, 2010

*Source:* Author's calculations based on JLMPS (2010).

a detailed analysis of sector and gender wage differentials by occupation, industry, and educational level. Together they show that gender gaps are most compressed for managers, for agricultural and industrial activities in the public sector, and for secondary and post-secondary-educated workers in the public sector. They are highest for sales and crafts workers, and those with basic and vocational education in the private sector. This is consistent with the expectation that gender gaps are usually more pronounced in informal private activities.

As for public–private wage differentials, males with lower education levels (basic education and lower) have the greatest disadvantage in the public sector and in agriculture, professional, trade, and crafts activities. Female public-sector advantages are greatest in the industrial sector, for vocational

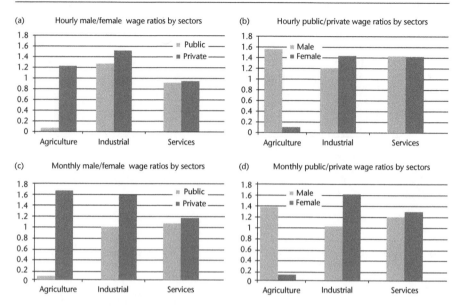

**Figure 5.7.** Hourly and monthly wage ratios by sector, male/female, public/private, 2010
*Source:* Author's calculations based on JLMPS (2010).

and postgraduates and for sales and services workers. This may reflect that the private sector is inhospitable, or may even discriminate against women in those categories. In Jordan, the gaps are much more compressed in the public sector and female disadvantages rise for those with low education level and for those who work in crafts, trade, and clerical positions in the private sector. As for public–private gaps, the greatest public advantage exists for both males and females with lower education and up to the secondary level who work in blue-collar occupations. Advantages in the private sector are more pronounced for professionals, managers, and university graduates or higher.

In sum, the latest data on distribution of wage differentials in Jordan after the crisis portrays a very similar picture of higher gender-based inequality among the less educated and blue-collar (possibly informal) private activities. They also show that despite falling real wages, the public sector maintains its wage advantage, especially for males at lower educational groups and females in the industrial sector, and in clerical occupations and middle education levels. The private sector offers wage advantages for workers with high skills and higher levels of education.

## 5.3 Empirical Methodology and Estimation

All the wage comparisons above ignore productivity-related factors specific to workers. For example, the comparison does not discriminate between

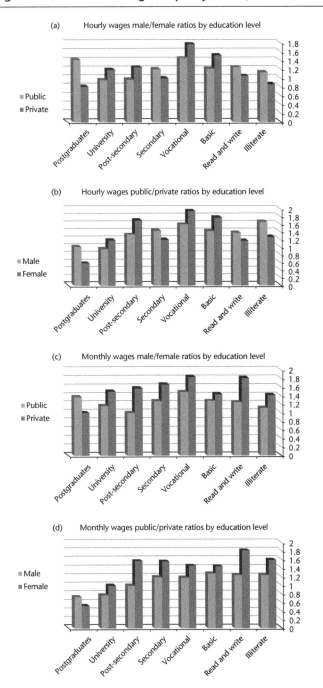

**Figure 5.8.** Hourly and monthly wage ratios by education levels, male/female, public/private, 2010

*Source:* Author's calculations based on JLMPS (2010).

workers with experience and educational attainment and those without. The next step is therefore to correct for these factors. Using multivariate regression analysis, five log hourly wage equations were estimated (for male wage workers, and for males and females across the two sectors, government and non-government).

The empirical analysis in this chapter proceeds in two stages. In the first stage, ordinary least squares (weighted by sampling weights as described later) are used to estimate separate wage equations for workers in the public (p), and private (r) sectors as follows:

$$\text{Ln}\,(w_{is}) = X_{is}b_s + u_s\,(s = p,\, r) \tag{1}$$

Where Ln $(w_{is})$ is log hourly wages of individual i in sector s and X is the vector of individual and job-related characteristics seen to be of relevance for wage determination. This was estimated twice, once for males and once for females, yielding a system of six equations.

Given the parameter estimates from (1), public–private wage differentials are evaluated at the mean of the sample using the following decomposition formula:

$$D_s = \overline{\ln(w_s)} - \overline{\ln(w_r)} = \frac{(\beta_s + \beta_r)(\overline{X_s} - \overline{X_i})}{2} + \frac{(\beta_s - \beta_r)(\overline{X_s} + \overline{X_i})}{2} \quad (s = p) \tag{2}$$

$D_s$ refers to the wage differential between the public and the private sector. $\overline{\ln(w)}$ refers to the mean of Ln wages.

The formula decomposes the wage differential into two main components. The first term, which is "explained," is the part of the differential attributable to differences in observed characteristics of workers (X's). The second term, which is "unexplained," is the part of the differential resulting from differences in the pay structure, or unobserved characteristics. Note that the unexplained component also includes the differential in base wage (the constant term) that can be interpreted as a premium or pure rent from attachment to a particular sector. Similarly, the same formula can be used to decompose the male–female wage gap as follows:

$$D_f = \overline{\ln(w_m)} - \overline{\ln(w_f)} = \frac{(\beta_m + \beta_f)(\overline{X_m} - \overline{X_f})}{2} + \frac{(\beta_m - \beta_f)(\overline{X_m} + \overline{X_f})}{2} \tag{3}$$

Here the unexplained component (second term on the right-hand-side) is broadly taken to refer to gender-based discrimination.

The second stage of estimation is essential because the parameter estimates in equation (1) are likely to suffer from sample selection bias, especially when the unobservable characteristics of the work decision are correlated with the unobservable characteristics affecting wages ($\varepsilon i$). The sample selection problem can be stated as follows:

The standard treatment for the sample selection problem is Heckman's two-step estimate (Heckman, 1979). It initially uses the entire sample to model the choice to work by a probit method. The results of work-choice equations are then used in the second stage to construct estimates of the selection variables (the inverse Mill's ratio $\lambda i^{\wedge}$). Lee (1982 and 1983) proposed a generalization of the two-step selection bias correction method introduced by Heckman (1979) that allows for any parameterized error distribution. His method extends to the case where selectivity is modeled as a multinomial logit decision (Bourguignon et al., 2007). His extension to Heckman's correction method is used in this chapter as a multinomial logistic regression, which allows us to examine selection into different sectors of participation, as will be discussed.

Thus the second stage of estimation is the following selectivity-corrected wage equation based on Lee's extension (1982 and 1983) of Heckman's selection model to the multinomial case.

$$\text{Ln}(w_{sl}) = \beta_s X + \sigma_s \lambda_s + e_s \ (s = p, r) \tag{4}$$

To examine the main aspects of wage inequality, the chapter presents estimates of a range of inequality and related indices commonly used by economists, plus decompositions of a subset of these indices by population subgroup. Inequality decompositions by subgroups are useful for providing inequality profiles at a point in time, and also for analyzing secular trends using shift-share analysis.

In this chapter, the Gini coefficient, the percentile ratios p90/p10 and general entropy (GE) inequality indices are estimated. Despite all of the criteria that make the Gini coefficient a useful measure of inequality, it fails in two criteria: it is not easily decomposable or additive across subgroups in a society and it is not easily tested for statistical significance of changes over time. Generalized entropy measures are a family of indices that satisfy such criteria besides those satisfied by the Gini coefficient. The formula for the general GE index is given by:

$$GE(a) = \frac{1}{a(a-1)} \left[ \frac{1}{N} \sum_{i=1}^{N} \left( \frac{y_i}{\bar{y}} \right)^{\infty} - 1 \right]$$

Consider a population of persons (or households...) $I = 1, \ldots, N$, with individual income y, and arithmetic mean of income $\bar{y}$, (in what follows all sums are overall values of whatever is subscripted). The most commonly used values for (a) are 0, 1, and 2. GE(0) is the mean logarithmic deviation, GE(1) is the Theil's T index and GE(2) is half the square of the coefficient of variation.

The inequality indices differ in their sensitivities to income differences in different parts of the distribution. The higher the value of (a), the more sensitive GE(a) is to income differences at the top of the distribution; the lower the value of (a), the more sensitive it is to differences at the bottom of the distribution.

$$GE(1) = \frac{1}{N}\left[\sum_{i=1}^{n} \frac{y_i}{y} \ln\left(\frac{y_i}{y}\right)\right]$$

$$GE(0) = \frac{1}{N}\sum_{i=1}^{N} \ln\left(\frac{y_i}{\bar{y}}\right)$$

The values of GE measures fall between 0 and ∞ where 0 represents perfectly equal distribution of income, whereas higher levels of GE indicate a higher level of inequality (Haughton, 2009).

Each GE(a) index can be additively decomposed as

GE(a) = GE_W(a) + GE_B(a)

where GE_W(a) is within-group inequality and GE_B(a) is between-group inequality.

The Gini coefficient is most sensitive to income differences around the middle (more precisely, the mode). It is given by

$$Gini = 1 - \frac{1}{N}\sum_{i=1}^{N}[y_i + y_{i-1}]$$

where persons are ranked in ascending order of $y_i$.

The Gini coefficient (and the percentile ratios) can be written as the sum of a term summarizing within-group inequality and a term summarizing between-group inequality (Jenkins, 2006).

## 5.4 Estimating Hourly Wage Differentials Using Wage Equations for Jordan, 2010

As mentioned earlier, comparisons based on raw or uncorrected wage ratios do not take account of productivity differences between workers and can be misleading as to the actual differentials between comparable individuals in terms of human capital characteristics. To estimate wage differentials that correct for differences in such characteristics, log hourly wage regressions for 2010 were estimated by both methods (OLS and selectivity correction) and results are reported in Tables 5A.5 to 5A.7 in the appendix. In each case, five regressions were estimated for the following: all wage workers, males in the private sector, males in the public sector, females in the private sector, and females in the public sector.

### 5.4.1 Sample of Study and Variable Specification

The sample of the study is confined to individuals who are not currently enrolled in school and belong to the working age group (15–64). Means and standard deviations for all variables used in the regressions are reported in Table 5A.4. As can be seen from this table, wage regressions controlled for experience and experience squared to account for non-linearity in the wage–experience profile. They also controlled for levels of educational attainment and region of residence. The sample on which the wage regression analysis is based consists of 4,903 males and females who worked for both the public and private sectors in 1998.

The work–status selection model also uses other non-wage, unemployed, and non-participating individuals within the working-age sample (7,505 males and 7,600 females). Additional household level and family background variables are also used to identify the sector selection equation from the wage equation. These include number of preschool children, children above six years of age, father's and mother's educational attainment, and father's work status variable. In addition, a measure of non-labor income (total monthly earnings of male members of the household) was used in the female work–5. status equation.

### 5.4.2 Ordinary Least Square Estimates

Gender and sector differentials are estimated from OLS regressions using two methods. The first method uses a dummy for being female and another for working in the public sector is included in the aggregate wage equation. This method accounts only for differences in the intercept and assumes similar returns to characteristics for males and females, both sectors (public and private). The second method uses the separate estimates across the four other equations to calculate wage decompositions that also allow for differences in the education, experience, and regional parameters to be included in the calculations.

155

Regression results for the aggregate wage equation estimates for Jordan based on the aggregate wage equation in 2010 indicate a disadvantage of 10% for women and an advantage of 20% for the public sector. These estimates are only indicative as they only consider differences in intercepts and not coefficients of the wage equation.

Using the second method, Table 5.1 and Figure 5.9 present corrected gender and sector wage differentials for Jordan based on the second method outlined. Thus corrected sector wage differentials are calculated as the differences between predicted log hourly wages for public-sector employees using the public-sector wage equation and their predicted log hourly wages using the private-sector wage equation (expressed as a proportion of the former). Similarly, corrected gender wage differentials are the differences between

**Table 5.1.** Gender and sector wage differentials, 2010

|  | Female–male in public sector | Female–male in private sector | Public–private for males | Public–private for females |
|---|---|---|---|---|
| Crude | 0.13 | −0.01 | 0.26*** | 0.40*** |
| Corrected (OLS) | −0.08*** | −0.14*** | 0.17*** | 0.24*** |
| Corrected (selection model) | 0.13 | 0.00 | −0.08*** | 0.17*** |

*Note*: *** denotes significance at the 1% level.

*Source:* Author's calculations based on JLMPS (2010).

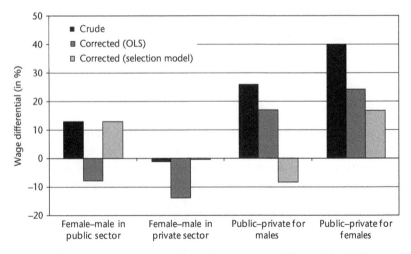

**Figure 5.9.** Crude and corrected gender and sector wage differentials, 2010
*Source:* Author's calculations based on JLMPS (2010).

predicted female wages using the female equation and their predicted wages using the male equation.

Results based on OLS correction reveal that significant public-sector wages advantages still exist in Jordan in 2010, and amount to 17% for males and 24% for females. Gender-based wage gaps are also significant and much larger in the private sector (14%) compared to the public sector (8%). However, once correction based on a selectivity model is used, these gender gaps are no longer significant.

### 5.4.3 Joint Model of Work Status and Wage Determination

DETERMINANTS OF CHOICE (MULTINOMIAL LOGIT MODEL)
In the first stage, four multinomial logit regressions are estimated to study selection into non-participation, unemployment, non-wage work, non-government work, and government-wage work in comparison to non-participation by gender. In each equation, the dependent variable is a categorical variable represented by the five different work statuses mentioned. The identification variables (that affect participation but not wages) are represented by household-related variables that determine participation in the labor force, which consequently affects the choice of employment status. Parameter estimates are then used to compute the four selection variables or inverse ($\lambda$) Mill's ratios to correct for selectivity bias, which are then included as regressors in the selectivity corrected wage equations.

Table 5A.6 shows the parameter estimates of the sector-gender-specific selection equations. The reference category is an illiterate, non-participant individual living in Amman. The results show that education increases a male's probability of being a wage worker in the government sector, but it decreases a male's chance of being a non-wage worker or a non-government-wage worker in most cases. Thus, the government remains the favored employer for males because of its job security and retirement schemes, in addition to the short working hours. For females, education increases a female's probability of being a wage worker in general, but especially in the government sector. One interpretation is that females prefer to work for the government sector, even more so than males, for the short working hours and convenient working conditions. As expected, higher education reduces a female's probability of being a non-wage worker.

Other patterns are found by examining the coefficients on the identification variables. As expected, presence of young children negatively affects the probability of being a wage worker for women but positively affects this probability for men. A father with an intermediate education or higher has a significant negative impact on choosing to work for the government sector. A mother with an intermediate education or higher has a significant and positive effect only on females' choice of becoming non-government workers. The father's employment status (whether self-employed, employer, or government employee) seems to also positively influence the probability that his son or daughter will follow in his path. Finally, non-labor income exerts influence only in preventing women from becoming non-wage workers.

SELECTIVELY CORRECTED WAGE EQUATION ESTIMATES

In the second stage, wage equations for males and females across economic sectors are estimated based on the standard Mincerian wage determination model. Log hourly wage is assumed to depend on many explanatory variables such as: educational attainment; age; age squared; and a set of controlling dummy variables for location. Table 5A.7 in the appendix presents the selectivity-corrected estimates for the wage equations for males and females in the government and non-government sectors. Except for negative significance, selection terms are insignificant for all equations, yet they affected the calculation of wage differentials.

After correcting for both productivity differences as well as sector selection bias, Figure 5.9 illustrates that public-sector wage advantages still exist in Jordan in 2010, but only for females, and amount to 17%. In contrast, the figure shows public-sector wage disadvantages of 8% for males. Gender-based wage gaps are compressed by international standards in the private sector and are almost non-existent in the public sector, In fact, they show a premium (of 13%) for women in the public sector.

## 5.5 Overall Wage Inequality in Jordan

Finally, Tables 5.2 and 5.3, and Figures 5.10 and 5.11 present different measures of overall observed inequality (or dispersion) of hourly wages, as described. All measures indicate that hourly wage dispersion is higher in the private sector than in the public sector, and that in the private sector it is

**Table 5.2.** Measures of inequality of hourly wages, 2010

|         |        | Decile Ratio p90/p10 | Mean log variation G (0) | Thile G(1) | Gini |
|---------|--------|----------------------|--------------------------|------------|------|
| Public  | Male   | 3.26                 | 0.28                     | 0.41       | 0.39 |
|         | Female | 3.11                 | 0.22                     | 0.30       | 0.35 |
| Private | Male   | 7.62                 | 0.74                     | 1.14       | 0.64 |
|         | Female | 8.53                 | 0.74                     | 1.04       | 0.64 |
| Total   | Male   | 5.89                 | 0.56                     | 0.89       | 0.57 |
|         | Female | 6.28                 | 0.49                     | 0.72       | 0.53 |

*Source:* Author's calculations based on JLMPS (2010).

**Table 5.3.** Thile index measures of inequality of hourly wages, within and between groups, 2010

|  |  | Education | | Occupation | | Industry | |
|---|---|---|---|---|---|---|---|
|  |  | Within | Between | Within | Between | Within | Between |
| Males | Public | 0.39 | 0.02 | 0.40 | 0.01 | 0.40 | 0.01 |
|  | Private | 1.03 | 0.10 | 1.00 | 0.14 | 1.09 | 0.05 |
|  | Total | 0.83 | 0.06 | 0.82 | 0.07 | 0.85 | 0.04 |
| Females | Public | 0.26 | 0.03 | 0.26 | 0.03 | 0.29 | 0.01 |
|  | Private | 0.97 | 0.08 | 0.92 | 0.13 | 0.85 | 0.20 |
|  | Total | 0.67 | 0.04 | 0.66 | 0.06 | 0.62 | 0.10 |
| Total | Public | 0.36 | 0.02 | 0.37 | 0.02 | 0.38 | 0.01 |
|  | Private | 1.03 | 0.09 | 1.01 | 0.11 | 1.06 | 0.06 |
|  | Total | 0.81 | 0.05 | 0.80 | 0.06 | 0.82 | 0.04 |

*Source:* Author's calculations based on JLMPS (2010).

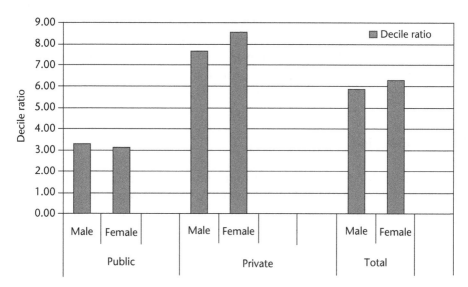

**Figure 5.10.** Inequality as measured by Decile Ratio p90/p10
*Source*: Author's calculations based on JLMPS (2010).

higher for females than for males. The level of inequality, as measured by the Decile Ratio p90/p10, is much higher in the private sector. The highest male (female) percentile wages are 7.5 (8.5)-fold the wages of the lowest percentile. Wages for the highest percentile in the public sector are only three-folds the wages of the lower percentile for both males and females.

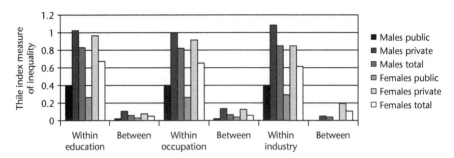

**Figure 5.11.** Thile index measures of inequality of hourly wages, within and between groups

*Source:* Author's calculations based on JLMPS (2010).

In each case, an attempt was made to decompose measured inequality into two components: a component attributable to changes "within" and another attributable to changes "between" important socio-economic groups. Most of the observed inequality for males and females in the three years can be attributed to changes "within" rather than to changes "between" groups. This signifies that the standard human capital variables (experience, education, and region) are no longer sufficient on their own to explain major wage variation and dispersion in Jordon

## 5.6 Conclusion

Recent empirical evidence on transition and emerging economies indicates that episodes of financial crises are bound to have profound impacts on the level and structure of labor earnings. This chapter adds to this literature by examining the impact of such transitions on pay differentials in Jordan, using data from JLMPS 2010.

Analyses of the occupational, sectoral, and educational distribution of wages after the crisis portray a picture of greater gender-based inequality among the less educated and blue-collar (possibly informal) private activities. They also show that the public sector maintains its wage advantage, especially for males of lower education and for females in the industrial sector, clerical occupations, and medium education levels. The private sector offers higher wages for workers with high skills and high education.

The empirical analysis employs a joint model of sector allocation and wage determination to examine public–private and gender dynamics of pay inequality in the aftermath of the world financial crisis. Results reveal that public-sector pay advantages still exist in Jordan in 2010, but only for women.

Gender-based wage gaps remain compressed by international standards in the private sector, and are either non-existent, or represent a premium for women in the public sector. The results confirm the importance of correcting for sector selection when estimating pay differentials in public-sector-dominated economies. Finally, overall hourly wage dispersion is much higher in the private than in the public sector, and it is overwhelmingly due to "within" as opposed to "between" socio-economic group inequality.

These results call for continued monitoring of the Jordanian labor market as the economy further adjusts to the aftermath of the financial crisis. The recent episodes of popular revolutions in the Arab region are likely to have profound structural labor market outcomes. Like many countries in the region, Jordan may have engaged in raising nominal wages for public-sector employees and increasing public-sector employment opportunities, particularly for young graduates, as a first reaction to the crisis. Such interventions are often criticized on the grounds that they are untargeted and ill designed, with limited pro-poor impact, as civil servants are typically not poor (World Bank, 2009).

The limitations of such short-term policies have been obvious, especially in countries such as Egypt and Morocco, where limited budgetary resources ultimately result in a severe compression of the wage structure. Moreover, raising the expectations of graduates for guaranteed public-sector jobs will ultimately result in massive queuing, higher rates in wait, and structural unemployment. Long-term solutions for youth unemployment and sector wage differentials ultimately lie in improving the demand in the private sector. An overhaul in education and acquired-skill systems may also help the labor force to meet the requirements of employment in the private sector.

# APPENDIX

**Table 5A.1.** Hourly and monthly wage ratios by occupation, 2010

| Occupations | Hourly wages | | | | Monthly wages | | | |
|---|---|---|---|---|---|---|---|---|
| | Male/female ratio | | Public/private ratio | | Male/female ratio | | Public/private ratio | |
| | Public | Private | Male | Female | Public | Private | Male | Female |
| Managers | 1.22 | 1.42 | 1.01 | 1.18 | 1.41 | 1.40 | 0.74 | 0.74 |
| Professionals | 0.95 | 1.45 | 0.89 | 1.36 | 1.11 | 1.67 | 0.67 | 1.00 |
| Technicians and associate professionals | 0.94 | 1.04 | 1.00 | 1.11 | 0.98 | 1.25 | 0.84 | 1.07 |
| Clerical support workers | 1.09 | 1.39 | 0.97 | 1.23 | 1.12 | 1.75 | 0.80 | 1.25 |
| Service and sales workers | 1.13 | 1.06 | 1.96 | 1.84 | 1.00 | 1.33 | 1.50 | 2.00 |
| Skilled agriculture, forestry, and fisheries | 0.56 | 0.82 | 1.56 | 2.31 | 0.68 | 1.73 | 0.94 | 2.40 |
| Crafts and trades workers | 1.50 | 1.73 | 1.51 | 1.73 | 1.44 | 1.85 | 1.25 | 1.60 |
| Plant, machine operators and assembly | – | 1.47 | 1.34 | 0.00 | – | 1.35 | 1.14 | 0.00 |
| Elementary occupation | 1.10 | 1.20 | 1.26 | 1.37 | 1.11 | 1.31 | 1.24 | 1.46 |

*Source:* Author's calculations based on JLMPS (2010).

**Table 5A.2.** Hourly and monthly wage ratios by sector, 2010

| Sectors | Hourly wages | | | | Monthly wages | | | |
|---|---|---|---|---|---|---|---|---|
| | Male/female ratio | | Public/private ratio | | Male/female ratio | | Public/private ratio | |
| | Public | Private | Male | Female | Public | Private | Male | Female |
| Agriculture | – | 1.1 | 1.6 | 0 | –5 | 1.7 | 1.4 | 0 |
| Industrial | 1.2 | 1.4 | 1.2 | 1.5 | 1.0 | 1.6 | 1.0 | 1.7 |
| Services | 0.8 | 0.8 | 1.5 | 1.5 | 1.1 | 1.2 | 1.2 | 1.3 |

*Source:* Author's calculations based on JLMPS (2010).

**Table 5A.3.** Hourly and monthly wage ratios by education level, 2010

| Education levels | Hourly wages | | | | Monthly wages | | | |
|---|---|---|---|---|---|---|---|---|
| | Male/female ratio | | Public/private ratio | | Male/female ratio | | Public/private ratio | |
| | Public | Private | Male | Female | Public | Private | Male | Female |
| Illiterate | 1.14 | 0.87 | 1.66 | 1.27 | 1.11 | 1.42 | 1.25 | 1.60 |
| Reads and writes | 1.25 | 1.05 | 1.38 | 1.17 | 1.25 | 1.82 | 1.25 | 1.82 |
| Basic | 1.22 | 1.52 | 1.42 | 1.78 | 1.28 | 1.44 | 1.29 | 1.45 |
| Vocational | 1.46 | 1.78 | 1.60 | 1.95 | 1.50 | 1.85 | 1.18 | 1.46 |
| Secondary | 1.20 | 1.00 | 1.44 | 1.20 | 1.28 | 1.67 | 1.20 | 1.56 |
| Post-secondary | 0.98 | 1.25 | 1.33 | 1.71 | 1.00 | 1.58 | 1.00 | 1.57 |
| University | 0.96 | 1.19 | 0.96 | 1.19 | 1.17 | 1.50 | 0.78 | 1.00 |
| Postgraduates | 1.43 | 0.82 | 1.02 | 0.58 | 1.38 | 1.00 | 0.74 | 0.53 |

*Source:* Author's calculations based on JLMPS (2010).

**Table 5A.4.** Means and standard deviation of variables used in regressions, 2010

| Variable | Male | | | | Female | | | | Total | |
|---|---|---|---|---|---|---|---|---|---|---|
| | Public | | Private | | Public | | Private | | | |
| | Mean | S.D. | Mean | S.D. | Mean | S.D. | Mean | S.D. | Mean | S.D. |
| Log real hourly wages | 0.62 | 0.59 | 0.36 | 0.89 | 0.75 | 0.56 | 0.35 | 0.98 | 0.50 | 0.78 |
| Real wages | 2.42 | 3.34 | 2.82 | 9.11 | 2.62 | 2.96 | 3.27 | 10.49 | 2.68 | 7.05 |
| Monthly wages | 369.85 | 464.66 | 526.02 | 2193.04 | 310.68 | 241.51 | 397.61 | 1150.3 | 432.2 | 1499.25 |
| Experience | 14.01 | 9.80 | 15.73 | 11.39 | 10.82 | 8.22 | 9.31 | 8.71 | 14.02 | 10.48 |
| Experience Sq | 292.07 | 362.28 | 377.09 | 481.79 | 184.46 | 250.05 | 162.41 | 291.68 | 306.33 | 410.54 |
| Illiterate | 0.01 | 0.12 | 0.04 | 0.20 | 0.01 | 0.12 | 0.05 | 0.22 | 0.03 | 0.17 |
| Reads and writes | 0.06 | 0.23 | 0.10 | 0.30 | 0.03 | 0.16 | 0.05 | 0.22 | 0.07 | 0.26 |
| Basic | 0.41 | 0.49 | 0.46 | 0.50 | 0.08 | 0.27 | 0.19 | 0.39 | 0.38 | 0.49 |
| Vocational | 0.01 | 0.08 | 0.02 | 0.15 | 0.00 | 0.04 | 0.00 | 0.07 | 0.01 | 0.11 |
| Secondary | 0.20 | 0.40 | 0.16 | 0.37 | 0.09 | 0.28 | 0.11 | 0.32 | 0.16 | 0.37 |
| Post-secondary | 0.11 | 0.31 | 0.08 | 0.28 | 0.23 | 0.42 | 0.22 | 0.41 | 0.12 | 0.32 |
| University | 0.17 | 0.38 | 0.12 | 0.32 | 0.48 | 0.50 | 0.33 | 0.47 | 0.19 | 0.39 |
| Postgraduate | 0.03 | 0.18 | 0.02 | 0.15 | 0.08 | 0.27 | 0.04 | 0.19 | 0.03 | 0.18 |
| Amman | 0.11 | 0.32 | 0.36 | 0.48 | 0.13 | 0.34 | 0.40 | 0.49 | 0.24 | 0.43 |
| Balqa | 0.08 | 0.26 | 0.07 | 0.26 | 0.11 | 0.31 | 0.12 | 0.32 | 0.08 | 0.27 |
| Zarqa | 0.09 | 0.29 | 0.19 | 0.39 | 0.09 | 0.28 | 0.13 | 0.33 | 0.14 | 0.34 |
| Madaba | 0.05 | 0.22 | 0.02 | 0.16 | 0.05 | 0.22 | 0.03 | 0.18 | 0.04 | 0.19 |
| Irbid | 0.19 | 0.39 | 0.14 | 0.35 | 0.15 | 0.36 | 0.15 | 0.36 | 0.16 | 0.37 |
| Mafreq | 0.11 | 0.31 | 0.04 | 0.20 | 0.09 | 0.29 | 0.04 | 0.19 | 0.07 | 0.26 |
| Jarash | 0.08 | 0.27 | 0.04 | 0.20 | 0.05 | 0.22 | 0.02 | 0.15 | 0.06 | 0.23 |
| Ajloun | 0.06 | 0.23 | 0.02 | 0.14 | 0.05 | 0.21 | 0.02 | 0.15 | 0.04 | 0.19 |
| Karak | 0.10 | 0.30 | 0.04 | 0.19 | 0.15 | 0.36 | 0.05 | 0.22 | 0.08 | 0.26 |
| Tafileh | 0.05 | 0.21 | 0.02 | 0.12 | 0.07 | 0.25 | 0.01 | 0.10 | 0.03 | 0.18 |
| Ma'an | 0.05 | 0.22 | 0.03 | 0.16 | 0.04 | 0.20 | 0.01 | 0.10 | 0.04 | 0.19 |
| Aqaba | 0.04 | 0.19 | 0.02 | 0.15 | 0.02 | 0.15 | 0.02 | 0.14 | 0.03 | 0.16 |
| Female | | | | | | | | | 0.19 | 0.39 |
| Public sector | | | | | | | | | 0.49 | 0.50 |
| Observations | 1,901 | | 2,801 | | 511 | | 410 | | 4,903 | |

*Source:* Author's calculations based on JLMPS (2010).

**Table 5A.5.** OLS log hourly wage regressions by sector and gender, 2010

| | All wage workers | Male | | Female | |
|---|---|---|---|---|---|
| | | Private | Public | Private | Public |
| Experience | 0.026*** | 0.033*** | 0.019*** | 0.033** | 0.011 |
| | (0.003) | (0.005) | (0.004) | (0.013) | (0.009) |
| Experience square | −0.000*** | −0.000*** | −0.000*** | −0.000 | −0.000 |
| | (0.000) | (0.000) | (0.000) | (0.000) | (0.000) |
| Reads and writes | 0.070 | 0.136 | 0.169 | −0.123 | 0.004 |
| | (0.072) | (0.107) | (0.117) | (0.282) | (0.236) |
| Basic education | 0.230*** | 0.268*** | 0.347*** | −0.222 | 0.192 |
| | (0.065) | (0.099) | (0.110) | (0.227) | (0.212) |
| Vocational education | 0.153 | 0.180 | 0.332* | −0.512 | 0.284 |
| | (0.112) | (0.155) | (0.199) | (0.639) | (0.546) |
| General secondary | 0.331*** | 0.393*** | 0.398*** | 0.004 | 0.216 |
| | (0.068) | (0.105) | (0.112) | (0.237) | (0.209) |
| Post-secondary | 0.518*** | 0.602*** | 0.534*** | 0.240 | 0.488** |
| | (0.070) | (0.114) | (0.115) | (0.221) | (0.200) |
| University | 0.844*** | 1.058*** | 0.749*** | 0.707*** | 0.765*** |
| | (0.068) | (0.110) | (0.112) | (0.218) | (0.199) |
| Postgraduate | 1.088*** | 1.288*** | 1.042*** | 1.155*** | 0.873*** |
| | (0.083) | (0.151) | (0.127) | (0.294) | (0.211) |
| Balqa | −0.090** | −0.068 | 0.030 | −0.391*** | −0.028 |
| | (0.042) | (0.073) | (0.060) | (0.148) | (0.093) |
| Zarqa | −0.117*** | −0.113** | −0.009 | −0.368*** | 0.103 |
| | (0.035) | (0.051) | (0.056) | (0.137) | (0.101) |
| Madaba | −0.028 | 0.093 | −0.024 | −0.092 | −0.014 |
| | (0.057) | (0.119) | (0.068) | (0.245) | (0.120) |
| Irbid | −0.112*** | −0.174*** | 0.051 | −0.516*** | 0.098 |
| | (0.033) | (0.057) | (0.048) | (0.129) | (0.086) |
| Mafraq | −0.082* | −0.213** | 0.104* | −0.750*** | −0.159 |
| | (0.044) | (0.093) | (0.054) | (0.233) | (0.099) |
| Jarash | −0.054 | −0.073 | 0.046 | −0.072 | −0.092 |
| | (0.049) | (0.092) | (0.060) | (0.293) | (0.116) |
| Ajloun | 0.150** | 0.154 | 0.278*** | −0.362 | 0.093 |
| | (0.058) | (0.134) | (0.066) | (0.309) | (0.122) |
| Karak | 0.082* | 0.122 | 0.122** | 0.228 | 0.131 |
| | (0.044) | (0.096) | (0.055) | (0.210) | (0.087) |
| Tafileh | 0.013 | 0.463*** | −0.063 | −0.838* | 0.058 |
| | (0.062) | (0.150) | (0.071) | (0.433) | (0.109) |
| Ma'an | −0.003 | 0.131 | 0.001 | −0.414 | 0.082 |
| | (0.058) | (0.116) | (0.067) | (0.435) | (0.126) |
| Aqaba | 0.130** | 0.369*** | 0.054 | −0.012 | 0.148 |
| | (0.066) | (0.126) | (0.077) | (0.312) | (0.166) |

*(Continued)*

**Table 5A.5.** (Continued)

| | All wage workers | Male | | Female | |
|---|---|---|---|---|---|
| | | Private | Public | Private | Public |
| Female | −0.104*** | | | | |
| | (0.029) | | | | |
| Public sector | 0.196*** | | | | |
| | (0.023) | | | | |
| Constant | −0.191*** | −0.343*** | −0.046 | 0.013 | 0.019 |
| | (0.070) | (0.108) | (0.118) | (0.229) | (0.214) |
| Observations | 4877 | 2071 | 1897 | 402 | 507 |
| R-squared | 0.174 | 0.158 | 0.142 | 0.293 | 0.214 |

*Note*: Standard errors in parentheses; *** p<0.01.

**Table 5A.6.** Multinomial logit estimates of work status selection equations

| | Male | | | | Female | | | |
|---|---|---|---|---|---|---|---|---|
| | Non-wage worker | Private-wage worker | Public-wage worker | Unemployed worker | Non-wage worker | Private-wage worker | Public-wage worker | Unemployed worker |
| Age | 0.704*** | 0.613*** | 0.659*** | 0.433*** | 0.339*** | 0.427*** | 0.571*** | 0.418*** |
| | (0.028) | (0.021) | (0.024) | (0.031) | (0.069) | (0.043) | (0.053) | (0.082) |
| Age squared | -0.008*** | -0.008*** | -0.009*** | -0.006*** | -0.004*** | -0.006*** | -0.008*** | -0.008*** |
| | (0.000) | (0.000) | (0.000) | (0.000) | (0.001) | (0.001) | (0.001) | (0.001) |
| Reads and writes | 0.866*** | 0.490** | 0.999*** | 0.488 | -0.181 | -0.523 | 0.519 | 0.097 |
| | (0.248) | (0.204) | (0.269) | (0.343) | (0.429) | (0.333) | (0.502) | (1.237) |
| Basic education | 2.077*** | 1.520*** | 2.349*** | 1.605*** | -0.017 | -0.433 | 0.563 | 1.558 |
| | (0.235) | (0.189) | (0.248) | (0.311) | (0.387) | (0.272) | (0.448) | (1.019) |
| Vocational education | 2.653*** | 2.410*** | 2.326*** | 2.842*** | | 1.753* | 3.978*** | 1.747* |
| | (0.544) | (0.432) | (0.532) | (0.532) | | (0.974) | (1.218) | (1.025) |
| General secondary | 0.986*** | 0.282 | 1.581*** | 0.539* | 0.215 | -0.788*** | 1.263*** | |
| | (0.241) | (0.194) | (0.251) | (0.323) | (0.411) | (0.295) | (0.448) | |
| Post-secondary | 1.577*** | 1.377*** | 2.739*** | 1.216*** | 0.419 | 0.993*** | 2.992*** | 4.025*** |
| | (0.286) | (0.239) | (0.288) | (0.392) | (0.430) | (0.271) | (0.431) | (1.017) |
| University | 1.807*** | 1.639*** | 3.220*** | 2.346*** | 0.981** | 1.619*** | 4.512*** | 4.888*** |
| | (0.273) | (0.224) | (0.274) | (0.343) | (0.485) | (0.279) | (0.435) | (1.017) |
| Postgraduate | 1.529*** | 1.827*** | 3.274*** | 0.707 | 2.200*** | 2.665*** | 5.661*** | 5.390*** |
| | (0.436) | (0.381) | (0.415) | (0.825) | (0.836) | (0.478) | (0.552) | (1.128) |
| North regions | -0.512*** | -0.805*** | 0.347*** | -0.091 | 0.134 | -0.604*** | 0.406*** | 0.565*** |
| | (0.104) | (0.086) | (0.089) | (0.118) | (0.231) | (0.134) | (0.129) | (0.161) |
| South regions | -0.887*** | -0.646*** | 0.798*** | 0.447*** | -0.111 | -0.575*** | 1.384*** | 1.745*** |
| | (0.161) | (0.120) | (0.115) | (0.146) | (0.356) | (0.199) | (0.148) | (0.175) |
| Pre-school children | 0.312*** | 0.178*** | 0.276*** | 0.012 | -0.115 | -0.727*** | -0.234*** | -0.517*** |
| | (0.058) | (0.050) | (0.051) | (0.070) | (0.131) | (0.077) | (0.063) | (0.082) |

*(Continued)*

Table 5A.6 (Continued)

| | Male | | | | Female | | | |
|---|---|---|---|---|---|---|---|---|
| | Non-wage worker | Private-wage worker | Public-wage worker | Unemployed worker | Non-wage worker | Private-wage worker | Public-wage worker | Unemployed worker |
| Children age above six years | -0.122*** | -0.174*** | -0.142*** | -0.039 | -0.009 | -0.218*** | -0.109*** | -0.017 |
| | (0.029) | (0.024) | (0.025) | (0.033) | (0.065) | (0.039) | (0.037) | (0.045) |
| Father education intermediate and above | -0.042 | -0.336*** | -0.636*** | -0.669*** | -0.043 | -0.058 | -0.531*** | -0.361** |
| | (0.146) | (0.102) | (0.107) | (0.139) | (0.337) | (0.149) | (0.149) | (0.165) |
| Mother education intermediate and above | -0.019 | -0.152 | -0.581*** | -0.515*** | 0.457 | 0.499*** | -0.133 | -0.148 |
| | (0.173) | (0.109) | (0.117) | (0.149) | (0.403) | (0.162) | (0.178) | (0.180) |
| Father self-employed or employer | 0.399*** | -0.253*** | 0.001 | -0.228* | 0.148 | -0.012 | 0.015 | 0.063 |
| | (0.113) | (0.092) | (0.102) | (0.129) | (0.252) | (0.146) | (0.153) | (0.173) |
| Father government employee | -0.365*** | -0.618*** | 0.235** | -0.376*** | -0.158 | 0.177 | 0.403*** | -0.019 |
| | (0.125) | (0.094) | (0.097) | (0.127) | (0.277) | (0.135) | (0.136) | (0.159) |
| Wages of males in household | | | | | -0.001** | 0.000 | -0.000 | -0.000 |
| | | | | | (0.000) | (0.000) | (0.000) | (0.000) |
| Constant | -14.780*** | -9.800*** | -12.392*** | -8.226*** | -10.931*** | -8.607*** | -14.455*** | -10.748*** |
| | (0.601) | (0.416) | (0.489) | (0.606) | (1.374) | (0.753) | (1.013) | (1.567) |
| Observations | 7,505 | 7,505 | 7,505 | 7,505 | 7,600 | 7,600 | 7,600 | 7,600 |

Source: Author's calculations based on ILMPS (2010).

Note: Standard errors in parentheses.

**Table 5A.7.** Selectivity corrected wage equation estimates, 2010

| | Males | | Females | |
|---|---|---|---|---|
| | in private sector | in public sector | in private sector | in public sector |
| Experience | 0.025*** | 0.019*** | 0.028** | 0.005 |
| | (0.006) | (0.005) | (0.014) | (0.010) |
| Experience squared | −0.000* | −0.000** | −0.000 | 0.000 |
| | (0.000) | (0.000) | (0.000) | (0.000) |
| Reads and writes | 0.151 | 0.175 | −0.144 | 0.103 |
| | (0.110) | (0.119) | (0.289) | (0.239) |
| Basic | 0.269*** | 0.354*** | −0.190 | 0.216 |
| | (0.101) | (0.113) | (0.228) | (0.212) |
| Vocational | 0.128 | 0.333* | −0.537 | 0.321 |
| | (0.157) | (0.200) | (0.653) | (0.554) |
| Secondary | 0.432*** | 0.406*** | 0.022 | 0.239 |
| | (0.108) | (0.116) | (0.239) | (0.211) |
| Post-secondary | 0.613*** | 0.545*** | 0.241 | 0.511** |
| | (0.116) | (0.122) | (0.230) | (0.211) |
| University | 1.061*** | 0.760*** | 0.705*** | 0.802*** |
| | (0.112) | (0.120) | (0.233) | (0.229) |
| Postgraduate | 1.298*** | 1.053*** | 1.136*** | 0.916*** |
| | (0.155) | (0.135) | (0.311) | (0.253) |
| Balqa | −0.053 | 0.027 | −0.401*** | −0.023 |
| | (0.074) | (0.060) | (0.148) | (0.093) |
| Zarqa | −0.113** | −0.013 | −0.374*** | 0.131 |
| | (0.052) | (0.056) | (0.138) | (0.102) |
| Madaba | 0.095 | −0.028 | −0.100 | −0.011 |
| | (0.119) | (0.068) | (0.246) | (0.119) |
| Irbid | −0.099 | 0.052 | −0.509*** | 0.103 |
| | (0.062) | (0.053) | (0.133) | (0.087) |
| Mafreq | −0.140 | 0.106* | −0.723*** | −0.152 |
| | (0.097) | (0.059) | (0.242) | (0.099) |
| Jarash | 0.036 | 0.047 | −0.052 | −0.081 |
| | (0.098) | (0.064) | (0.300) | (0.117) |
| Ajloun | 0.208 | 0.279*** | −0.357 | 0.090 |
| | (0.135) | (0.070) | (0.311) | (0.123) |
| Karak | 0.218** | 0.123* | 0.208 | 0.139 |
| | (0.100) | (0.064) | (0.235) | (0.096) |
| Tafileh | 0.564*** | −0.059 | −0.827* | 0.064 |
| | (0.153) | (0.079) | (0.438) | (0.115) |
| Ma'an | 0.219* | 0.005 | −0.411 | 0.092 |
| | (0.120) | (0.075) | (0.437) | (0.130) |
| Aqaba | 0.435*** | 0.058 | 0.011 | 0.159 |
| | (0.128) | (0.083) | (0.316) | (0.169) |
| Selection term male private | −0.213*** | | | |
| | (0.067) | | | |

*(Continued)*

**Table 5A.7.** (Continued)

| | Males | | Females | |
|---|---|---|---|---|
| | in private sector | in public sector | in private sector | in public sector |
| Selection term male public | | 0.013 | | |
| | | (0.059) | | |
| Selection term female private | | | −0.049 | |
| | | | (0.109) | |
| Selection term female public | | | | 0.015 |
| | | | | (0.080) |
| Constant | −0.105 | −0.070 | 0.098 | −0.022 |
| | (0.129) | (0.172) | (0.313) | (0.313) |
| Observations | 2,047 | 1,892 | 398 | 506 |
| R-squared | 0.158 | 0.141 | 0.299 | 0.215 |

*Note:* Standard errors in parentheses; *** $p<0.01$; ** $p<0.05$; * $p<0.1$.

*Source:* Author's calculations based on JLMPS (2010).

### References

Assaad, R. and M. Amer, 2008. *Labor Market Conditions in Jordan, 1995–2006: An Analysis of Microdata Sources*. Amman, Jordan: National Center for Human Resource Development.

Bourguignon, F., M. Fournier, and M. Gurgand, 2007. Selection bias corrections based on the multinomial logit model: Monte Carlo comparisons. *Journal of Economic Surveys* 21(1): 174–205.

Cazes S., S. Verick, and C. Heuer, 2009. Labor market policies in times of crisis. Employment Working Paper No. 35, International Labor Office, Geneva.

Department of Statistics (Jordan), 2013. *Employment and Unemployment Survey*. Amman, Jordan: Department of Statistics, <http://www.dos.gov.jo> (accessed December 27, 2013).

Department of Statistics (Jordan), 2009. *National Accounts*. Amman, Jordan: Department of Statistics.

The Economic Research Forum, 2010. *Jordan Labor Market Panel Survey of 2010 Dataset (JLMPS 2010)*. Cairo, Egypt: The Economic Research Forum.

Haughton, Jonathon and Shahidur R. Khandker, 2009. *Handbook on Poverty and Inequality*. The International Bank for Reconstruction and Development/The World Bank, chapter 6.

Heckman, J., 1979. Sample selection as specification error. *Econometrica* 47: 153–61.

Jenkins, S. P., 2006. Estimation and interpretation of measures of inequality, poverty, and social welfare using Stata. Presentation at the North American Stata Users' Group Meetings 2006, Boston MA, <http://econpapers.repec.org/paper/bocasug06/16.htm> (accessed December 27, 2013).

Lee, L., 1982. Some approaches to the correction of selectivity bias. *Review of Economic Studies* 49 (July): 355–72.

—— 1983. Generalized econometric models with selectivity. *Econometrica* 51 (March): 507–12.

Population Council, 2010. The impact of the world financial crisis on the labor market in Jordan. Report submitted to the World Bank. Cairo: Population Council WANA Regional Office.

Verick, S., 2010. Unraveling the impact of the global financial crisis on the South African labor market. Employment Working Paper No. 48, International Labor Office, Geneva.

World Bank, 2009. How should labor market policy respond to the financial crisis? A note by Human Development (HD) and Poverty Reduction and Economic Management (PREM) Labor Market Teams, <http://siteresources.worldbank.org/INTLM/Resources/Note-LM_Crisis_Response_26April.pdf> (accessed December 27, 2013).

# 6

# Immigration, Emigration, and the Labor Market in Jordan

*Jackline Wahba*

## 6.1 Introduction

The Jordanian economy, like most countries in the Middle East and North Africa (MENA), has been affected by labor migration. In particular, Jordan has been a country of both labor emigration and immigration. Since the oil price increases of 1973, a significant proportion of mainly high-skilled Jordanians have emigrated to work in the neighboring Gulf Corporation Council (GCC) countries. Estimates of Jordanians currently overseas are scarce and fragmented. Di Bartolomeo et al. (2010) estimated that 4.9% of the total Jordanian population lived outside Jordan in 2008. In the meantime, Jordan is the recipient of unskilled and semi-skilled labor destined to fill the gaps in agriculture, construction, and services sectors. In 2004, the population census carried out by Jordan's Department of Statistics (DoS) recorded that 7.7% of the total population, or alternatively 13.2% of the working population, were foreign nationals (Department of Statistics, 2004). Recent figures by the Ministry of Labor indicate that in 2009 some 8% of Jordan's 5.98 million population were foreign nationals (Ministry of Labor, 2010).

The Jordanian economy has one of the world's highest levels of remittances as a proportion of GDP (23% in 2009), and remittances are a key source of income and foreign exchange for Jordan (World Bank, 2011). Table 6.1 shows the significance of remittances for Jordan: in 2008 the net foreign direct investment (FDI) inflows were US$2.0 billion; overseas development aid (ODA) received was US$0.7 billion; the total international reserves were US$8.9 billion; exports of goods and services were US$12.4 billion. Yet despite Jordan appearing to be a net immigration country it is worth noting that outward remittance flows are very small in comparison to inward remittance flows.

**Table 6.1.** Remittances flows

| US$ millions | 2003 | 2004 | 2005 | 2006 | 2007 | 2008 | 2009 |
|---|---|---|---|---|---|---|---|
| Inward remittance flows | 2,201 | 2,330 | 2,500 | 2,883 | 3,434 | 3,794 | 3,597 |
| of which | | | | | | | |
| Workers' remittances | 1,981 | 2,059 | 2,179 | 2,514 | 2,994 | 3,159 | 3,119 |
| Compensation of employees | 220 | 272 | 321 | 369 | 440 | 635 | 478 |
| Outward remittance flows | 227 | 272 | 349 | 402 | 479 | 472 | 502 |
| of which | | | | | | | |
| Workers' remittances | 200 | 240 | 308 | 354 | 423 | 416 | 443 |
| Compensation of employees | 27 | 32 | 41 | 47 | 57 | 56 | 59 |

*Source:* The World Bank (2011).

The strong economic growth of the 1970s and 1980s was based almost entirely on emigrants' remittances. Between 1999 and 2009, the average annual GDP growth rate was 6.7% and remittances averaged 23% of GDP (World Bank, 2011). However, this economic growth did not translate into job creation or a vibrant labor market. In fact, Jordan has significantly low rates of labor market participation (Saif and El-Rayyes, 2010). In particular, female labor force participation has always been pretty low (16% in 2009 and 12% in 2008), yet male labor force participation was 84% in 2009 (Ministry of Labor, 2009). Furthermore, Jordan suffers from high unemployment rates. According to the Ministry of Labor (2009), the unemployment rate was 12.9% in 2009. Female unemployment rates were especially high at 24.1%, despite females' low level of economic activity. It is also worth noting that unemployment rates are highest among university graduates, at around 16%.

Finally, Jordanian unemployment is very concentrated in youth, both in terms of absolute numbers and in terms of unemployment rates (Assaad, 2012).

## 6.2 Data

This chapter uses data obtained from the first wave of the Jordan Labor Market Panel Survey of 2010 (JLMPS 2010), which collected micro-level information from February to April 2010. The survey was designed and carried out by the Economic Research Forum (ERF) in cooperation with the Department of Statistics in Jordan (DoS) and the National Centre for Human Resources Development (NCHRD). JLMPS incorporates detailed information on education, labor market experiences and behavior, and demographic characteristics (e.g., employment status, household composition, income, parental education, education history, ownership of assets, monetary transfers, remittances, migration, and marriage history). The survey covers about 5,000 households incorporating about 25,000 individuals, applying appropriate sampling methods to make gathered data nationally representative.

It is worth noting, however, that JLMPS 2010 underestimates labor migration in both directions: emigrants and immigrants. Assaad (2012) refers to this: "Since JLMPS 2010 has the same sampling strategy as the regular Employment and Unemployment (EUS) survey conducted quarterly by the Department of Statistics (DoS), it focuses exclusively on the population residing in regular households rather than in collective residential units. This makes it equally likely as the EUS to under-sample the foreign worker population in Jordan. This version of the data makes no attempt to try to correct for this potential under-representation of foreign workers by using Ministry of Labor information on foreign worker licenses, and so on. The accurate estimation of the role of foreign workers in the Jordanian labor market therefore remains a challenge, although we can get some sense of what kinds of jobs they are likely to be concentrated in."

## 6.3 Outward Migration

### 6.3.1 Current Jordanian Emigrants

Despite these concerns, JLMPS 2010 does provide some insights about migrants currently living overseas. In 2010, some 2.1% of households had at least one member working overseas. However, it is important to remember that this is an underestimate, since it does not include migrant households who are wholly overseas, that is, it does not include migrants who have their whole families residing with them overseas.

Approximately 38% of current migrants had left Jordan in the two years preceding the JLMPS 2010 and 80% had visited. Most emigrants are highly educated (62% have a university degree), which highlights that it is mostly the high-skilled workers that migrate from Jordan. Current emigrants are predominately urban—95% of their households are located in urban areas. Interestingly, 94% of the current migrants were employed before migrating and 79% were working in the private sector.

Figure 6.1 shows the overseas destinations of current emigrants. More than half are in Saudi Arabia (32%) and the UAE (24%) and around a quarter are in Western countries, with the USA being the main destination (9%).

Examining the jobs of current emigrants reveals that 91.8% are waged workers, 7.8% are employers, and that the majority (89%) works in the private sector. In addition, Figure 6.2a, which illustrates the overseas occupations of

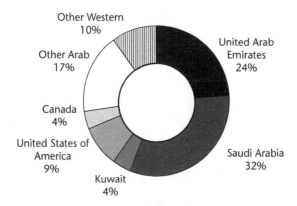

**Figure 6.1.** Destination of current emigrants (%)
*Source:* Author's calculation based on JLMPS (2010).

current migrants, indicates that over half are engaged in skilled occupations. In terms of economic activity, Jordanian emigrants tend to be engaged in construction, wholesale and retail trade, professional and technical activities, and accommodation and food industries (Figure 6.2b).

### 6.3.2 Remittances

Remittances are integral to the Jordanian economy. Around 3.3% of Jordanian households (or 4.9% of the Jordanian population) received remittances from household members or other relatives overseas in 2010. Some 69% of households received remittances from migrants in Arab countries and 31% from migrants in Western countries. Remittances are mostly received by female household heads living in urban areas (92%). In addition, more than half the remittances are sent to either a spouse (25%) or an offspring (33%) (Figure 6.3). Different methods are employed to send remittances from overseas (Figure 6.4). Money order is the most popular way, and 44% of current migrants use this service to send remittances to Jordan. Only 27% send their transfers through the banking system, but almost one-third send remittances through informal channels (by hand or through friends and relatives).

The average amount of remittances received over the previous 12 months in 2010 was approximately JD 2,055 (median = JD 1,200). The mean amount of remittances sent by migrants in Western countries was higher than that sent by migrants in Arab countries (JD 2,254 compared to JD1,663), but the median from migrants in Arab countries was higher at JD1,200 relative to JD 1,000 from migrants in Western countries). Only 5% of household heads receiving overseas transfers were currently employed, but this is mainly because those households are female-headed and more than 55% of those

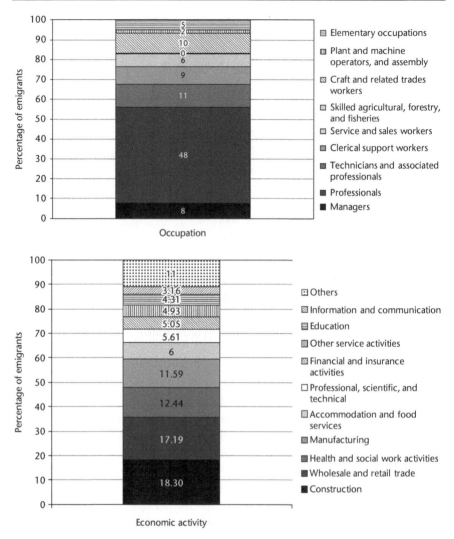

**Figure 6.2.** Overseas occupation and economic activity of current emigrants (%)
*Source:* Author's calculation based on JLMPS (2010).

females are above 40 years of age. In fact, on examining labor force participation, there is evidence that individuals in households in receipt of remittances are less likely to participate in the labor market, suggesting that remittances might lead to higher reservation wages. For example, the labor market participation rate of males above 24 years of age is 69% in households receiving remittances compared to 80% in households not receiving remittances. For females, the participation rate is 14% for those in households receiving remittances compared to 20% in non-recipient households. Interestingly, there

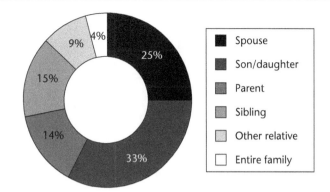

**Figure 6.3.** Relationship between remittance receiver and donor
*Source:* Author's calculation based on JLMPS (2010).

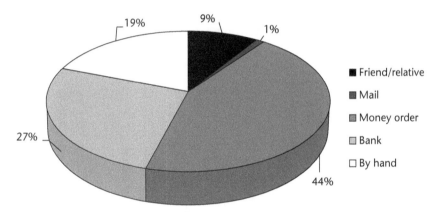

**Figure 6.4.** Method of sending overseas remittances
*Source:* Author's calculation based on JLMPS (2010).

is no significant difference in the educational level of individuals of both groups (Figure 6.5). Also, Figure 6.6 shows that households receiving overseas transfers were more likely to belong to the top two wealth quintiles (4 and 5).

### 6.3.3 Return Migration

Almost 10.9% of the households have a return migrant. Around 18% returned in 1990–92 after the first Gulf War. Some 10% returned in 2008–10, possibly in the aftermath of the global economic crisis. The majority of returnees (95.6%) live in urban areas.

Analyzing the educational levels of current and return migrants reveals that current migrants are on average better educated than returnees (Figure 6.7).

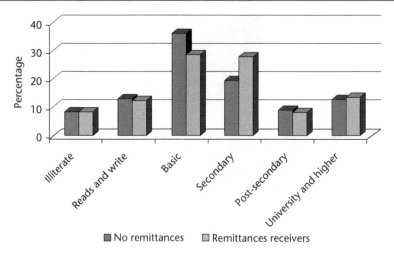

**Figure 6.5.** Educational level of individuals, 15 years of age and above (%)
*Source:* Author's calculation based on JLMPS (2010).

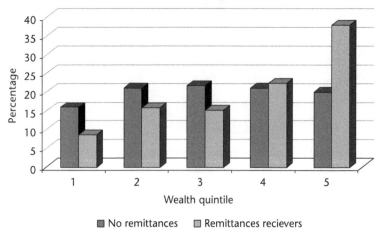

**Figure 6.6.** Household wealth quintiles
*Source:* Author's calculation based on JLMPS (2010).

This could either be a selection issue, less successful migrants return, or an age effect, given that returnees are older than current migrants. However, return-ees are still more educated than non-migrants, which again highlights that it is most often the high-skilled Jordanians that migrate.

Figure 6.8 shows the destinations from which migrants had returned: Saudi Arabia was the main destination, followed by Kuwait and the UAE. In total,

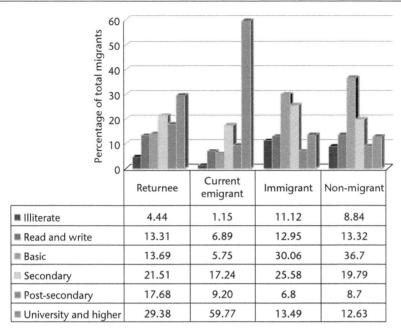

| | Returnee | Current emigrant | Immigrant | Non-migrant |
|---|---|---|---|---|
| ■ Illiterate | 4.44 | 1.15 | 11.12 | 8.84 |
| ■ Read and write | 13.31 | 6.89 | 12.95 | 13.32 |
| ■ Basic | 13.69 | 5.75 | 30.06 | 36.7 |
| ■ Secondary | 21.51 | 17.24 | 25.58 | 19.79 |
| ■ Post-secondary | 17.68 | 9.20 | 6.8 | 8.7 |
| ■ University and higher | 29.38 | 59.77 | 13.49 | 12.63 |

**Figure 6.7.** Educational levels by migration status (%)
*Source:* Author's calculation based on JLMPS (2010).

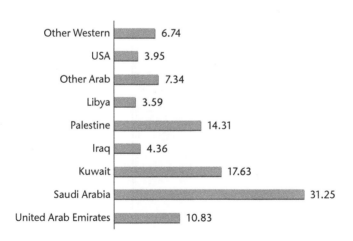

Overseas destinations of return migrants (%)

**Figure 6.8.** Overseas destinations of return migrants
*Source:* Author's calculation based on JLMPS (2010).

almost 90% of Jordanian returnees came back from the GCC and other Arab countries. The main Western destination from which Jordanian migrants returned was the USA.

Examining the characteristics of returnees by destination shows no significant difference in terms of educational level. Jordanian emigrants to the West have similar educational levels to those who went to Arab countries: almost 40% of Jordanian emigrants to both destinations have secondary education or higher (Figure 6.9). The majority of Jordanians were employed as waged workers overseas. Meanwhile 20% of Jordanian returnees from the West and 7% of returnees from Arab countries were employers or self-employed (Figure 6.10).

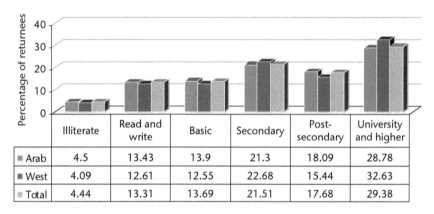

| | Illiterate | Read and write | Basic | Secondary | Post-secondary | University and higher |
|---|---|---|---|---|---|---|
| Arab | 4.5 | 13.43 | 13.9 | 21.3 | 18.09 | 28.78 |
| West | 4.09 | 12.61 | 12.55 | 22.68 | 15.44 | 32.63 |
| Total | 4.44 | 13.31 | 13.69 | 21.51 | 17.68 | 29.38 |

**Figure 6.9.** Educational level of returnees by previous overseas destination (%)
*Source:* Author's calculation based on JLMPS (2010).

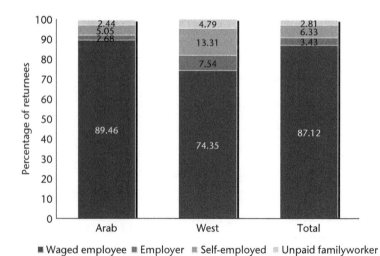

**Figure 6.10.** Overseas employment status of returnees by destination (%)
*Source:* Author's calculation based on JLMPS (2010).

One-third of Jordanian returnees were employed in the public sector in Arab countries, compared to only 7% in the West (Figure 6.11). There is also evidence that destination plays a role with regards to type of occupation. The biggest proportion of Jordanians in Arab countries (38%) was engaged in professional occupations, whereas the biggest proportion of Jordanians in the West (39%) was engaged in services and sales (see Figure 6.12). One last aspect of comparison between returnees from Arab countries and those from the West is their contract status. Of the first group, 37% worked without contract, 33% had permanent contracts, and 31% had temporary contracts, whereas of the second group 63% worked without contract, only 26% had permanent contracts, and 10% had temporary contracts (see Figure 6.13).

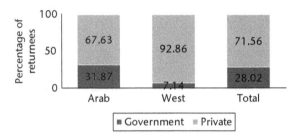

**Figure 6.11.** Overseas sector of employment of returnees by destination (%)
*Source:* Author's calculation based on JLMPS (2010).

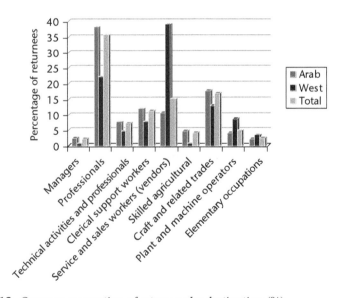

**Figure 6.12.** Overseas occupation of returnees by destination (%)
*Source:* Author's calculation based on JLMPS (2010).

181

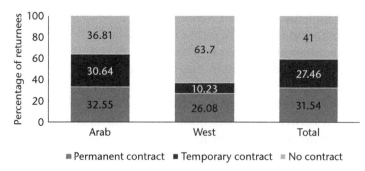

**Figure 6.13.** Overseas contract status of returnees by destination (%)
*Source:* Author's calculation based on JLMPS (2010).

## 6.4 Inward Migration

One of the reservations on JLMPS 2010, and other surveys like the EUS 2010 is that they underestimate the proportion of non-Jordanians because their samples include only traditional households and not collective places of residence (Assaad, 2012). JLMPS 2010 reports that foreigners make up 8% of the working-age population and 10% of overall employment (Figure 6.14a). As shown in Figure 6.14b, of those foreigners, the largest single nationality group is Egyptians (29%). However, the group "other Arabs," which includes Palestinians without Jordanian citizenship, is collectively larger (46%). Iraqis and Syrians represent 17% and 7% of the foreigners in Jordan, respectively. Interestingly, the educational levels of non-Jordanians vary; Iraqis are the most educated (Figure 6.15).

Table 6.2 shows the gender mix of non-Jordanians—in comparison to that of Jordanians, which is almost evenly split between males and females. Most Egyptians immigrants are male (78%), while most Syrian immigrants are female (71.3%). Meanwhile the gender mix of the other nationalities is evenly balanced. The gender composition of the non-Jordanian population appears to have an impact on each group's respective labor market participation rates. Three-quarters of Egyptians are employed, but the employment rate for other groups is much lower.

There is no significant difference between Jordanians and non-Jordanians in terms of marital status. However, it might also be the case that not all immigrants have their spouses living with them in Jordan (Table 6.3). Non-Jordanians, like Jordanians, live predominately in urban areas.

Focusing on Jordanian non-migrants and the non-Jordanian labor force, we now examine the characteristics of each group. Figure 6.16 shows that immigrant workers are on average less educated than native Jordanian workers, which suggests that Jordan mainly imports unskilled labor, while exporting

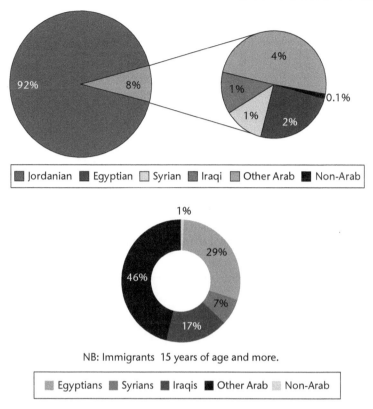

NB: Immigrants 15 years of age and more.

**Figure 6.14.** Nationality of working population (%)
*Source:* Author's calculation based on JLMPS (2010).

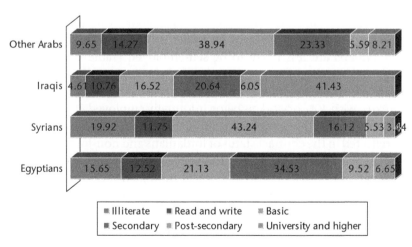

**Figure 6.15.** Educational level of all immigrants by nationality (%)
*Source:* Author's calculation based on JLMPS (2010).

183

**Table 6.2.** Characteristics of Jordanians and non-Jordanians by nationality (15 years and older)

|  | Jordanians | Egyptians | Syrians | Iraqis | Other Arabs | Total non-Jordanians |
|---|---|---|---|---|---|---|
| *Gender* |  |  |  |  |  |  |
| Male | 49.24 | 77.70 | 28.70 | 50.78 | 54.28 | 58.42 |
| Female | 50.76 | 23.30 | 71.30 | 49.22 | 45.72 | 41.58 |
| *Employed* |  |  |  |  |  |  |
| Total | 41.89 | 76.92 | 30.02 | 27.57 | 44.70 | 49.78 |
| Male | 66.95 | 97.73 | 92.10 | 44.04 | 68.42 | 76.54 |

*Source:* Author's calculation based on JLMPS (2010).

**Table 6.3.** Demographic characteristics of immigrants and Jordanians

|  | Jordanians | Non-Jordanians |
|---|---|---|
| *Marital status* |  |  |
| Single | 39.06 | 38.03 |
| Married | 55.63 | 58.03 |
| Other | 5.30 | 3.94 |
| *Location* |  |  |
| Urban | 81.19 | 90.16 |
| *Housing* |  |  |
| Apartment | 68.01 | 78.01 |
| House/*dar* | 31.22 | 21.39 |

*Source:* Author's calculation based on JLMPS (2010).

skilled workers (as discussed in section 6.3). Although the proportion of waged workers is approximately the same for Jordanians and non-Jordanians (80%), non-Jordanians are less likely to be self-employed (Table 6.4). And while 40% of Jordanians work in the public sector, almost 96% of non-Jordanians are employed by the private sector. Although informal work is common to Jordanians, with 40% of workers being informally employed, it is almost twice as common among non-Jordanians (86% are informally employed). This is again reflected in the contract status of Jordanians and non-Jordanians. Of the first group, 38% have no contract, and of the second, 65% have no contract. In addition, non-Jordanians do not benefit from paid vacations (almost 80% do not have this benefit). Furthermore, non-Jordanians are mainly employed in the trade, services, construction, manufacturing, and agriculture sectors (Figure 6.17), but even in those sectors they are basically employed in occupations that reflect their low skill and education, such as elementary occupations, craft workers, services and sales workers, and so on (Figure 6.18). This

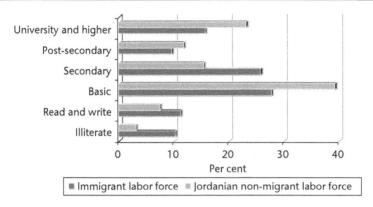

NB: Educational level of those currently in the labor force.

**Figure 6.16.** Educational levels of immigrants and the Jordanian labor force (%)
*Source:* Author's calculation based on JLMPS (2010).

**Table 6.4.** Employment characteristics of immigrants and Jordanians

|  | Jordanians | Non-Jordanians |
|---|---|---|
| *Employment status* | | |
| Waged employee | 81.07 | 79.35 |
| Employer | 7.38 | 10.77 |
| Self-employed | 10.62 | 2.81 |
| *Sector* | | |
| Public | 38.83 | 2.29 |
| Private | 60.30 | 96.42 |
| *Formality* | | |
| Informal | 40.11 | 85.77 |
| Formal | 59.89 | 14.23 |
| *Contract* | | |
| Permanent contract | 54.29 | 17.40 |
| Temporary contact | 8.22 | 18.11 |
| No contract | 37.50 | 64.49 |
| *Paid vacation* | | |
| No | 38.64 | 79.16 |
| Yes | 61.36 | 20.84 |

*Source:* Author's calculation based on JLMPS (2010).

evidence suggests that immigrants are employed in less attractive jobs compared to natives.

Finally, comparing the median monthly wage from the primary job, Table 6.5 suggests that on average immigrants earn less than Jordanians. The median monthly wage for an immigrant worker is JD 200, compared to JD

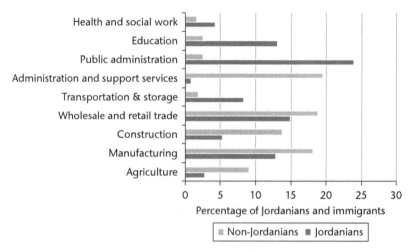

**Figure 6.17.** Economic activity of Jordanians and immigrants (%)
*Source:* Author's calculation based on JLMPS (2010).

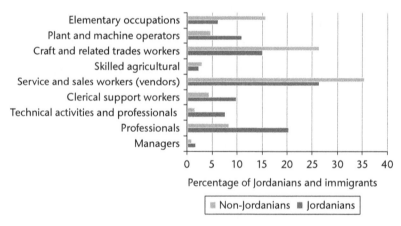

**Figure 6.18.** Occupation of Jordanians and immigrants (%)
*Source:* Author's calculation based on JLMPS (2010).

280 for Jordanian non-migrants. However, Jordanian returnees earn more than non-migrants, suggesting a possible human capital accumulation when abroad. Controlling for education and age, the same pattern is observed (immigrants earn the lowest wage). Interestingly, on average current emigrants earn around four times as much as stayers, and the gap becomes much bigger for those with university degrees—almost ten times as much.

**Table 6.5.** Median monthly wages (primary job) of natives and migrants (in Jordanian dinars)

|  | All educational levels | University graduate | Above 40 years of age |
|---|---|---|---|
| *In Jordan* |  |  |  |
| Non-migrants | 280 | 350 | 300 |
| Returnees | 350 | 470 | 358 |
| Immigrants | 200 | 260 | 217 |
| *Overseas* |  |  |  |
| Emigrants | 1,000 | 4,000 | . . . |

*Source:* Author's calculation based on JLMPS (2010).

## 6.5 Conclusion

This book uses a new and original dataset, the Jordan Labor Market Panel Survey of 2010 (JLMPS 2010) to study migration and the labor market in Jordan. The chapter documents the characteristics of outward migration and describes both current Jordanian emigrants and return migrants. It then compares immigrant workers to natives. Although the JLMPS 2010 underestimates both the number of emigrants and immigrants, it is still very useful in describing the main patterns of Jordanian migration. The findings suggest that Jordan is exporting high-skilled workers but importing low-skilled labor. There is evidence that immigrant workers undercut Jordanian wages. However, immigrant workers are employed in low-skilled jobs in the informal sector with very little benefits or security. On the other hand, Jordanian emigrants are able to earn at least four times the Jordanian wage and remit substantial amount of remittances, thereby increasing the domestic reservation wages, which may have given rise to the rentier state phenomena.

### References

Assaad, R., 2012. The structure and evolution of employment in Jordan. ERF Working Paper No. 674. Cairo, Egypt: The Economic Research Forum.

Department of Statistics (Jordan), 2004. *Jordan Population and Housing Census 2004*. Amman, Jordan: Department of Statistics.

Di Bartolomeo, T. Fakhoury, and D. Perrin, 2010. CARIM Migration Profile: Jordan. CARIM European University Institute, Robert Schuman for Advanced Studies.

Saif I. and T. El-Rayyes, 2010. Labor markets performance and migration flows in Jordan. In *Labor Market Performance and Migration Flows in Arab Mediterranean Countries: Determinants and Effects*. European Economy, European Commission Occasional Paper 60, Volume III, Directorate-General for Economic and Financial Affairs, EC.

Ministry of Labor, 2009. *Jordanian Labor Market in Figures 2009*. Jordan: Ministry of Labor.

—— 2010. *Study on the Jordanian Labor Market, Policies and Strategic Planning Unit*. Jordan: Ministry of Labor.

World Bank, 2011. *The Migration and Remittances Factbook 2011*. Washington DC: World Bank.

# 7

# Trends and Differentials in Jordanian Marriage Behavior: Marriage Timing, Spousal Characteristics, Household Structure, and Matrimonial Expenditures

*Rania Salem*

## 7.1 Background and Introduction

In recent decades, Jordanian society has undergone dramatic change in the realm of marriage and the family, and many of these changes are consistent with the classical demographic transition undergone by Western industrialized countries. The international social science literature on Jordanian marriage has been dominated thus far by studies of the continued practice of kin marriage and its effects on population health (Khoury and Massad, 1992; Sueyoushi and Ohtsuka, 2003; Hamamy et al., 2005; Obeidat et al., 2010). Popular discourse in Jordan as represented by articles in the press, on the other hand, has been more concerned with the late age at which many young people find themselves financially capable of marrying, and the resulting rates of celibacy (Badran and Sarhan, 1995; Alasmar, 2007; Shaker, 2008; Khalifa, 2009; Alshuwayki, 2011). Although information on age at marriage in Jordan has thus far been limited to women (Department of Statistics Jordan and ICF Macro, 2010), Jordan is located in the region which records the oldest male singulate mean age at marriage among all world regions (Mensch et al., 2005).

This chapter employs the first wave of the Jordan Labor Market Panel Survey (JLMPS), fielded in 2010, to analyze patterns in marriage timing and marriage behavior over time and across socio-demographic groups in Jordan. The JLMPS also includes a module of questions about marriage costs in Jordan, and the analysis given here incorporates a description of how marriage expenditures have varied across marriage cohorts and different socio-demographic groups.

## 7.2 Duration of Engagement

The marriage process in Jordan encompasses several stages. For the majority Muslim population, the first step in getting engaged is an event called the *qirayet fatiha*, followed by an event called the *tolba*, followed by an engagement party, followed by the signing of the legal marriage contract (*katb kitab*), and finally there is a wedding party (*'urs*) and the start of cohabitation by the new couple (Khuraisat, 1990). Two or more of these events can be combined and held on the same day, or they may be separated by several months or years. This chapter investigates the duration of engagement in Jordan by examining the time elapsed between the *fatiha* and the *katb kitab* on the one hand, and between the *katb kitab* and the start of cohabitation on the other. The questions regarding the duration of engagement were posed to ever-married women aged 15–60 in the JLMPS.

While some women reported having been engaged for months or years, the average length of the *fatiha* stage in the JLMPS sample as a whole is approximately 1.1 months. Approximately 45.3% of respondents had the *fatiha* and the *katb kitab* in the same week, and 28.4% held the two events one week apart. As for the *katb kitab* stage, its average length was considerably longer (7.2 months).

To illustrate differentials in the length of the *fatiha* and *katb kitab* stages across socio-demographic characteristics,[1] a variable was created that combines the two stages. Overall, the average time between the start of engagement and the start of cohabitation was 8.4 months. The time to marriage is slightly longer in urban areas compared to rural areas, and the time to marriage is longest in central Jordan (Table 7.1). Table 7.1 also shows that there are minimal differentials according to wealth, and that those with intermediate levels of education have the longest engagement durations.

What about the evolution of engagement duration over time? By disaggregating respondents according to their date of marriage, we may observe trends in engagement duration over time. As illustrated by Figure 7.1, the average months to marriage decreased somewhat between the mid-1960s and the mid-1980s, and since then, engagements have become slightly lengthier in Jordan.

---

[1] Socio-demographic characteristics are based on current reports. Unfortunately, the JLMPS does not contain measures of respondents' residence, wealth, or education at the time of marriage.

**Table 7.1.** Mean months from engagement to marriage by socio-demographic characteristic of the wife, ever-married women aged 15–60

|  | Months from engagement to marriage | No. |
|---|---|---|
| *Residence* |  |  |
| Rural | 8.1 | 1,205 |
| Urban | 8.4 | 3,306 |
| *Region* |  |  |
| Central | 8.6 | 2,371 |
| Northern | 8.0 | 1,473 |
| Southern | 7.9 | 667 |
| *Wealth* |  |  |
| Poorest | 8.3 | 1,423 |
| Middle wealth | 8.4 | 1,546 |
| Wealthiest | 8.4 | 1,542 |
| *Education* |  |  |
| Less than basic | 7.0 | 1,035 |
| Basic | 8.6 | 1,550 |
| Secondary | 9.3 | 780 |
| Post-secondary | 8.5 | 1,146 |
| *Total* | 8.4 | 4,511 |

*Source:* JLMPS (2010).

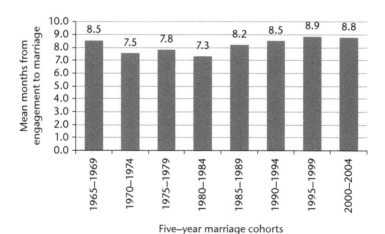

**Figure 7.1.** Mean months from engagement to marriage across five-year marriage cohorts, ever-married women aged 15–60
*Source:* JLMPS (2010).

## 7.3 Current Marital Status

Marriage is virtually universal for Jordanian women and men alike. In the JLMPS 2010 sample, 6.5% of women aged 45-49 had never married, and 1.9% of men aged 45-49 had never married. This may be compared to the 2009 Jordan Population and Family Health Survey (JPFHS), which found that 8.5% of women had never married by the same age (Figure 7.2) (Department of Statistics Jordan and ICF Macro, 2010). Although current concerns regarding high rates of celibacy among Jordanian women are largely unfounded, the popular perception that celibacy among women is more common than it is among men is borne out by the JLMPS data.

Table 7.2 shows the age pattern of other marital statuses, such as divorced or separated and widowed. It is important to bear in mind that the JLMPS only collected data on respondents' *current* marital status. So for example, if a woman had married, divorced, and remarried, and was thus in her second marriage at the time of the JLMPS interview, she would be classified as married by the survey. Therefore, the proportions of divorced or separated in the JLMPS are an underestimate of the total divorce rate in Jordan. One would expect divorce and separation to increase steadily with exposure to marital disruption, but the percentage of those in this category does not rise within successively older age groups. Rather, the proportion divorced or separated is highest among those currently aged 35–39 in Jordan (Table 7.2). This might suggest an increase in divorce rates over time, though this would have to be confirmed with data from vital statistics.

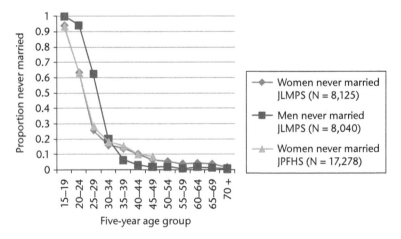

**Figure 7.2.** Proportion of women and men never married by age group
*Source:* JLMPS (2010) and JPFHS (2009).

**Table 7.2.** Current marital status of women and men by five-year age group

| Five-year age group | Marital status | | | | | | | | | |
|---|---|---|---|---|---|---|---|---|---|---|
| | Never-married | | Married | | Divorced/ separated | | Widowed | | No. | |
| | Women | Men | women | Men | Women | Men | Women | Men | Women | Men |
| 15–19 | 94.0 | 100.0 | 6.0 | 0.1 | 0.1 | 0.0 | 0.0 | 0.0 | 1,486 | 1,488 |
| 20–24 | 63.4 | 94.2 | 35.8 | 5.8 | 0.8 | 0.1 | 0.1 | 0.0 | 1,194 | 1,240 |
| 25–29 | 26.0 | 62.5 | 72.0 | 36.9 | 2.0 | 0.6 | 0.0 | 0.1 | 1,006 | 1,050 |
| 30–34 | 16.0 | 19.8 | 81.9 | 79.7 | 1.7 | 0.5 | 0.4 | 0.0 | 905 | 858 |
| 35–39 | 13.8 | 6.3 | 81.0 | 92.1 | 3.9 | 1.6 | 1.3 | 0.0 | 870 | 800 |
| 40–44 | 10.4 | 3.1 | 84.8 | 95.8 | 1.9 | 0.8 | 2.9 | 0.2 | 679 | 698 |
| 45–49 | 6.5 | 1.9 | 82.0 | 97.7 | 2.4 | 0.4 | 9.1 | 0.0 | 504 | 516 |
| 50–54 | 5.4 | 2.0 | 76.5 | 96.6 | 2.9 | 1.4 | 15.1 | 0.0 | 406 | 328 |
| 55–59 | 4.0 | 0.7 | 75.5 | 98.0 | 0.8 | 0.9 | 19.7 | 0.4 | 296 | 292 |
| 60–64 | 4.3 | 1.8 | 57.2 | 93.5 | 2.6 | 1.3 | 35.9 | 3.4 | 265 | 244 |
| 65–69 | 3.9 | 1.2 | 55.6 | 97.3 | 2.6 | 0.0 | 38.0 | 1.5 | 187 | 213 |
| 70+ | 1.6 | 0.6 | 31.3 | 86.0 | 1.4 | 0.8 | 65.6 | 12.6 | 327 | 313 |
| Total | 34.4 | 43.6 | 56.5 | 55.2 | 1.7 | 0.6 | 7.5 | 0.7 | 8,125 | 8,040 |
| Total both sexes | 39.0 | | 55.8 | | 1.1 | | 4.1 | | 16,165 | |

*Source:* JLMPS (2010).

## 7.4 Marriage Timing

The fact that men marry considerably later than women is apparent from the age pattern of first marriage displayed in Figure 7.2. Men's median age at first marriage[2] in the JLMPS sample stands at 28.7 years overall. Women's median age at first marriage in Jordan is 23.8 years of age. We see in Table 7.3 that both men and women marry earlier in urban areas compared to rural areas. Moving on to other socio-demographic differentials in age at first marriage, minimal variation in age is found at first marriage across Jordan's three regions. Women and men living in central Jordan, however, marry younger than their counterparts in northern and southern Jordan. Table 7.3 indicates that the wealth gradient in age at first marriage is steepest among women, with the poorest Jordanian women marrying at age 21.9, those in the middle third marrying at age 23.0, and the wealthiest marrying at age 25.5. Men's wealth differentials in marriage timing are less pronounced, with the poorest Jordanian men marrying at age 28.2 and the wealthiest marrying at age 29.9. Women's age pattern of first marriage by education mirrors the wealth

---

[2] The measure utilized here—the indirect median age at first marriage—is calculated in a manner that takes into account the fact that some of those who will marry have not yet entered into their first union (Siegel and Swanson, 2004).

**Table 7.3.** Median age at first marriage for women and men by socio-demographic characteristic

| | Women's median age at first marriage | No. | Men's median age at frst marriage | No. |
|---|---|---|---|---|
| *Residence* | | | | |
| Rural | 24.5 | 2,283 | 29.1 | 2,259 |
| Urban | 23.6 | 5,842 | 28.7 | 5,781 |
| *Region* | | | | |
| Central | 23.6 | 4,073 | 28.5 | 4,026 |
| Northern | 24.1 | 2,765 | 29.2 | 2,797 |
| Southern | 24.1 | 1,287 | 29.3 | 1,217 |
| *Wealth* | | | | |
| Poorest | 21.9 | 2,606 | 28.2 | 2,627 |
| Middle wealth | 23.0 | 2,659 | 28.1 | 2,571 |
| Wealthiest | 25.5 | 2,860 | 29.9 | 2,842 |
| *Education* | | | | |
| Less than basic | 22.3 | 2,197 | 29.7 | 1,651 |
| Basic | 20.8 | 2,664 | 27.6 | 3,264 |
| Secondary | 24.1 | 1,568 | 29.1 | 1,571 |
| Post-secondary | 25.0 | 1,696 | 29.6 | 1,553 |
| *Total* | 23.8 | 8,125 | 28.7 | 8,040 |

*Source:* JLMPS (2010).

pattern of first marriage, with the more educated marrying later than the least educated (women with basic education are an exception to this general pattern, marrying earliest of all). Among men, however, those with the lowest and the highest educational attainment marry at the oldest ages (Table 7.3).

Another set of measures can be used to examine marriage timing, namely the proportions of men and women married by ages 18, 20, 25, and 30. These measures confirm many of the patterns in marriage universality and marriage timing revealed by the median age at first marriage. Among women in the JLMPS sample, 22.6% had married by age 18; 37.8% had married by age 20; 72.9% had married by 25; and 85.4% had married by 30. Consistent with Table 7.2, Table 7.3 shows that rural women begin entering into marriage later than urban women, and a higher proportion appears never to wed. In addition, a greater proportion of women in central Jordan had married by every age than in northern or southern Jordan. Although the poorest women in Jordan are the ones most likely to marry in their teens, a larger proportion remain unmarried at age 30 compared to those in the middle or highest wealth categories. Table 7.2 indicates that the wealthiest women marry the latest, but this is not because a large portion of them remain unmarried. It seems from Table 7.4 that the wealthiest women are *least* likely never to have married by age 30, followed by those in the middle wealth category, and finally the poorest women. Finally, the largest proportion of women to have married by age 30 according to educational attainment are those with less than basic education, and the smallest proportion of women to have married by 30 are those with post-secondary education (Table 7.4).

**Table 7.4.** Proportions married by various ages by socio-demographic characteristic

| | Proportion married by 18 | Proportion married by 20 | Proportion married by 25 | Proportion married by 30 | No. |
|---|---|---|---|---|---|
| All women | 0.226 | 0.378 | 0.729 | 0.854 | 7,169 |
| *Residence* | | | | | |
| Rural | 0.211 | 0.352 | 0.699 | 0.829 | 1,986 |
| Urban | 0.230 | 0.383 | 0.735 | 0.860 | 5,183 |
| *Region* | | | | | |
| Central Jordan | 0.231 | 0.384 | 0.735 | 0.860 | 3,602 |
| Northern Jordan | 0.225 | 0.379 | 0.720 | 0.845 | 2,438 |
| Southern Jordan | 0.201 | 0.337 | 0.714 | 0.845 | 1,129 |
| *Wealth* | | | | | |
| Poorest | 0.275 | 0.430 | 0.718 | 0.835 | 2,305 |
| Middle wealth | 0.242 | 0.400 | 0.737 | 0.856 | 2,319 |
| Wealthiest | 0.182 | 0.326 | 0.730 | 0.865 | 2,545 |
| *Education* | | | | | |
| Less than basic | 0.453 | 0.622 | 0.827 | 0.902 | 1,805 |
| Basic | 0.326 | 0.515 | 0.770 | 0.853 | 2,102 |
| Secondary | 0.097 | 0.288 | 0.730 | 0.854 | 1,566 |
| Post-secondary | 0.022 | 0.082 | 0.580 | 0.787 | 1,696 |
| All men | 0.018 | 0.055 | 0.365 | 0.764 | 7,128 |
| *Residence* | | | | | |
| Rural | 0.018 | 0.056 | 0.395 | 0.802 | 1,990 |
| Urban | 0.018 | 0.055 | 0.359 | 0.757 | 5,138 |
| *Region* | | | | | |
| Central Jordan | 0.014 | 0.047 | 0.362 | 0.760 | 3,575 |
| Northern Jordan | 0.022 | 0.070 | 0.372 | 0.775 | 2,463 |
| Southern Jordan | 0.027 | 0.059 | 0.363 | 0.760 | 1,090 |
| *Wealth* | | | | | |
| Poorest | 0.031 | 0.083 | 0.432 | 0.794 | 2,320 |
| Middle wealth | 0.016 | 0.051 | 0.375 | 0.766 | 2,310 |
| Wealthiest | 0.010 | 0.037 | 0.306 | 0.742 | 2,498 |
| *Education* | | | | | |
| Less than basic | 0.061 | 0.147 | 0.535 | 0.825 | 1,257 |
| Basic | 0.013 | 0.056 | 0.421 | 0.806 | 2,751 |
| Secondary | 0.008 | 0.029 | 0.322 | 0.748 | 1,567 |
| Post-secondary | 0.006 | 0.014 | 0.204 | 0.675 | 1,553 |
| *Total* | 0.122 | 0.216 | 0.548 | 0.810 | 14,297 |

*Source:* JLMPS (2010).

As for men in the JLMPS sample, 1.8% had married by age 18; 5.5% had married by age 20; 36.5% had married by age 25; and 76.4% had married by age 30 (Table 7.4). Early marriage is rare among both rural and urban men, but urban men appear to postpone or forgo marriage to a greater extent compared to rural men, contrary to the findings reported in Table 7.2. There are minimal differences in men's marriage timing by region. Men in central Jordan are very unlikely to marry in their teens, but in all regions men enter into marriage predominantly between the ages of 25 and 30 and are about as likely to have married by age 30. The poorest men in Jordan tend to marry earlier than their wealthier counterparts, and they are more likely to have married by age 30. Table 7.3 also shows that the greater the educational attainment of a Jordanian man, the later he is likely to marry.

Several sources have documented rising ages at first marriage in Jordan in recent decades, although few have been able to make gender comparisons. According to the JPFHS, for example, the percentage of women who had never married has grown over successive waves of the survey, particularly in the period 1990–2002. Since 2002, the upward trend in women's ages at first marriage has leveled off, and among those aged 20–34, there are even signs of a slight dip in the age at first marriage (Department of Statistics Jordan and ICF Macro, 2010). This pattern is not apparent in the JLMPS 2010. Utilizing measures of the proportion married by certain ages, Figure 7.3 shows that Jordanian women's age at marriage has generally been rising across birth cohorts. The proportion marrying by each age considered has dropped over time. However, a temporary return to earlier ages at marriage is evident

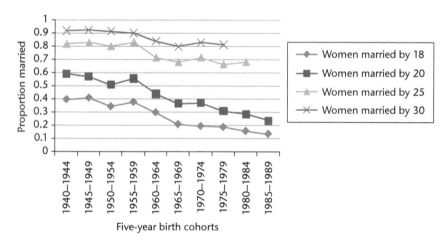

**Figure 7.3.** Proportion of women married by age 18, 20, 25, and 30 across five-year birth cohorts

*Source:* JLMPS (2010).

among the 1955–59 birth cohorts, and the 1970–74 birth cohorts of women. Figures 7.4 and 7.5 show that this pattern is driven largely by rural women. It is not clear what may have led to these spikes in early marriage. These women would have been marrying in the late 1970s and early 1990s, periods that contrast in terms of the geopolitical climate and levels of migration and remittances. In addition, Figures 7.4 and 7.5 indicate that trends in the

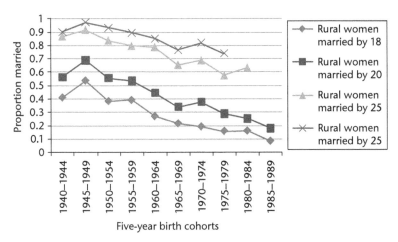

**Figure 7.4.** Proportion of rural women married by age 18, 20, 25, and 30 across five-year birth cohorts
*Source:* JLMPS (2010).

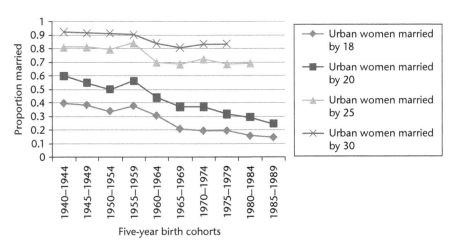

**Figure 7.5.** Proportion of urban women married by age 18, 20, 25, and 30 across five-year birth cohorts
*Source:* JLMPS (2010).

postponement of marriage over time have been more pronounced among rural women compared to urban women. In Figures 7.6 to 7.9, trends are disaggregated in the proportion of women married by educational attainment. These trends likely reflect changes in women's marriage timing behavior, as well as changes in the composition of various educational groups over time.

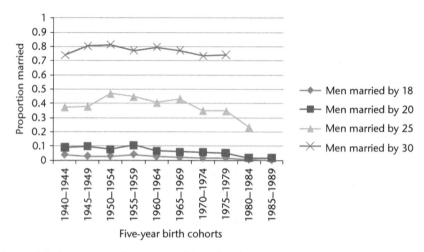

**Figure 7.6.** Proportion of women with less than basic education married by age 18, 20, 25, and 30 across five-year birth cohorts
*Source:* JLMPS (2010).

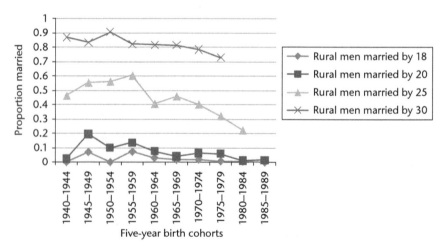

**Figure 7.7.** Proportion of women with basic education married by age 18, 20, 25, and 30 across five-year birth cohorts
*Source:* JLMPS (2010).

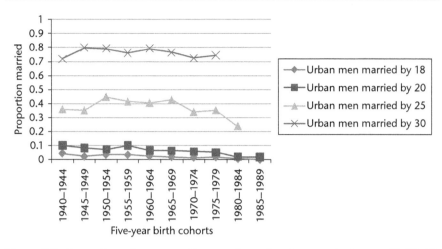

**Figure 7.8.** Proportion of women with secondary education married by age 18, 20, 25, and 30 across five-year birth cohorts
*Source:* JLMPS (2010).

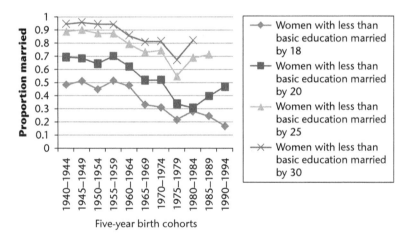

**Figure 7.9.** Proportion of women with post-secondary education married by age 18, 20, 25, and 30 across five-year birth cohorts
*Source:* JLMPS (2010).

Trends in the proportion of men married by ages 18, 20, 25, and 30 show that men's marriage under the age of 20 has always been, and remains, uncommon in Jordan (Figure 7.10). Over time, a larger proportion of Jordanian men are postponing marriage to their late twenties. Comparing Figures 7.3 and 7.10 reveals that successive generations of Jordanian men have been delaying marriage at a slower rate than women have. Among all men represented in the

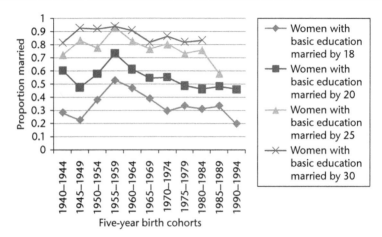

**Figure 7.10.** Proportion of men married by age 18, 20, 25, and 30 across five-year birth cohorts

*Source:* JLMPS (2010).

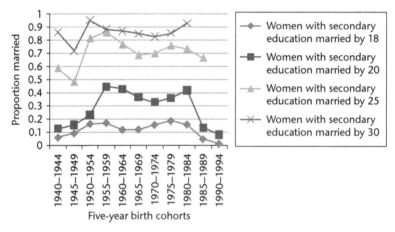

**Figure 7.11.** Proportion of rural men married by age 18, 20, 25, and 30 across five-year birth cohorts

*Source:* JLMPS (2010).

JLMPS, those born in the early 1940s and those born after the early 1970s had postponed marriage the most. If we disaggregate these trends by rural/urban residence, we find that rural men had undergone the most dramatic delay in their marriage transitions from the birth cohorts of the late 1940s to the early 1960s. Urban men's age at marriage appears to have declined less steeply than rural men's age (Figures 7.11 and 7.12). Trends in men's marriage timing according to educational attainment can be seen in Figures 7.13 to 7.16.

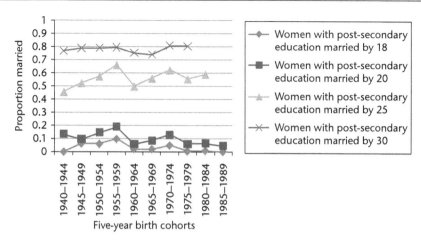

**Figure 7.12.** Proportion of urban men married by age 18, 20, 25, and 30 across five-year birth cohorts
*Source:* JLMPS (2010).

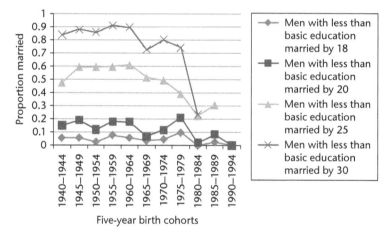

**Figure 7.13.** Proportion of men with less than basic education married by age 18, 20, 25, and 30 across five-year birth cohorts
*Source:* JLMPS (2010).

## 7.5 Spousal Age and Education Gaps

I next consider spousal characteristics such as age, education, and kinship status. Age seniority of the husband is preferred in many countries, and Arab societies are no exception to this general pattern. For currently married women, those whose husbands were present in the household were identified and interviewed by the JLMPS in order to calculate the age difference between husbands

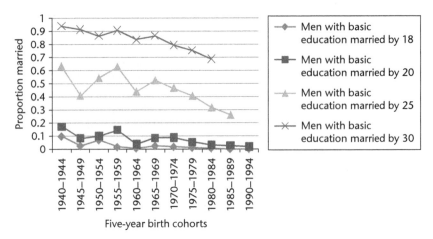

**Figure 7.14.** Proportion of men with basic education married by age 18, 20, 25, and 30 across five-year birth cohorts

*Source:* JLMPS (2010).

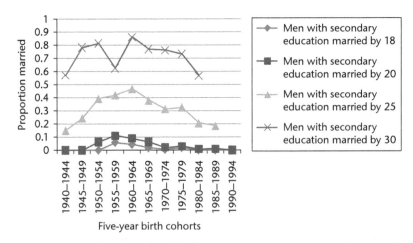

**Figure 7.15.** Proportion of men with secondary education married by age 18, 20, 25, and 30 across five-year birth cohorts

*Source:* JLMPS (2010).

and wives. Across Jordanian society, women were married to men 6.1 years their seniors in age on average, according to the JLMPS. No difference in husband's age seniority could be observed in rural versus urban areas, but husbands tended to be older than their wives in southern Jordan, followed by central Jordan and finally northern Jordan. The poorest Jordanian couples had the smallest age gap between them, but those women with less education generally had a smaller spousal age gap than those women with more education (Table 7.5).

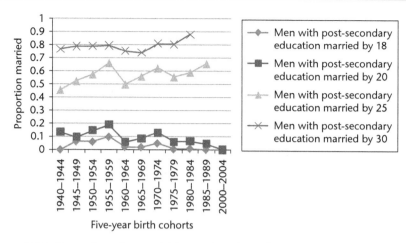

**Figure 7.16.** Proportion of men with post-secondary education married by age 18, 20, 25, and 30 across five-year birth cohorts
*Source:* JLMPS (2010).

**Table 7.5.** Husband's mean age advantage by socio-demographic characteristic of the wife, ever-married women aged 15–60

|  | Husband's mean age advantage | No. |
|---|---|---|
| *Residence* |  |  |
| Rural | 6.1 | 1,169 |
| Urban | 6.1 | 3,108 |
| *Region* |  |  |
| Central | 6.2 | 2,189 |
| Northern | 5.9 | 1,446 |
| Southern | 6.4 | 642 |
| *Wealth* |  |  |
| Poorest | 5.9 | 1,343 |
| Middle wealth | 6.0 | 1,460 |
| Wealthiest | 6.3 | 1,474 |
| *Education* |  |  |
| Less than Basic | 6.6 | 1,091 |
| Basic | 6.8 | 1,406 |
| Secondary | 5.9 | 716 |
| Post-Secondary | 5.0 | 1,064 |
| *Total* | 6.1 | 4,277 |

*Source:* JLMPS (2010).

Jordanians' trends in marriage timing suggest that men and women's ages at marriage may be converging in Jordan, but Figure 7.17 indicates that there has been no such narrowing of the spousal age gap over successive marriage cohorts. Jordanian husbands' age advantage has followed a cyclical pattern, and after declining in the late 1970s and 1980s, it has generally increased since the marriage cohorts of the early 1990s. When spousal age gaps are broken down by rural/urban residence, it becomes clear that this pattern is driven largely by urban couples (Figure 7.17).

Boys' educational attainment has historically exceeded girls' educational attainment in many Arab societies, and Arab culture dictates that the husband's education should be equivalent to or greater than his wife's. However, spousal education gaps are quite narrow in Jordan. On average, Jordanian husbands have only 0.4 years more education than their wives. Table 7.5 displays differentials in husband–wife educational gaps by socio-demographic group. Differentials are generally quite small, but what is noteworthy is the fact that Jordanian wives with secondary and post-secondary degrees have *more* years of education on average than their husbands, a pattern that does not hold for less educated women in the JLMPS (Table 7.6).

Figure 7.18 shows that couples in which the wife has more years of education than her husband are becoming more common over time in Jordan. In the earliest marriage cohorts represented in the JLMPS, husbands had about three years more of education than their wives, but by the 1990–1994 marriage cohort, the mean spousal education gap was zero. Since then, Jordan's most recently married women have achieved a slight educational advantage over

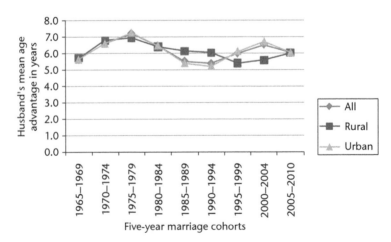

**Figure 7.17.** Husband's mean age advantage by rural/urban residence across five-year birth cohorts, ever-married women aged 15–60
*Source:* JLMPS (2010).

**Table 7.6.** Husband's mean educational advantage by socio-demographic characteristic of the wife, ever-married women aged 15–60

|  | Husband's mean educational advantage | No. |
|---|---|---|
| *Residence* |  |  |
| Rural | 0.5 | 1,169 |
| Urban | 0.3 | 3,107 |
| *Region* |  |  |
| Central | 0.3 | 2,188 |
| Northern | 0.5 | 1,446 |
| Southern | 0.2 | 642 |
| *Wealth* |  |  |
| Poorest | 0.3 | 1,343 |
| Middle wealth | 0.0 | 1,459 |
| Wealthiest | 0.7 | 1,474 |
| *Education* |  |  |
| Less than basic | 3.3 | 1,091 |
| Basic | 0.2 | 1,406 |
| Secondary | −0.5 | 716 |
| Post-secondary | −1.2 | 1,063 |
| Total | 0.4 | 4,277 |

*Source:* JLMPS (2010).

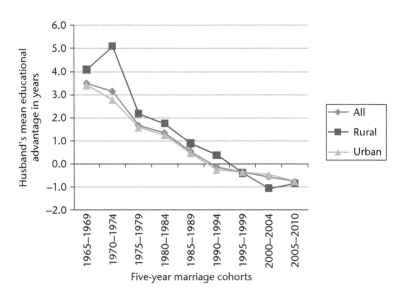

**Figure 7.18.** Husband's mean educational advantage by rural/urban residence across five-year birth cohorts, ever-married women aged 15–60
*Source:* JLMPS (2010).

their husbands, on average. This pattern holds in both urban and rural areas (Figure 7.18). In marriages contracted since 1990, the JLMPS shows that 41.9% of all wives had exceeded their husbands in educational attainment, and 25.4% of wives were equivalent in years of education to their husbands.

## 7.6 Consanguinity

The JLMPS contains questions regarding the kinship relation between husbands and wives, which were posed to all ever-married women aged 15–60. Overall, 35.3% of all ever-married women interviewed for the survey reported that their first marriages were consanguineous. Of these consanguineous marriages, 44.4% involved a union with a paternal cousin, 26.9% involved a union with a maternal cousin, 24.6% involved a union with another blood relative, and 4.1% involved a union with a relative by marriage.

In the JLMPS sample as a whole, kin marriages account for 42% of all rural marriages and 33.9% of all urban marriages. Consanguinity is also practiced most often in northern Jordan, followed by southern Jordan, and finally central Jordan. If consanguineous marriage is broken down by socio-economic status, we find that kin marriages are most common among the least wealthy and least common among the wealthiest. Those with modest educational attainment are more likely to marry relatives than those with more education (Table 7.7).

My analysis also shows that the practice of kin endogamy has declined steadily over time for the Jordanian population as a whole. A full 41.4% of all marriages contracted in 1965–69 were between relatives, but by 2005–10 this percentage had declined to 26.1% (Figure 7.19). However, this belies important differences in the trajectory of consanguinity by residence. Since the marriage cohorts of the 1960s, consanguineous marriages have dwindled in urban areas. In rural areas, however, kin marriage followed a general upward trend until the marriage cohorts of the late 1990s, after which it followed a downward trend.

## 7.7 Household Structure

The JLMPS contains a question posed to ever-married women aged 15–60 regarding the structure of the household they entered upon marriage, which allows us to explore nuclear versus extended family living arrangements. In the JLMPS sample as a whole, 64.2% of these women reported that they had established an independent nuclear family when they entered into their first union. Nearly all of the remaining women went to live with their husband's

**Table 7.7.** Percentage of marriages consanguineous by socio-demographic characteristic of the wife, ever-married women aged 15–60

|  | Percentage of marriages consanguineous | No. |
|---|---|---|
| *Residence* | | |
| Rural | 42.0 | 1,205 |
| Urban | 33.9 | 3,306 |
| *Region* | | |
| Central | 33.2 | 2,372 |
| Northern | 39.5 | 1,472 |
| Southern | 37.3 | 1,472 |
| *Wealth* | | |
| Poorest | 41.8 | 1,424 |
| Middle wealth | 36.8 | 1,546 |
| Wealthiest | 29.5 | 1,541 |
| *Education* | | |
| Less than basic | 45.5 | 4,511 |
| Basic | 40.5 | 1,551 |
| Secondary | 32.0 | 780 |
| Post-secondary | 23.6 | 1,145 |
| *Total* | 35.3 | 4,511 |

*Source:* JLMPS (2010).

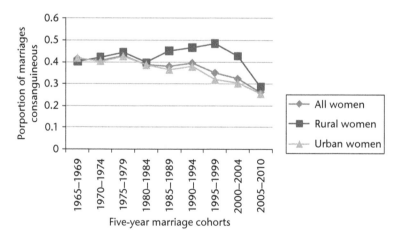

**Figure 7.19.** Proportion of marriages that were consanguineous by rural/ urban residence across five-year marriage cohorts, ever-married women aged 15–60
*Source:* JLMPS (2010).

family. Surprisingly, nuclear family living at the start of marriage was reported slightly more frequently among women living in rural areas, compared to women living in urban areas. This may be because the high cost of purchasing or renting a home in the cities forces urban Jordanian newly weds to live with relatives at the start of their married lives. As we might expect, the rich are most likely to live in nuclear households at the start of marriage, and the poor are least likely to live in nuclear households. There is also a steep educational gradient in nuclear family living, with the most educated setting up independent living arrangements at the start of marriage nearly twice as often as the least educated. Furthermore, in the JLMPS sample as a whole, nuclear family living arrangements at the start of marriage are most common in southern Jordan, followed by northern Jordan and central Jordan (Table 7.8). Again, this may be due to expensive real estate prices in the central and northern regions, or it may be due to different customs in each of these regions.

The practice of extended family living has also diminished in favor of nuclear family living, which has increased in prevalence over time (Figure 7.20). In the 1960–64 marriage cohort, 39% of all Jordanian couples lived as a nuclear household at the start of their marriages. By the 2005–10 marriage cohort, twice as many couples lived as nuclear families upon marriage. If we compare

**Table 7.8.** Percentage of households nuclear at first marriage by socio-demographic characteristic of the wife, ever-married women aged 15–60

|  | Percentage of households nuclear at first marriage | No. |
| --- | --- | --- |
| *Residence* | | |
| Rural | 67.8 | 1,205 |
| Urban | 63.5 | 3,306 |
| *Region* | | |
| Central | 62.6 | 2,372 |
| Northern | 63.1 | 1,472 |
| Southern | 78.5 | 667 |
| *Wealth* | | |
| Poorest | 56.3 | 1,424 |
| Middle wealth | 61.9 | 1,546 |
| Wealthiest | 71.7 | 1,541 |
| *Education* | | |
| Less than basic | 45.0 | 1,035 |
| Basic | 57.6 | 1,551 |
| Secondary | 70.3 | 780 |
| Post-secondary | 82.6 | 1,145 |
| *Total* | 64.2 | 4,511 |

*Source:* JLMPS (2010).

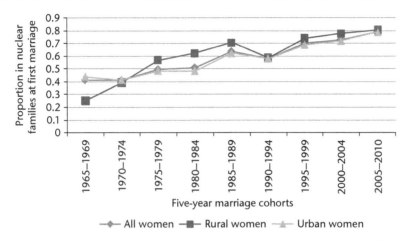

**Figure 7.20.** Proportion living as nuclear family at start of first marriage by rural/urban residence across five-year marriage cohorts, ever-married women aged 15–60
*Source:* JLMPS (2010).

the trajectory of nuclear family living in urban and rural areas, we find that nuclear family arrangements were much less common in rural areas than urban areas in the earliest marriage cohorts. Nuclear family living has grown in frequency among rural and urban residents, with the exception of the 1990–94 marriage cohort, in which extended family living spiked briefly. This may have been due to the 1991 Gulf War, which saw many Jordanians return to the Kingdom from the oil-rich countries of the Persian Gulf. This return migration may have driven up housing prices in Jordan, forcing newly wed couples to temporarily reside with relatives.

## 7.8 Marriage Expenditures

The JLMPS contains a number of questions posed to ever-married women aged 15–60 on expenditures related to their first marriages. Respondents were asked to report the Jordanian dinar (JD) value of the *mahr* (prompt dower) given by the groom to the bride,[3] the jewelry given by the groom to the bride, the furniture and appliances purchased for the conjugal home, the costs of housing, and the costs of celebrations, including the engagement and wedding parties. Information was collected on two other items that are not included in the calculation of the total costs of marriage, namely the value of

---

[3] The *mahr* (also called the *mahr mua'ajjal*) is only practiced among Muslims.

the furniture recorded in the marriage contract and the value of the *muakhar* (deferred dower) recorded in the marriage contract.[4]

First, the average cost of each of the expenditures made at the time of marriage is explored in marriages contracted since 1990, disaggregating these expenditures by socio-demographic characteristics of the respondent. Jordanian dinars are standardized to 2010 values, and therefore are adjusted for inflation.[5] Table 7.9 shows that the average cost of marriage in Jordan is approximately JD9,900 or about $14,000.[6] If we compare average marriage costs by socio-demographic characteristics, we see that total marriage costs are actually slightly higher in rural Jordan compared to urban Jordan, primarily due to higher expenditures on jewelry and housing in rural areas (Figures 7.21 and 7.22). Not surprisingly, the poor spend less on marriage in absolute terms than wealthier Jordanians. There are also some differentials in marriage outlays across Jordan's three main regions. Respondents in northern and southern Jordan reported spending nearly equal sums on marriage overall, and respondents in central Jordan spent the least among all regions. Figure 7.22 shows that generally, the most costly component of marriage expenditures is furniture and appliances, which represents 35% of total marriage costs on average. This is followed by celebrations (24%), jewelry (15%), and finally housing and *mahr* (each accounting for 14%).

Finally, using retrospective reports on marriage costs from marriage cohorts dating back to the 1970s,[7] trends in matrimonial expenditures in Jordan are examined. Contrary to popular discourse, the costs of marriage have *not* increased in Jordan in recent years. When marriage expenditures are standardized to current values, the total cost of marriage rises and then falls over the forty-year period under consideration (Figure 7.23). Compared to those who married in 1970–74, those who married in 1985–89 spent about 30% more on their marriage preparations. Marriage costs for those who married in 1980–84 were significantly higher than for those who married five years earlier, and although those who married in 1985–89 spent even more than those who

---

[4] The *muakhar* (also called the *mahr mu'ajjal*) is a sum of money, agreed upon at the time of marriage, which Muslim brides can claim if they are widowed or divorced. Because it is not actually paid to the bride at the time of marriage it is excluded from the calculation of the total costs of marriage. Similarly, the JD value of furniture recorded in the (Muslim) marriage contract is meant to document the property to which the bride would be entitled upon divorce. In this analysis, it is assumed that this furniture represents the value (perhaps inflated) of the furniture and other household goods purchased by the bride and groom (Moors, 1994), which is captured in another question in the JLMPS questionnaire.

[5] Outliers in the costs of marriage data were also eliminated by using the Cook's D statistic. This ensures that the reported means are not unduly influenced by exceptionally large values of the costs of marriage.

[6] An exchange rate of $1.4117 to JD1 was used (<http://www.oanda.com/currency/historical-rates/>)

[7] A longer-time trend could not be constructed because historical inflation rates for the Jordanian dinar are not available earlier than 1967.

**Table 7.9.** Mean total cost of marriage in 2010 (Jordanian dinars) by socio-demographic characteristic of the wife, among ever-married women aged 15–60 who married in 1990 or later

|  | Total costs of marriage (JD) | No. |
|---|---|---|
| *Residence* | | |
| Rural | 10,575 | 726 |
| Urban | 9,756 | 2,041 |
| *Region* | | |
| Central | 9,808 | 1,473 |
| Northern | 10,046 | 927 |
| Southern | 10,048 | 367 |
| *Wealth* | | |
| Poorest | 7,749 | 947 |
| Middle wealth | 9,941 | 999 |
| Wealthiest | 11,765 | 821 |
| *Education* | | |
| Less than basic | 6,850 | 255 |
| Basic | 8,954 | 1,123 |
| Secondary | 10,409 | 541 |
| Post-secondary | 11,551 | 848 |
| *Total* | 9,895 | 2,767 |

*Source:* JLMPS (2010).

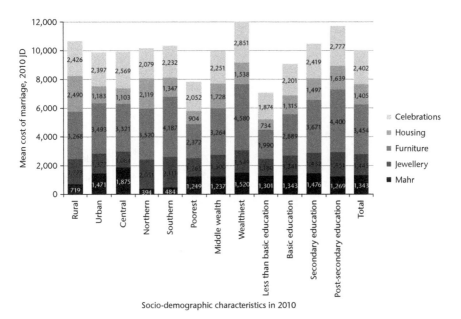

**Figure 7.21.** Mean spending on marriage cost components by socio-demographic characteristic of the wife, among ever-married women aged 15–60 who married in 1990 or later

*Source:* JLMPS (2010).

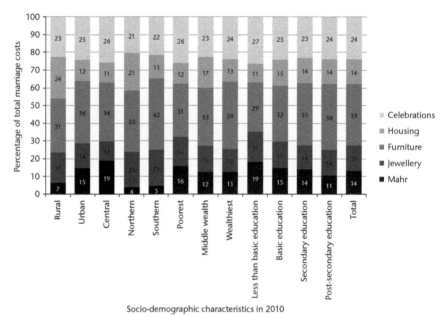

**Figure 7.22.** Proportional spending on marriage cost components by socio-demographic characteristic of the wife, among ever-married women aged 15–60 who married in 1990 or later

*Source:* JLMPS (2010).

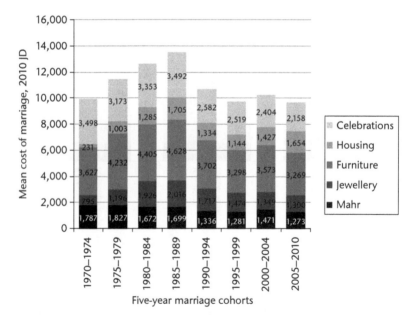

**Figure 7.23.** Mean spending on marriage cost components across five-year marriage cohorts, ever-married women aged 15–60

*Source:* JLMPS (2010).

married five years earlier, this increase was not statistically significant. After the 1985–89 marriage cohorts, however, marriage costs dropped precipitously and significantly, and have hovered around JD10,000 ever since the marriages of the early 1990s (see Table 7.10). Figure 7.24 shows that the trend of increasing then diminishing marriage costs is most pronounced in rural areas. The inflation in marriage costs witnessed in the 1980s was steepest

**Table 7.10.** Mean total cost of marriage in 2010 (Jordanian dinars) across five-year marriage cohorts, ever-married women aged 15–60

| Marriage cohort | Total costs of marriage | No. |
| --- | --- | --- |
| 1970–1974 | 9,707 | 161 |
| 1975–1979 | 10,813 | 255 |
| 1980–1984 | 12,391** | 287 |
| 1985–1989 | 13,088 | 380 |
| 1990–1994 | 10,601*** | 634 |
| 1995–1999 | 9,555*** | 624 |
| 2000–2004 | 10,093* | 728 |
| 2005–2010 | 9,418** | 781 |

*Source:* JLMPS (2010).

*Notes:* *p<.05; **p<.01; ***p<.001.

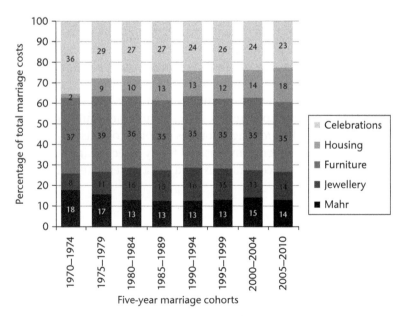

**Figure 7.24.** Mean spending on total marriage costs by urban/rural residence across five-year marriage cohort, ever-married women aged 15–60
*Source:* JLMPS (2010).

213

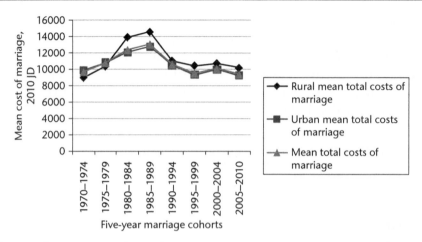

**Figure 7.25.** Proportional spending on marriage cost components across five-year marriage cohorts, ever-married women aged 15–60
*Source:* JLMPS (2010).

in rural areas, and even when it declined, it plateaued at a level higher than urban areas. The 1980s was a period of relatively high remittances from the oil-rich countries of the Gulf, which might account for more lavish spending on marriage during those years. Overall, the pattern in average total marriage costs provides little evidence to suggest that the rising age at first marriage for Jordanian men or women is a response to inflation in the costs of marriage.

Examining proportional spending on marriage cost components over time reveals that housing has grown most as a proportion of total marriage costs. Housing expenses comprised 2% of marriage costs among those marrying in 1970–74, and 18% among those marrying in 2005–10. Considering that more and more young couples report living as nuclear family households at the start of marriage, the growing resources devoted to housing expenses are not surprising. This has been compensated for by a decline in the proportion of expenditures made on celebrations, and, to a lesser extent, on the *mahr* (Figure 7.25).

## 7.9 Conclusions

This chapter has described marriage behavior in contemporary Jordan by utilizing a unique data source, the JLMPS 2010. Questions contained in the JLMPS questionnaire allow for the exploration of several facets of marriage behavior in the Jordanian population, including the duration of engagements, current marital status, marriage timing, spousal characteristics, household structure, and marriage expenditures.

Across Jordan, the average length of engagement among ever-married women was approximately eight months. Disaggregating engagement durations by socio-demographic characteristic revealed that engagements were longest among urban dwellers (those residing in central Jordan), among the wealthy, and among women who had intermediate education. Trends in engagement durations are such that engagements became shorter over successive marriage cohorts until 1980–84, after which time engagements have lengthened slightly in Jordan.

Virtually all Jordanians will enter into a marital union in the course of their lifetimes. Among those aged 45–49, only 2% of men and 7% of women had never married, according to the JLMPS. These rates of never-married indeed confirm that women are more likely than men to remain single, but they do not represent the emergence of a pressing social problem, as some sources would suggest.

Marriage timing in the JLMPS is examined here through the use of two measures: the median age at marriage, and the proportions married by ages 18, 20, 25, and 30. At the national level, the median age at marriage in Jordan is 24 for women and 29 for men. These two measures both indicate that women marry later in rural areas compared to urban areas, but they yield contradictory findings with regards to whether rural or urban men marry later. Both measures suggest that the transition to marriage occurs latest in north and south Jordan compared to central Jordan, although the differences among men are minimal. Women's median age at marriage increases with increasing wealth, but the proportion of married women at every age indicates that the poorest women begin marrying earliest, but at the same time a larger fraction of these women remain unmarried at age 30. Men's median age at marriage increases with increasing wealth according to both measures of marriage timing. Both measures also confirm that the more education women have attained, the later they tend to marry. However, the two measures disagree in terms of the education gradient in men's marriage timing. Transitions to marriage have generally been occurring at later ages over time in Jordan. Trends in the proportions married at certain ages show that the proportion of women who are married at certain ages have decreased over time, suggesting a rise in the female age at marriage. Men's ages at marriage also appear to have been delayed over successive birth cohorts, although the rise in men's ages at marriage is considerably flatter than women's. Comparing rural and urban populations, we see that rural women and men have undergone greater change in marriage timing than their urban counterparts.

Spousal characteristics were next examined, beginning with differences in age and education between husbands and wives. Across Jordan, husbands are six years older than their wives on average. There are no rural–urban differences in husbands' age seniority, but the greatest age advantage exists among southern Jordanian couples, among the wealthy, and among the least educated. The spousal age gap has fluctuated over time in Jordan, but has generally failed to narrow over successive marriage cohorts. As for educational differences between husbands and wives, they are minimal in Jordan, with wives having half a year less education on average than their husbands. Disaggregating educational differences by socio-demographic characteristic yields few contrasts, but highly educated women are distinct in that their education exceeds that of their husbands, on average. If we look at trends over time, we find that husbands' education exceeded their wives' in the earliest marriage cohorts. In the most recent marriage cohorts, however, wives have achieved a one-year educational advantage over their husbands on average. The final spousal characteristic explored in this chapter had to do with kinship. Thirty-five percent of all marriages represented in the JLMPS data were between relatives. Kin marriages are more common in rural areas, in northern Jordan, among the poorest Jordanians, and among the least educated. Consanguineous marriages have generally declined in prevalence over time, but still, approximately one-quarter of all marriages contracted in the most recent marriage cohort were between relatives.

There are important variations by socio-demographic characteristic in household structure in Jordan. Those living in rural Jordan, those residing in the south, wealthy Jordanians, and highly educated Jordanians are most likely to live in a nuclear family household (rather than an extended family household) at the start of marriage. Over time, nuclear family living has become more common in Jordan, as modernization accounts of economic development would predict.

Marriage expenditures are the final feature of marriage behavior investigated in this chapter. The various material requirements that accompany marriage in Jordan include a dower for the bride, jewelry, furniture, appliances, housing costs, and celebration costs. Together these items require an average outlay of about $14,000, with housing and celebrations being the most costly two components overall. Those in urban areas, those in central Jordan, those in the poorest third of the wealth distribution, and those with the least education spend the least on marriage. Variations in marriage expenditures over time are apparent in the JLMPS data, but they are not in the expected direction. The costs of marriage are found to have followed an upward trajectory between the marriage cohorts of the early 1970s and those of the late 1980s. However, marriage costs in Jordan subsequently declined by a factor of about 20%, and have remained more or less constant since the early 1990s. These findings are in contrast to Jordanians' popular perceptions, which hold that marriage costs have been rising dramatically over time. This dissonance between perception and reality is difficult to account for, and unlocking this puzzle will require further research.

## References

Alasmar, H., 2007. عنوسة. `Unoosa. [Spinsterhood]. *Addustour,* <http://www.addustour. com/ViewarchiveTopic.aspx?ac=\opinionandnotes\2007\04\opinionandnotes_ issue15439_day29_id248664.htm> (accessed October 14, 2013).

Alshuwayki, S., 2011. أسباب العزوف عن الزواج...دائرة متكاملة. *Asbab al`ozouf `an al`zawaj...da`ira mutakamilah.* [Reasons for reluctance towards marriage: an integrated circle]. *Al`raiy*<http://www.alrai.com/article/281526.html> (accessed December 27, 2013).

Badran, F. and M. Sarhan, 1995. تكاليف الزواج في الاردن. *Takaleef Al`zawaj Fi Al`urdun.* [Marriage costs in Jordan]. Amman, Jordan: *Jam`iyyat Al`afaf Al`khayriyyah,*

Department of Statistics (Jordan) and ICF Macro, 2010. *Jordan Population and Family Health Survey 2009.* Calverton, Maryland, USA: Department of Statistics and ICF Macro.

The Economic Research Forum, 2010. *Jordan Labor Market Panel Survey 2010 (JLMPS 2010).* Cairo, Egypt: The Economic Research Forum.

Hamamy, H., L. Jamhawi, J. Al-Darawsheh, and K. Ajlouni, 2005. Consanguineous marriages in Jordan: Why is the rate changing with time? *Clinical Genetics* 76:511–16.

Khalifa, J., 2009. المقبلون علي الزواج: عقبات كثيرة و هموم تعيقهم. *Al`muqbiloun `ala al`zawaj: `aqabat katheera wa humoum ta`eequhum.* [Couples wanting to get married: myriad hinderences and obstacles]. *Addustour,* <http://www.addustour. com/ViewarchiveTopic.aspx?ac=\miscellany\2009\09\miscellany_issue722_ day30_id178235.htm> (accessed October 14, 2013).

Khoury, S. A. and D. Massad, 1992. Consanguineous marriage in Jordan. *American Journal of Medical Genetics* 43:769–75.

Khuraisat, S., 1990. تقاليد الزواج في الاردن. *Taqaleed al`zawaj fi al`urdun.* [Marriage customs in Jordan]. Amman, Jordan: *Al`dar Al`arabiyya Lilnashr wa Al`tawzee`.*

Mensch, B., S. Singh, and J. Casterline, 2005. Trends in the timing of first marriage among men and women in the developing world. Population Council Policy Research Division Working Paper No. 202.

Moors, A., 1994. Women and dower property in twentieth-century Palestine: The case of Jabal Nablus. *Islamic Law and Society* 1(3): 301–31.

Obeidat, B., R. Yousef, S. Khader, Z. O. Amarin, M. Kassawneh, and M. Al Omari, 2010. Consanguinity and adverse pregnancy outcomes: The north of Jordan experience. *Maternal and Child Health Journal* 14:283–89.

Shaker, A. J., 2008. العنوسة...مسئولية المجتمع كله. *Al`unoosa...mas`uliyyat al`mujtama` kullu.* [Spinsterhood: society's responsibility]. *Addustour,* <http://www.addustour. com/ViewarchiveTopic.aspx?ac=\opinionandnotes\2008\06\opinionandnotes_ issue245_day09_id56700.htm> (accessed October 14, 2013).

Siegel, J. S. and D. A. Swa1son (eds), 2004. *The Methods and Materials of Demography.* San Diego, CA: Elsevier Academic Press.

Sueyoushi, S. and R. Ohtsuka, 2003. Effects of polygyny and consanguinity on high fertility in the rural Arab population in south Jordan. *Journal of Biosocial Science* 35:513–26.

# 8

# The Patterns of Early Retirement among Jordanian Men

*Ibrahim Al Hawarin*

## 8.1 Introduction

Labor force participation (LFP) contributes to the economy's capacity to produce goods and services. The prevalence of early retirement lowers LFP and has consequences on the economy (Gruber and Wise, 1994; Conde-Ruiz and Galasso, 2004; Glomm et al., 2009). Therefore, there is a growing interest in early retirement behavior and its patterns in developed economies (Oorschot and Jensen, 2009). However, existing studies on developing countries are rare (El-Hamidi, 2007; Glomm et al., 2009).

LFP in Jordan has been low even in comparison with developing countries. The average observed LFP is around 40% even during high growth periods. Both men and women over 40 contribute significantly to this phenomenon. The low level of female LFP (15%) has been the subject of many studies; however, little research has addressed the LFP of elderly males and the early exit of middle-aged male workers from the labor market.

Early withdrawal from the labor market for Jordanian men is striking and requires the attention of academics and policymakers alike. The available evidence shows that the incidence of early retirement has increased over time and has become the rule rather than the exception (Social Security Corporation (SSC), 2009). This is also confirmed in Assaad and Amer (2008), which documented that the decline in activity rates in Jordan starts as early as age 40, and the propensity toward early exit also seems to have been increasing over time. Figure 8.1 graphs male LFP trends by age group. It clearly illustrates that participation rates drop from 85% to 81% from 2001 to 2009 for the age group 40–54. The participation rates for the 55–64 age group remains low throughout the period, at around 45% on average.

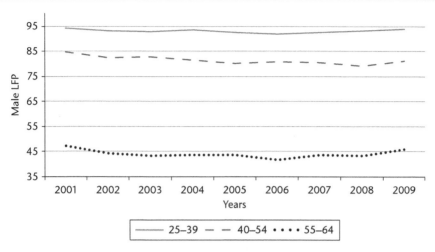

**Figure 8.1.** Male LFP for selected age groups (2001–2009) (%)
*Source:* EUS (2001–2009).

In light of the preceding discussion, this chapter examines early retirement among Jordanian male workers. To the best of my knowledge, it is the first study to use micro data to analyze the phenomenon of early retirement in Jordan. The results could be of particular interest to policymakers who are looking to implement successful labor market and social insurance reforms.

The chapter looks at the following questions:

1. What are the general characteristics of male early retirees?
2. What do early retirees do after retirement? Do they return to the labor force?
3. If they do, what kind of jobs do they occupy?
4. Do early retirees take up informal employment?
5. Is the phenomenon of early retirement limited to public and military employees and service members, or does it extend beyond those groups?
6. What differentiates economically active and inactive men receiving early retirement pensions?
7. What does the available data reveal about retirement decisions at the individual level?

Section 8.2 examines the legal background of retirement in Jordan. Section 8.3 discusses methodological and data issues. Section 8.4 is concerned with the data analysis. Section 8.5 employs the results of the study to explore potential determinants of early retirement decisions in Jordan.

## 8.2 Institutional Background

Currently, there are three major retirement legislations covering civil servants and workers in public and private sectors, as well as the military and public security forces. These are: the Military Retirement Law (MRL); the Civil Retirement Law (CRL); and the Social Security Law (SSL). Other occupational pension schemes also exist for a few labor unions (e.g. Jordan Engineers Association). Employer and employees' monthly monetary contributions constitute the main sources of financing pension funds in Jordan.

The MRL no. 33 (1959)—and its amendments—regulates retirement of the Jordanian armed and security forces. It permits early retirement after a minimum number of years in service (16, raised to 20 in mid-2004). Individuals with special circumstances, like those with partial disability, can retire after serving the military for at least ten years. On the other hand, the law does not allow those in service to continue in duty after the age of 60, except for very special exceptions. It also does not set a minimum age for a service member to obtain pension and other related benefits. Thereby military men may retire in their early thirties or even before. In 2003, a new government initiative moved new military entrants under the umbrella of the Social Security Corporation (SSC). However, the arrangements applicable to military forces in the MRL remained in place.

Most public-sector workers recruited before 1994 were covered by the CRL no. 34 (1959) and its amendments. Since 1994, new entrants to the public sector have been insured by the SSLs (see later). Under the CRL, early retirement for men was allowed after having spent at least twenty years in service (modified to twenty-five in 2006); no minimum age for retirement was identified; and the age for compulsory retirement was 60 years. However, the law remained flexible with regards to workers with special needs or partial/full disability.

A pivotal year in the formulation of social policy in Jordan, and particularly in the development of pension systems, was 1978, when the government introduced a social security law for the first time. Until that law was introduced, a significant proportion of private- and public-sector employees were not covered by either of the two laws mentioned. Therefore, it was of great importance for Jordan to widen social protection through the introduction of the SSL. The SSL was subject to some modifications in 2001 and to major restructuring and reshaping in 2010. The first SSL no. 30 (1978) was modified to SSL no. 19 (2001), which enhanced social protection; however, it was arguably considered too generous. SSL no. 7, introduced in 2010 and applicable primarily to new entrants, was considered less generous and more rational.

As far as male workers are concerned, SSL no. 30 and no. 19 set the early age of retirement and retirement pension at 45 and 60 years, respectively. Those who do not make enough contributions may continue working until

65 in order to collect a pension. The SSL 2010 adjusted retirement regulations by increasing the number of monthly accumulated contributions and the minimum age required to make one eligible for early retirement. Now new entrants to the labor market cannot retire before the age of 50, except for some specified categories of labor (e.g. those employed under severe working conditions, such as mining workers).

## 8.3 Data and Methodological Issues

This study uses the recent cross-sectional data obtained from the first wave of the Jordan Labor Market Panel Survey of 2010 (JLMPS 2010), which collected micro-level information during the period from February to April 2010. The survey and its procedures were designed and administered by the Economic Research Forum (ERF) in co-operation with the Department of Statistics in Jordan (DoS) and the National Centre for Human Resources Development (NCHRD). JLMPS involves gathering detailed information on education, labor market experiences and behaviors, and demographic characteristics (e.g. employment status, household composition and income, parental education, education history, ownership of assets and monetary transfers and remittances, migration, and marriage history). The survey covers about 5,000 households and about 26,000 individuals, and applies appropriate sampling methods for making the gathered data nationally representative.

In comparison to former surveys, the JLMPS contains, for the first time, novel features that make it suitable to study early retirement and elderly LFP. Surveyed individuals were asked to self-identify the amount and type of monetary transfers received by them or any of their household members, such as pension and other governmental transfers. The survey, furthermore, tracks retrospectively the employment status of workers. The participants in the survey, older than six, were asked to indicate in detail their current, previous, pre-previous, and employment status in 1999, together with dates of entry to and exit from each of those statuses. The survey also incorporates a variety of questions that directly address social security and pension coverage.

Those who receive pensions are classified as retirees, with full awareness of the possibility of other sources of pension (e.g. inherited pension for children and dependants). The age of 60, which is the legal age for retirement in Jordan, was considered as the cutoff point between early retirement and old age retirement. In effect, early retirees were defined as those retirees who received retirement pensions for the first time when they were below the age of 60.

## 8.4 Data Analysis

### 8.4.1 General Characteristics of Early Retirees

Having determined retirees in the representative data of JLMPS, they were consequently classified into three categories representing the three major pension systems in Jordan: retirees from the military and public security forces; retirees from the public sector, excluding the previous category; and retirees from the private sector.

Figure 8.2 illustrates the cumulative distribution of male retirees in Jordan by source of retirement pension and age of retirement. It appears clear that early retirement in Jordan is the rule rather than the exception. Most of the retirees, regardless of the sector, receive retirement pensions well before the age of 60. In general, male retirement starts from the early 30s, and noticeably after the age of 33 for service members in military and security forces and by the late 30s for civilian public- and private-sector workers. Male early retirees comprise about 86% of the Jordanian living male retirees. Those who retire under the age of 50 comprise about 86% of the total number of military retirees, while they comprise 40% and 45% of the total civilian public- and private-sector retirees, respectively.

Additionally, the data shows that the propensity towards early retirement has accelerated over time, as depicted in Figure 8.3. The ratio of early retirees to the total number of retirees increased by more than 25 percentage points for those born between 1945 and 1949, compared to those born before 1929. This finding matches well with the records of SSC, which records the same pattern among recent pensioners covered by social security (SSC 2009). It is possible that this is partly attributable to the generosity of pension regulations in Jordan. However, the retirement decision is more sophisticated, and requires deeper and more effective investigative research in the future. We

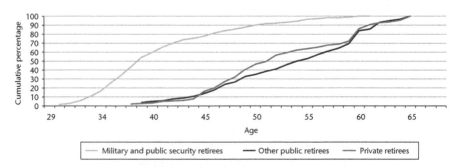

**Figure 8.2.** Cumulative distribution of male retirees by sector and age of retirement
*Source:* Author's calculations based on JLMPS (2010).

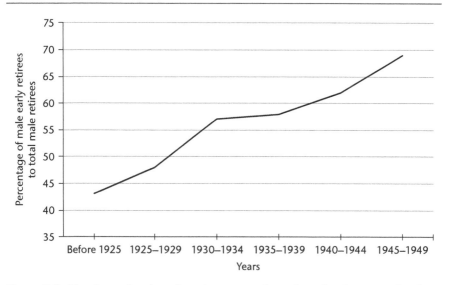

**Figure 8.3.** The share of male early retirees to total number of male retirees for those born before 1950

*Source:* Author's calculations based on JLMPS (2010).

will address some factors that contribute to the understanding of early withdrawal/inactivity of men in Jordan.

Table 8.1 displays the general characteristics of early retirees. Two noticeable features come to the forefront: approximately 78% of the early retirees have secondary education or lower, and more than two-thirds reside in urban areas.

### 8.4.2 Do Early Retirees Return to the Labor Market after Retirement?

The statistical analysis shows that a considerable fraction of male early retirees return to the labor market after receiving their retirement pension. On average, and regardless of the sector of retirement, nearly 45% of those classified as early retirees are currently economically active (see Figure 8.4). LFP is around 55% for early pensioners from military and other similar forces. Of course, this observation is not strange, as most of them retire relatively early, suggesting that there is an age factor in determining the economic activity behavior for this group. It appears that as a male pensioner in Jordan gets older, he is more likely to become inactive. In other words, LFP tends to decline dramatically as the age of pensioner increases, as shown in Figure 8.5. This pattern is confirmed by the LFP of male early retirement receivers from both the private and public sectors, who have a higher age of retirement on average, as presented in Figure 8.4. A little over 30% of the latter two

**Table 8.1.** Overall characteristics of male early retirees

|  | Category | Percentage |
| --- | --- | --- |
| Current education | Illiterate | 8 |
|  | Reads and writes | 24 |
|  | Basic | 28 |
|  | Secondary | 18 |
|  | Post-secondary | 10 |
|  | University and higher | 12 |
| Sector of retirement | Public (including military) | 84 |
|  | Private | 16 |
| Current area of residence | Urban | 71 |
|  | Rural | 29 |
| Current marital status | Single | 0.5 |
|  | Married | 97.5 |
|  | Divorced | 0.1 |
|  | Widowed | 1.9 |
| Current region of residence | Middle | 45 |
|  | North | 42 |
|  | South | 13 |

*Source:* Author's calculations based on JLMPS (2010).

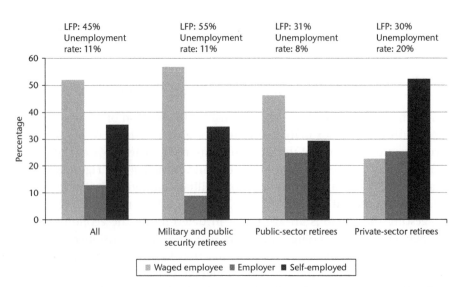

**Figure 8.4.** Employment status distribution of early retirement receivers after first retirement

*Source:* Author's calculations based on JLMPS (2010).

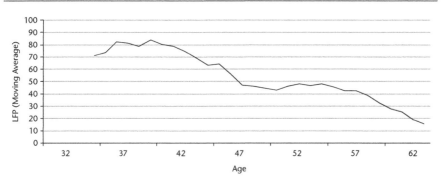

**Figure 8.5.** LFP of male early retirement pension receivers by current age (moving average trend)
*Source:* Author's calculations based on JLMPS (2010).

categories continue in the labor market after their early retirement. This age trend is also consistent with the overall LFP of men in Jordan, which drops as age increases, as reflected in Figure 8.1.

In addition, Figure 8.4 reveals the employment status of male early retirees in the case that they reappear in the labor market. Nearly 52% become waged employees, while 35% and 13% become self-employed or employers, respectively. The analysis also shows that waged employees come mostly from those returning from the public sector and particularly from military and security forces. On the other hand, self-employment appears to be the primary labor market route for private-sector early retirement receivers. Such a trend may indicate some labor market opportunity differences available for these different groups and may also reflect some deficiencies in pension systems in Jordan. For instance, public-sector workers and the armed forces covered by MRL and CRL retain the right to be socially covered by the SSL if they return to the labor market, unlike private-sector workers. Sections 4.3, 4.4, and 4.5 take a closer look at this.

It is also evident from Figure 8.4 that private-sector retirees are at a higher risk of unemployment if they return to the labor market. Their unemployment rate exceeds that of their counterparts from the other two categories (20% compared to 8% and 11% for public sector and military forces, respectively). Education tends to contribute to differences in unemployment and activity rates among returnees. Early retirees from the public sector, excluding military and security forces, are found to have higher education levels comparatively (see later).

As far as the economic activity is concerned, in addition to the results shown in Figures 8.4 and 8.5, there are other interesting observations. The following points summarize them:

1. LFP of early pension receivers is 57% for those aged below 60 at the time of the survey (66%, 42%, and 34% for military and security forces, other public and private sector, respectively).

2. Urban early pension receivers have a lower LFP (44 % compared to 51% for rural); however, they have lower unemployment rates (10.6% against 12.6%). This is possibly due to the fact that public and military careers comprise the main source of employment in rural areas.

3. Some 21% of inactive early retirement pension receivers identify illness, old age, and disability as the reasons they are out of the labor force, while 78% mention the availability of income as the chief factor for economic inactivity. Such patterns suggest that health and disability are somewhat responsible for the early withdrawal from the labor market and the inability of retirees to return to employment again. On the other hand, the availability of income may render support to the notion that retirement legislations are generous in Jordan.

4. Not many engage in secondary jobs (1.7%).

### 8.4.3 Economic Activities of Active Early Retirement Pension Receivers

Figure 8.6 presents the economic activities to which early retirees turn on returning to work, in comparison with other Jordanian workers, and reveals some interesting patterns. First, active early retirement pension receivers are concentrated in the trade (wholesale and retail), transportation, and storage

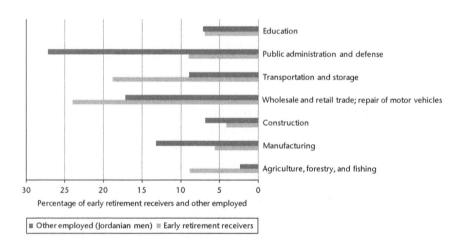

**Figure 8.6.** Distribution of economic activities returned to by early retirement receivers and other employed workers in the economy

*Source:* Author's calculations based on JLMPS (2010).

sectors. These activities involve private and informal occupations as examined later. Second, agriculture-related activities that typically incorporate foreign labor seem to attract Jordanians more after securing pension entitlements. However, construction activities, which are also foreign-labor intensive, are negligible in importance and do not attract active pensioners. This particular sector involves hard work and severe working conditions, which deter retirees and other workers alike from partaking in it, despite its reasonable wage levels compared to other sectors.

### 8.4.4 Occupations Taken Up by Active Male Early Retirement Pension Receivers

The analysis finds that a substantial proportion of early retirement receivers end up in informal occupations when they return to the labor market. The classification of the employed from this group according to major and sub-major occupations corroborates this observation (see Figure 8.7 and Table 8.2). More than 33% of the employed engage in service and sale occupations (vendors), while nearly 22% work as plant and machine operators and as assemblers (a category that includes drivers). Also, as mentioned, agricultural occupations employ a disproportionate number. These occupations seem to attract retirement pension receivers more than other categories of employed males and thus raise the core issue of unemployment in Jordan and the procedures necessary to formalize such occupations to make them more appealing to the working population in general. Early retirement receivers are more likely to end up in informal employment since some of them—particularly the private- and public-sector civilian retirees—cannot take up

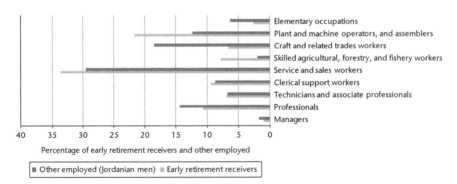

**Figure 8.7.** Major occupational distribution for jobs taken up by early retirement receivers after returning to the labor market compared with other employed workers in the economy

*Source:* Author's calculations based on JLMPS (2010).

**Table 8.2.** Sub-major occupational distribution of employed early pension receivers by sector

| Military and public security forces | Public sector | Private |
|---|---|---|
| Drivers and mobile plant operators 22.6% | Drivers and mobile plant operators 11.4% | Drivers and mobile plant operators 29.5% |
| Protective services workers 15.7% | Business and administration professionals 13.9% | Health professionals 9.6% |
| Sale workers 17.2% | Sale workers 17% | Sale workers 21.9% |
| The other workers are distributed on other 24 occupations | The other workers are distributed on other 18 occupations | The other workers are distributed on other 6 occupations |

*Source:* Author's calculations based on JLMPS (2010).

jobs covered by social security without losing their early retirement benefits. This concern is probably one of the main factors considered when selecting the type of occupation post early retirement, because retirement benefits in Jordan provide health insurance for workers and their dependents even after retirement.

The distribution of sub-major occupations, as reflected in Table 8.2, identifies more precisely the jobs captured by early retirees on returning to the labor market. There tends to be an occupational concentration among them, as they crowd into a limited number of jobs. More commonly they work as drivers and mobile plant operators, protective services workers and sale workers (vendors). When breaking down the distribution by sector of retirement, the analysis additionally finds that almost 14% of public-sector pension receivers become business and administration professionals, while 9.6% of private-sector pension receivers become health professionals. An important feature of the analysis presented in the table is the limited occupational choices available to those retiring from the private sector, compared with the other two groups. This is in line with the previous discussion on the role of social security regulations in distributing labor market opportunities. Of course, other variables, such as accumulated human capital, may intervene as well. Differences in educational levels exist between the three different groups; however, they are not enough to explain these differences in occupational choices (see later).

Further examination of the occupations that early retirees hold reveals that most of the jobs are informal. Some 73% work in unskilled jobs and 91% are not members of a syndicate or trade union. Half the jobs taken up by retirees from the public sector and military are covered by social security, but none

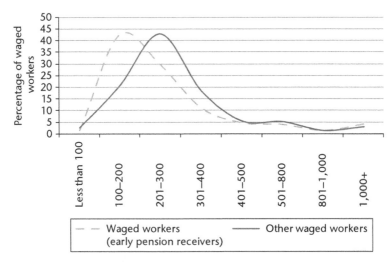

**Figure 8.8.** Wage categorical distribution of wage employed early retirement pension receivers and other counterparts aged 30+ in the economy
*Source:* Author's calculations based on JLMPS (2010).

of the private retirees are entitled to such coverage. Overall, 34% have health insurance packages in their new jobs, but almost 59% have no paid vacations.

It is also worth looking to the relative earnings of the jobs occupied by this group of workers. Figure 8.8 distributes current-wage workers by wage categories, taking into account whether or not they are early retirement pension receivers. There appears to be a clear disparity in favor of other wage workers in the economy aged 30 and over. In other words, those who return to the labor market after early retirement tend to accept comparatively lower wages. The investigation of earning differences certainly requires more rigorous estimation procedures. However, the results are suggestive of the general picture with important policy implications (discussed in section 8.5).

### 8.4.5 Economic Activity/Inactivity of Early Retirees

We have considered some of the variables that account for the decision of early retirees to become active. Participation in the labor market is more common to younger retirees, suggesting that age is an important determinant of activity. Economic activity is also apparently determined by the institutional source of retirement pensions; those formerly working in the army and security forces are more likely to remain active (see Figure 8.4). Similarly, living in rural areas appears to increase the probability of returning to the labor market, resulting, however, in a higher risk of unemployment. Moreover, the data shows that sickness and disability encourage inactivity, and may actually be causes of the early retirement itself.

This subsection further inspects other important factors that influence returning to economic activity after retirement. First and foremost is the amount due to an individual as pension for years served. Second is the level of educational attainment. In addition, it sheds some light on the potential influences of family size and household variables.

Income sufficiency, as reported above, is the principal factor that influences the decision of early retirees on whether or not to return to economic activity. The monthly pension is the primary source of income for most retirees in Jordan. On the other hand, education lies at the heart of labor market theories. It increases earnings through either enhancing productivity or signaling innate ability. In addition, educated workers are theorized to be more efficient in searching for jobs and on-the-job training and accumulating experience. Finally, the household's family size and the availability of other breadwinners, either active or retired, may interact with the previous variables to determine inactivity/retirement versus returning to labor market.

As far as early retirees are concerned, the descriptive analysis of JLMPS concludes that, on average, active pension receivers differ from inactive ones in terms of monthly pension entitlements. Monthly pension in Jordanian dinar (JD) is likely to influence the decision of early retirees to return to the labor market, as depicted in Figure 8.9. The figure shows the categorical cumulative distribution of pension by activity status. Sixteen per cent of the inactive early retirement receivers attain more than JD300 as pension payments, compared to 10% of the active ones. Similarly, those who obtain more than JD500 are 4% and 2% of inactive and active, respectively. These differences suggest that the probability of a retiree to return to work or search for work after early retirement is inversely related to pension payments.

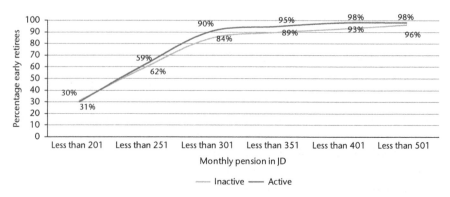

**Figure 8.9.** Cumulative distribution of monthly pension for active and inactive men early retirees

*Source:* Author's calculations based on JLMPS (2010).

Now we move to the effect of education on economic activity after retirement. Having more years of education appears to be associated with a higher propensity for returning to the labor market and higher LFP, as Figure 8.10 indicates. An exception is those with post-secondary education (intermediate diploma), who make up 10% of all early retirees. The LFP of those with fewer years of education, specifically the illiterate and those who can only read and write, is comparatively lower, as shown in Figure 8.10.

The role of education is less clear when one concentrates on unemployment of early retirees in relation to educational attainment (see Figure 8.11). More education does not particularly guarantee lower chances of unemployment. Yet, the figure indicates that early retirees with university education and higher are less likely to experience unemployment once they return to the labor market.

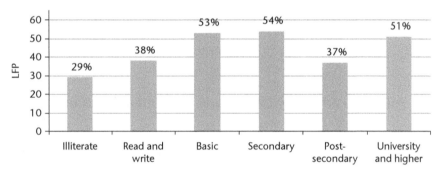

**Figure 8.10.** LFP for male early retirees by level of education
*Source:* Author's calculations based on JLMPS (2010).

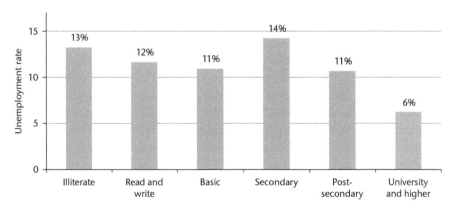

**Figure 8.11.** Unemployment rates for male early retirees by level of education
*Source:* Author's calculations based on JLMPS (2010).

Financial obligations (expenditure) facing households usually grow with a larger family size and therefore may influence individuals' decisions to retire early and also to return to the labor market after retirement. This factor interacts with other income variables, such as other sources of income, pension, and the number of workers or retirees in a household. The study finds that family size does influence retirees. The household size of a significant proportion of early retirees (58%) comprises more than five people, whereas only 52% of households of other labor force groups of the same age are as large. This implies a potential role for family size in the retirement decisions. Moreover, 52% of retirement receivers in households with this size become active again after retirement, while only 30% remain inactive. This means that family size may also increase the possibility of those retiring early from the labor market to return to it again.

Finally, the analysis shows that 93% of households of male early retirees contain only one retiree, with negligible differences between active and inactive, and in comparison with old-age retirees. Households of male early retirees also vary to some extent, based on whether or not their wives currently work. The results of the study indicate that 9% of active early retirees' wives are employed, compared to 10% for inactive early retirees.

## 8.5 Voluntary and Involuntary Early Retirement Decisions

The analysis of retirement decisions necessitates further in-depth analysis, principally through multivariate estimation. Such an analysis requires detailed data on monetary and non-monetary incentives and opportunities created for workers both by pension schemes and the labor market. Typically, the retirement decision variables are classified into push and pull (supply and demand) variables. Many financial, occupational, institutional, personal, and health factors determine early retirement decisions (Blundell et al., 2002). Macroeconomic cycles also intervene in shaping retirement decisions, particularly on the push side (El-Hamidi, 2007; Glomm et al., 2009). Employment policies that accompany macroeconomic restructuring and privatization are also reported to induce early exit from the labor market (El-Hamidi, 2007).

As emphasized in the introduction, this section further investigates the phenomenon of early retirement by means of descriptive statistics because the data needed for an econometric estimation of retirement decision at the individual level is not captured by the JLMPS (e.g. pension entitlements on retirement and push variables at the firm level). However, capitalizing on the results extracted from the JLMPS and other general information on the Jordanian economy, one can shed light on some of the driving forces of early retirement in Jordan.

First, it is evident from the analysis that the military and security forces are more likely to exit early. Future research on this issue must take into account that decisions vary by economic sector and more emphasis should be placed on those retiring involuntarily and those who fall outside the military sector. Excluding the military sector, where the vast majority retires early, about 70% of the retirees from the public and private sectors exit early from the labor market.

Second, as the private sector is weaker in rural areas and military and public sectors create most of the jobs available for rural residents, it is not surprising that the area of residence is a factor in early retirement decisions. Workers living in rural areas are more likely to retire early (more than 80%, compared with about 75% for urban areas). However, rural retirees are more likely to return to the labor market, but are placed at a slightly higher risk of unemployment, as reported earlier.

Third, inactive early retirement pension receivers identify illness and disability as reasons for remaining out of the labor force, which means that health variables may have induced them to withdraw from work originally.

Fourth, inactive early retirement pension receivers also report that income availability makes it easier for them to remain inactive after their early withdrawal. Nonetheless, solid conclusions on the role of monetary incentives and the generosity of early retirement pensions cannot definitely bring us to the current finding. Workers may retire before the formal age of retirement not because of sufficient pension entitlements, but rather because of the insufficiency of current earnings. This is supported by the results discussed in the section 8.4, which show that active early retirees are recipients of lower pensions.

Fifth, the analysis reveals that financial pressures and household expenditure obligations may also determine differences in retirement decisions, as well as post-retirement labor market participation at the individual level. More than 12% of normal-age male retirees have working spouses, while only 9% of early male retirees have working spouses. Additionally, households of early retirees are larger than other labor force groups of the same age. In effect, retirement and post-retirement labor force participation decisions are probably taken at the household level.

Finally, some other variables may have been partly responsible for the increasing propensity for male early retirement in Jordan. Privatization of government-owned projects is one such variable. For example, selling off the Jordanian Cement Factories Company involved generous early retirement schemes. These schemes extended to other institutions, particularly those in the overstaffed phosphate sector, which is undertaking similar arrangements for laying off workers. Such push variables are very significant, particularly in the aftermath of macroeconomic restructuring or recessions. During economic downturns, in general, one would expect firms to pressurize employees eligible for early retirement to agree to early retirement packages.

The scarcity of information hinders further research into the reasons for early retirement, and to take this research a step forward detailed quantitative data focused on retirement needs to be gathered, maybe through a self-reporting survey.

### References

Assaad, A. and M. Amer, 2008. *Labor Market Conditions in Jordan, 1995–2006: An Analysis of Microdata Sources*. Amman, Jordan: National Center for Human Resources Development, Al Manar Project.

Blundell R., C. Meghir, and S. Smith, 2002. Pension incentives and the pattern of early retirement. *Economic Journal* 112 (478): C153–70.

Conde-Ruiz, J. and V. Galasso, 2004. The macroeconomics of early retirement. *Journal of Public Economics* 88:1849–69.

Department of Statistics (DoS). 2010. *The Employment and Unemployment Survey (EUS) 2010*. Amman, Jordan: Department of Statistics.

El-Hamidi, F., 2007. Early retirement in the government sector in Egypt: Preferences, determinants and policy implications. ERF Working Paper No. 721. Cairo, Egypt: The Economic Research Forum.

Glomm, G., J. Juergen, and C. Tran, 2009. Macroeconomic implications of early retirement in the public sector: The case of Brazil. *Journal of Economic Dynamics and Control* 33: 777–97.

Gruber, J. and D. Wise, 1998. Social security and retirement: An international comparison. *The American Economic Review* 88 (2): 158–63.

Oorschot, W. and P. Jenson, 2009. Early retirement differences between Denmark and the Netherlands: A cross-national comparison of push and pull factors in two small European welfare states. *Journal of Aging Studies* 23: 267–78.

Social Security Corporation, 2009. *Annual Report 2009*. Amman, Jordan: Social Security Corporation.

# Index

235